Weathering Shakespeare

Environmental Cultures Series

Series Editors:

Greg Garrard, University of British Columbia, Canada
Richard Kerridge, Bath Spa University

Editorial Board:

Frances Bellarsi, Université Libre de Bruxelles, Belgium
Mandy Bloomfield, Plymouth University, UK
Lily Chen, Shanghai Normal University, China
Christa Grewe-Volpp, University of Mannheim, Germany
Stephanie LeMenager, University of Oregon, USA
Timothy Morton, Rice University, USA
Pablo Mukherjee, University of Warwick, UK

Bloomsbury's *Environmental Cultures* series makes available to students and scholars at all levels the latest cutting-edge research on the diverse ways in which culture has responded to the age of environmental crisis. Publishing ambitious and innovative literary ecocriticism that crosses disciplines, national boundaries, and media, books in the series explore and test the challenges of ecocriticism to conventional forms of cultural study.

Titles available:
Bodies of Water, Astrida Neimanis
Cities and Wetlands, Rod Giblett
Civil Rights and the Environment in African-American Literature, 1895–1941, John Claborn
Climate Change Scepticism, Greg Garrard, George Handley, Axel Goodbody, Stephanie Posthumus
Climate Crisis and the 21st-Century British Novel, Astrid Bracke
Colonialism, Culture, Whales, Graham Huggan

Ecocriticism and Italy, Serenella Iovino
Fuel, Heidi C. M. Scott
Literature as Cultural Ecology, Hubert Zapf
Nerd Ecology, Anthony Lioi
The New Nature Writing, Jos Smith
The New Poetics of Climate Change, Matthew Griffiths
This Contentious Storm, Jennifer Mae Hamilton
Climate Change Scepticism, Greg Garrard, Axel Goodbody,
George B. Handley, and Stephanie Posthumus
Ecospectrality, Laura White
Teaching Environmental Writing, Isabel Galleymore
Radical Animism, Jemma Deer
Cognitive Ecopoetics, Sharon Lattig
Digital Vision and the Ecological Aesthetic (1968–2018), Lisa FitzGerald
Environmental Cultures in Soviet East Europe, Anna Barcz
The Living World, Samantha Walton

Forthcoming Titles:
Imagining the Plains of Latin America, Axel Pérez Trujillo Diniz
Ecocriticism and Turkey, Meliz Ergin

Weathering Shakespeare

Audiences and Open-air Performance

Evelyn O'Malley

BLOOMSBURY ACADEMIC
LONDON • NEW YORK • OXFORD • NEW DELHI • SYDNEY

BLOOMSBURY ACADEMIC
Bloomsbury Publishing Plc
50 Bedford Square, London, WC1B 3DP, UK
1385 Broadway, New York, NY 10018, USA
29 Earlsfort Terrace, Dublin 2, Ireland

BLOOMSBURY, BLOOMSBURY ACADEMIC and the Diana logo are
trademarks of Bloomsbury Publishing Plc

First published in Great Britain 2021
This paperback edition published in 2022

Copyright © Evelyn O'Malley, 2021

Evelyn O'Malley has asserted her right under the Copyright, Designs and
Patents Act, 1988, to be identified as Author of this work.

For legal purposes the Acknowledgments on pp. xi–xii represent an
extension of this copyright page.

Cover design by Burge Agency
Cover photograph © Shutterstock

All rights reserved. No part of this publication may be reproduced or transmitted in any form
or by any means, electronic or mechanical, including photocopying, recording, or any information
storage or retrieval system, without prior permission in writing from the publishers.

Bloomsbury Publishing Plc does not have any control over, or responsibility for,
any third-party websites referred to or in this book. All internet addresses given
in this book were correct at the time of going to press. The author and publisher
regret any inconvenience caused if addresses have changed or sites have ceased
to exist, but can accept no responsibility for any such changes.

A catalogue record for this book is available from the British Library.

Library of Congress Cataloging-in-Publication Data
Names: O'Malley, Evelyn, author.
Title: Weathering Shakespeare : audiences and open-air performance / Evelyn O'Malley.
Description: London ; New York : Bloomsbury Academic, 2021. | Series: Environmental cultures |
Includes bibliographical references and index. | Summary: "From The Pastoral Players' 1884 performance
of As You Like It to contemporary productions in London's Regents Park, there is a rich history of open
air performances of Shakespeare's plays. Weathering Shakespeare reveals how new insights from
the environmental humanities can transform our understanding of this popular performance practice.
Drawing on audience accounts of outdoor productions of those plays most commonly chosen for
open air performance - including A Midsummer Night's Dream and The Tempest - the book examines
how performers and audiences alike have reacted to unpredictable natural environments. Weathering
Shakespeare goes on to explore the ways in which contemporary concerns about the environment have
informed new and emerging performance practices"– Provided by publisher.
Identifiers: LCCN 2020040940 (print) | LCCN 2020040941 (ebook) | ISBN
9781350078062 (hardback) | ISBN 9781350202443 (paperback) | ISBN
9781350078079 (ePDF) | ISBN 9781350078086 (eBook)
Subjects: LCSH: Shakespeare, William, 1564-1616–Dramatic production. |
Shakespeare, William, 1564-1616–Stage history. | Shakespeare, William,
1564-1616–Appreciation. | Theater, Open-air. | Ecocriticism.
Classification: LCC PR3091 .O53 2021 (print) | LCC PR3091 (ebook) | DDC 792.09–dc23
LC record available at https://lccn.loc.gov/2020040940
LC ebook record available at https://lccn.loc.gov/2020040941

ISBN:	HB:	978-1-3500-7806-2
	PB:	978-1-3502-0244-3
	ePDF:	978-1-3500-7807-9
	eBook:	978-1-3500-7808-6

Series: Environmental Cultures

Typeset by Integra Software Services Pvt. Ltd.

To find out more about our authors and books visit www.bloomsbury.com
and sign up for our newsletters.

for ma, and the glaciers

Contents

List of Figures	x
Acknowledgments	xi
Introduction	1

Part One

1	Performing Pastoral: A New Form of Poetic Representation	45
2	"Light them at the fiery glow-worm's eyes": Max Reinhardt's *A Midsummer Night's Dream* and the Regent's Park Open Air Theatre	71

Part Two

3	Shakespeare-Inspired Nature-Theaters: Minack and the Willow Globe	95
4	Wandering in Woods: The Natural Place for the Play	123

Part Three

5	Green Atmospheres: Nature Playing (Along, Sometimes)	151
6	Shakespeare for a Changing Climate	177

Afterword	201
Bibliography	204
Index	220

List of Figures

2.1	Audience hats at Max Reinhardt's *A Midsummer Night's Dream* in Oxford, 1933	76
2.2	*A Midsummer Night's Dream* at Oxford, 1933	78
2.3	"During the Interval. Spectators Examine the Pitch"	85
3.1	The Minack Theatre	97
3.2	The Willow Globe, May 2014	109
4.1	Alison Halstead and Connor Allen in Taking Flight's *As You Like It*, 2014	137
4.2	Natasha Magigi and Tom Ross Williams as Mirando and Ferdinand in Teatro Vivo's *After The Tempest*, 2013	142
6.1	Eleanor Dillon Reams and Lucy Green in *As You Like It*, Maumbury Rings, Dorchester, 2017	182
6.2	Darragh Martin, Michelle Tylicki and James Atherton in BP or not BP's Mischief Festival, 2018	186
6.3	Projection onto the Royal Shakespeare Theatre, Stratford Upon Avon, June 2018	193

Acknowledgments

I am grateful to the UK Arts and Humanities Research Council for the PhD funding, which enabled this project. The University of Exeter also assisted with a period of study leave for which I am thankful.

Thanks also to Richard Kerridge and Greg Garrard for supporting the book; to David Avital, Ben Doyle, and Lucy Brown for their editorial expertise at Bloomsbury; and to the anonymous readers who made this work much better than it would have been. Remaining mistakes are mine.

In Drama at Exeter Cathy Turner offered opening supervision; friends and colleagues read drafts and shared light at Thornlea—special thanks to Bec Benzie, Katie Beswick, Adrian Curtin, Jerri Daboo, Sarah Goldingay, Kate Holmes, Rebecca Loukes, Jane Milling, Kate Newey, Michael Pearce, and Konstantinos Thomaidis; JP, Andy and Lewis helped with dramatech; in English, Pascale Aebischer and Chloe Preedy were grounding; Mick Mangan, Chris McCullough, and Peter Thomson offered early encouragement; and scienceweather conversations with Peter Stott and the Climate Stories crew were illuminating.

Beyond Exeter, I had the good fortune of conversations with and insights from Swati Arora, Todd Borlik, Aiden Condron, Heidi Dorschler, N. Eda Erçin, Jennifer Mae Hamilton, Helen John, Gwilym Jones, Ilaria Pinna, Stephen Purcell, Sally Mackey, Randall Martin, Danielle Meunier, Sharanya Murali, Conor O'Malley, Eoin Price, Kirsty Sedgman, Laura Smith, Jon Venn, Wei-Hsien Wan, Nora Williams, Penelope Woods, Lisa Woynarski, and valuable input from colleagues in working groups at ASLE, SAA, and TaPRA.

For archival assistance, I am thankful to the University of Binghamton, Bristol Theatre Archive, Folger Shakespeare Library, University of Southern California, Victoria and Albert Museum, British Institute of Florence, Natural History Museum, and Santa Clara University. Funding from the Society for Theatre Research enabled me to get to Binghamton. Richard Anders, Sophie Austin, David Leddy, Helen Lawson, Jorge Lizalde Cano, The Minack Theatre Archive, Mark Nesbitt, and Feral X gave permission to reproduce their photographs and writing. Extracts from the Introduction and Chapters 3 and 4 appear in *Shakespeare Bulletin*, *Performance Research*, and *Participations Journal of Audience and Reception Studies*, and I appreciate the opportunity to rework them here.

Heartfelt gratitude to the theater people who make this kind of thinking possible through their work: Sue Best, Phil Bowen, and everyone at the Willow Globe; Phil Jackson, Anne and Zoë Curnow, and all at Minack; Elise Davison, Beth House, and Taking Flight; Sophie Austin and Teatro Vivo; Chris Chambers and Another Way; Maddy Kerr and Heartbreak; Hester and Liam Evans-Ford at Sprite; Emma Gersch and Moving Stories; Paul Moss, Tom Dixon, and The HandleBards; actorvists at BP or not BP; and many others. To the generous audience members whose words run through this book, I hope there's something here you recognize.

Best days to Andie, Bec, Kim, Jacqui, Joe, Nora, Róisín—for friendship across times and places; sharanya—there is no work without you; Mark—quiet logistics; Oscar—impetus agus aimsir; Ma, Da, Eoghan, Clare—grá always, home.

Introduction

I remember waiting for a performance of A Midsummer Night's Dream *to begin, sitting under a tree and listening to the curator of the Botanic Gardens in Dublin, Ireland, introduce the play. Expecting to hear the usual sort of preamble, comparing the touring company to a merry Elizabethan troupe, I was surprised instead to hear him note the audience's opportunity to observe the gardens' specialist plants on a summer's night. Trees, shrubs, and flowers behave differently in the cool of the evening, he explained, and the audience should make the most of their after-hours access to the gardens at the end of a hot day. And hadn't it been a hot day? They would see a funny and magical play by Shakespeare too, he added—as an afterthought. I spent most of that performance newly alert to the gardens in the dropping temperature and changing light, preoccupied by movement, smells, and shadows, as lively as any Athenian lovers, mechanicals, fairies, or human audience. Turning to tend to my damp bum, I learned that the tree I had been sitting under was a* Sorbus mougeotii *or Mougeot's Whitebeam, native to the Austrian Alps, and as out of place in Glasnevin as a 400-year-old play by an English playwright.*

This book considers the reception of a limited repertoire of canonical plays by a 400-year-old playwright, exposed to the weather. A bright enactment of the defunct culture/nature dualism is at once attempted and undone in open-air Shakespeares—and high culture by way of Shakespeare and capital "N" Nature at that.[1] Both Shakespeare and nature are cultural, of course, but the persistence of thinking about nature as distinct from culture endures at the heart of today's many tragedies. As the "whirl" of living in the anthropocene[2]

---

[1] To acknowledge the diversity of contemporary practice, "Shakespeares" follows the contention first made in the *Alternative Shakespeares*' series that there are not "one" but "many" Shakespeares. John Drakakis, ed., *Alternative Shakespeares: Volume 1* (London: Routledge, 1985).

[2] Greg Mitman, "Reflections on the Plantationocene: A Conversation with Donna Haraway and Anna Tsing," June 18, 2019, https://edgeeffects.net/haraway-tsing-plantationocene/. Discussing the controversies surrounding the "Anthropocene," Anna Tsing seeks to "add" complexity and nuance to the term. In her spirit, I use the term cautiously, signaling an acknowledgment of its conceptual limitations with a lower case "a" throughout.

sediments into just another epistemological layer, what might theater audiences for outdoor performances of Shakespeare's plays tell us about environmental cultures, beyond conjuring the image of a soggy gathering, stoically enduring *A Midsummer Night's Dream* as the tide comes in?[3] What might matter ecologically in responses to these popular and peculiar theatrical events? Whether or not the theater-makers of this book conceive of themselves as collaborating with the environment when they work in the "open" air (and often they do so only superficially, irrespective of whether they consider themselves collaborating with their environments or not), the weather is an important part of the lived theater experience for audiences, highlighting exposure and profoundly affecting how people respond to the plays.

In a world certain humans have put under threat, the risks of not paying attention to all forms of performance in relation to their more-than-human counterparts are too high to ignore. One strand running through research concerned with climate change inaction is a consensus that scientific facts and crisis narratives—for reasons that philosophers and social scientists claim are variously to do with scale, tangibility, overwhelm, helplessness, fear, denial, imagination, economics, and ideology—have not been sufficiently mobilizing to avert the catastrophe that many are already living.[4] That a cultural, imaginative, and philosophical upheaval is needed if humans are to contend with the changes already in motion, forestall the worst of what's to come, and adapt to a profoundly altering habitat with compassion for the flourishing of all life on earth is clear. In "heart-breaking"[5] times, Alison Tickell's catchy provocation that "Creativity is the most sustainable and renewable energy source on the planet" feels worth clinging onto.[6] Art and culture, capaciously conceived, have the potential to

---

[3] Jeffrey Jerome Cohen and Lowell Duckert, eds., *Veer Ecology* (Minneapolis and London: University of Minnesota Press, 2017), 3, welcome readers to the *"whirled"* in their ecocritical companion for environmental thinking, theory, and practice [original emphasis].

[4] John Cook and Haydn Washington, *Climate Change Denial: Heads in the Sand* (London: Earthscan, 2011);Timothy Clark, *Ecocriticism on the Edge: The Anthropocene as a Threshold Concept* (London and New York: Bloomsbury, 2015), 159–73; Naomi Klein, *This Changes Everything* (London and New York: Allen Lane, Penguin Books, 2014), 15–18; Martin Lack, *The Denial of Science: Analysing Climate Change Scepticism in the UK* (Bloomington: AuthorHouse, 2013); Timothy Morton, *Hyperobjects: Philosophy and Ecology after the End of the World* (Minneapolis: University of Minnesota Press, 2013); Kari M. Norgaard, *Living in Denial: Climate Change, Emotions, and Everyday Life* (Cambridge, MA: MIT Press, 2011); Naomi Oreskes and Erik M. Conway, *Merchants of Doubt: How a Handful of Scientists Obscured the Truth on Issues from Tobacco Smoke to Global Warming* (New York: Bloomsbury, 2010).

[5] Wendy Arons and Theresa J. May, eds., *Readings in Performance and Ecology* (Basingstoke: Palgrave Macmillan, 2012).

[6] Alison Tickell, "Sustainability Should Be at the Heart of Our Collective Artistic Vision," *Guardian*, October 25, 2012, http://www.theguardian.com/culture-professionals-network/culture-professionals-blog/2012/oct/25/sustainability-arts-council-julies-bicycle.

foster creative engagement with an endangered planet—so one hopeful story goes. Indeed, creativity's capacity to respond to this unprecedented moment is the premise upon which much ecotheater and performance, environmental art, literary ecocriticism, ecopoetry, and new nature writing are founded. Paradoxically, environmental criticism also and often reveals that art and culture have been complicit in the making of the problem all along; culpable either through obfuscation or representing untenable relations between humans and nonhuman nature.[7] Irrespective of disputes over the best way to proceed, differing theoretical attachments, and despite having no shared image of what a saved planet would actually look like and for whom, environmentally attuned art and culture share the desire for less harmful ways of being in a multispecies "weather-world".[8]

Understanding how people negotiate their responses to cultural events is always an important ethical undertaking, but living in the anthropocene renders it all the more pressing. Although assumptions about the transformative power of theater and performance have been widespread for centuries, less scholarship attends to the stated affects of these works upon the people who encounter them. Despite nuanced ecocritical analyses of works of art and literature, little criticism incorporates the responses of people—other than academics and students—especially where environmental claims are made for the works' affective capacities. In the context of ecopedagogies, David Mazel asks for evidence about whether "students who read and write about green texts turn into more thoughtful and effective environmentalists than they might have been otherwise?"[9] Greg Garrard likewise queries the "widespread, untested and untheorized assumption that education *about* the environment [...] delivered *through* the environment [...] will automatically be education *for* the environment."[10] Similar questions apply, still largely unanswered—and, to a large extent, this is because they are unanswerable—to "green" forms of theater. Theater, performance, and, of course, all kinds of art and culture yield anticipated

---

[7] Baz Kershaw, *Theatre Ecology: Environments and Performance Events* (Cambridge and New York: Cambridge University Press, 2007), 10, queries the ways in which theatre is "embroiled in the ecological mess that is climate change." See also, Arons and May, *Readings in Performance and Ecology*, 3; Amitav Ghosh, *The Great Derangement: Climate Change and the Unthinkable* (Chicago and London: University of Chicago Press, 2016).

[8] Tim Ingold, "Earth, Sky, Wind, and Weather," *Journal of the Royal Anthropological Institute* 13, no. 1 (2007): 32.

[9] David Mazel in Simon C. Estok, *Ecocriticism and Shakespeare: Reading Ecophobia* (New York: Palgrave Macmillan, 2011), 50–42; Greg Garrard, "Foreword," in *Ecocritical Shakespeare*, eds. Dan Brayton and Lynne Bruckner (Farnham and Burlington: Ashgate, 2011), xxii.

[10] Timothy Clark, *Ecocriticism on the Edge: The Anthropocene as a Threshold Concept* (London and New York: Bloomsbury, 2015), 168.

and unexpected affects, contingent upon many different factors. Thinking about environmental cultures with some of these affects is the objective of this book. I'll open with a hunch—hopefully not too self-defeating a revelation with which to begin—that instrumental approaches to performance-making *and* reception will always be hopelessly reductive, but that doesn't diminish the imperative to try, to listen to what people have to say and to enter into conversations that might accommodate a biodiversity of voices.

Driven by spiraling urgency, *Weathering Shakespeare* doesn't travel very far and travels slowly. It looks back, looks around, and contemplates ahead within the parochial context of open-air Shakespeares in the UK.[11] It listens carefully to what people have had to say in response to these performances and thinks about what they have had to say discloses about cultural events framed by nature, teasing out their national specificity and treating it as of global concern.[12] It is one thing to sit on a bench with midges biting and sunlight forcing squinted vision, as clouds pass and changing temperatures demand a sunhat one moment and a blanket the next: "thou mayest see a sunshine and a hail / In me at once. But to the brightest beams / Distracted clouds give way" (*All's Well That Ends Well* 5.3.34–5). It is another to sit in a black plastic bag in a puddle, as rain blurs vision, seeps into shoes, and hoods stifle the sound of actors' voices: "then was I as a tree/ Whose boughs did bend with fruit: but in one night, / A storm or robbery, call it what you will, Shook down my mellow hangings, nay, my leaves, And left me bare to weather" (*Cymbeline* 3.3.62–4). As Una Chaudhuri points out, theater is one place where what Timothy Clark calls "derangements of scale" can be made perceptible.[13] Next to the end of the world Shakespeare performed outdoors is frivolous. And yet disaster on a planetary scale means revaluating everything, including poking around in language, gesture, and performance, however trivial they seem, hoping to learn about how we have arrived at where we are and to dream about where we might be better.

---

[11] This book does not feature examples from Northern Ireland or Scotland, which have their own specific conditions for response, although some of the theater companies I include tour to these places.

[12] For calls to slow down in response to the escalating crises of the anthropocene, see Timothy Morton, *Ecology without Nature: Rethinking Environmental Aesthetics* (Cambridge, MA, Harvard University Press, 2007), 28; Sharon O'Dair, "Slow Shakespeare: An Eco-critique of 'Method,'" in *Early Modern Literary Studies: From Florentine Codex to Shakespeare*, eds. Thomas Hallock, Ivo Kamps, and Karen L. Raber (Basingstoke: Palgrave Macmillan, 2008); Deborah Bird Rose, "Slowly ~ Writing into the Anthropocene," *TEXT* Special Issue 20: Writing Creates Ecology and Ecology Creates Writing, eds. Matthew Harrison, Deborah Bird Rose, Lorraine Shannon, and Kim Satchell (October 2013).

[13] Una Chaudhuri, "Anthropo-Scenes: Theater and Climate Change," *JDCE* 3, no. 1 (2015): 13.

Open-Air Shakespeares

Michael Dobson jokes that "from June to August it is still practically impossible to be more than twenty miles from an open-air Shakespearean venue in mainland Britain without fleeing to the moorlands of Scotland," highlighting the pervasiveness of small-scale performances of plays by Shakespeare on all kinds of green plots across the UK every summer.[14] Besides multitudinous amateur Shakespeares in outdoor settings, small professional touring companies visit village greens, heritage properties, public parks, and private gardens, performing mostly once before moving to the next venue. Few smaller companies receive any form of public funding and many exist only for a year or two, hinting at the challenges of successive wet summers and the sheer stamina and enthusiasm required for a rigorous schedule as reasons for faltering. Then there are productions specially produced at purpose-built amphitheaters. Of these, the most well-known include the reconstructed Shakespeare's Globe and the Open Air Theatre at Regent's Park, both in London. Regional amphitheaters also accommodate productions of Shakespeare's plays: most spectacularly the Minack—the first of Amber Massie-Blomfield's *Twenty Theatres to See before You Die* (2018)—carved into the cliffs on the edges of Cornwall and facing the Atlantic Ocean.[15] Some of these amphitheaters produce their own work and others host traveling theater. Beyond particular sites for outdoor performance, one-off, experimental productions are occasionally staged in "found spaces" outdoors, leaving little trace after the event.[16]

Given that open-air Shakespeares tend to take place during the summer and often during school holidays, the repertoire of plays performed is mostly limited to comedies and to what Downing Cless calls Shakespeare's "most nature-laden plays."[17] *As You Like It*, *A Midsummer Night's Dream*, and *The Tempest* are popular for obvious reasons. *Macbeth*'s Birnam Wood is also commonly performed outdoors, as are *Lear*'s heath, *Juliet*'s balcony, and *Henry V*'s nationalism. There are very few instances of plays by other early modern playwrights performed in outdoor settings today. Rather, many of the companies

---

[14] Michael Dobson, *Shakespeare and Amateur Performance* (Cambridge: Cambridge University Press, 2011), 155.

[15] Amber Massie-Blomfield, *Twenty Theatres to See before You Die* (London: Penned in the Margins, 2018).

[16] Richard Schechner, "6 Axioms for Environmental Theatre," *The Drama Review* 12, no. 3 (1968): 54 differentiates between "transformed" and "found space" as settings for environmental performance, and argues that in "found space [...] the challenge is to acknowledge the environment and *cope* with it as best one can" (my emphasis).

[17] Downing Cless, *Ecology and Environment in European Drama* (New York: Routledge, 2010), 91.

who perform Shakespeare outdoors also adapt classic novels, children's stories, and light operettas, especially where the sources contain some pastoral content, broadly construed. The material is usually culturally conservative and out of copyright.

Such long-standing appetite for Shakespeare in the open-air begs the question of why, when John Russell Brown proposes looking to outdoor performance to retrieve the original "spirit" of Elizabethan theater, he alights upon contemporary street performance companies such as Welfare State International and Bread and Puppet Theatre without mentioning open-air Shakespeares at all.[18] The answer likely relates to an unspoken equation Brown makes between early modern Shakespeares in their original contexts and a vision of a socially inclusive, democratic outdoor performance space, at odds with perceptions of contemporary open-air Shakespeares inherited from Victorian pastorals.[19] However much today's open-air Shakespeares resemble or deviate from their early modern counterparts in their spatial configurations, they emerge from a political heritage that is anathema to that which precedes twentieth- and twenty-first-century experimental, street-based, site-specific, and, most recently, various eco-theater and performance forms. Michael Dobson offers that "in a climate like this [...] the popularity of outdoor Shakespeares probably has less to do with what outdoor performance in such locations does aesthetically for the plays than with what the plays do ideologically for the locations."[20] Certainly, as Stephen Purcell observes, while "open-air performance [...] may seem free from the trappings of a Victorian proscenium arch theatre [...,] the presence among its audience of expensive picnic hampers and popping champagne corks can cast it in a very different light."[21] I venture that the muddiness of this distinction—and the contradictory environmental histories stuck in this mud—encourages caution when it comes to claims for theater's affective potential, with broader attendant lessons for arts-based approaches to environmental education or climate change communication.

---

[18] John Russell Brown, *Shakespeare and the Theatrical Event* (Basingstoke: Palgrave Macmillan, 2002), 11–18. Nor does Brown mention that Welfare State International worked with Shakespeare's texts as stimulus for some of their outdoor performances. WSI's *Tempest on Snake Island* and *The Wagtail and the Wasteland* are based on *The Tempest* and *King Lear*, respectively. See Tony Coult and Baz Kershaw, eds., *Engineers of the Imagination: The Welfare State Handbook*, 2nd ed. (London: Methuen, 1990), 164–81; and John Fox, *Eyes on Stalks* (London: Methuen, 2002), 64–8.

[19] See Bettina Boecker, *Imagining Shakespeare's Original Audience: 1660-2000: Groundlings, Gallants, Grocers* (Basingstoke and New York: Palgrave, 2015), for an extensive history of how this myth of an Elizabethan audience has morphed and endured over centuries.

[20] Dobson, *Shakespeare and Amateur Performance*, 187.

[21] Stephen Purcell, "A Shared Experience: Shakespeare and Popular Theatre," *Performance Research* 10, no. 3 (2005): 83.

Open-Air or Outdoor Theater?

Unravelling the following micro-example from British arts funding politics helps me to alight upon what is of global environmental interest in the reception of Shakespeare in the open-air. In July 2012, Arts Council England published details of a commission to create outdoor performance for small children. The brief stated that open-air *theater* practitioners were not to apply, supplying the following rationale:

> Q. Why are we not interested in "open-air theatre" or indoor theatre re-created in an outdoor setting?
> Outdoor Arts is an area of presentation in its own right. It requires a different way of working in order to meet the many demands working outdoors brings. We are not looking for passive audience experiences; the work must stand up to the rigours of the outdoor festival environment. Work designed for an indoor theatre space, is extremely difficult to transfer outdoors bearing in mind we are usually working with very little infrastructure and cannot re-create theatre conditions outdoors.[22]

The nuance here is that the brief conflates open-air and indoor *theater* as passive experiences and offers outdoor *arts* as an antidote to both. That different forms of performance-making require different approaches seems fair enough. What is odd is that the wording of the question considers open-air theater and indoor theater re-created in an outdoor setting to be synonymous ("we are *not* interested in 'open air *theatre*'"). Because the suggestion is that open-air *theater*-makers do not understand the requirements of working in the open-air—in the way that outdoor *arts* practitioners do—the brief presupposes a reader-practitioner cognizant with the semantics of their obliquely coded and culturally-specific terminology. There is more here than a nod to aesthetics or formal detail. Although the commission sought a newly devised piece of children's theater, my suggestion is that twentieth-century performances of *Shakespeare* are responsible for this way of classifying open-air theater as "indoor-theater-performed-outdoors" (despite the irony that much early modern drama was written for outdoor amphitheaters). The brief's implicit expectation is that its reader/practitioner will understand differences that pertain to what a performance does socially, politically, and environmentally: they will infer that "open-air theater" is a safe middle-brow activity, likely consisting of an iteration of some kind of historical, canonical text that engages its audiences in a "passive" manner ("passive" here

---

[22] Arts Council England, "Small Wonders Frequently Asked Questions" (2012): 1.

invokes now-dated ways of thinking about theater audiences watching a play in a darkened auditorium, detached, despite considerable resistance—via Jacques Rancière's *The Emancipated Spectator* (2009)—to the assertion that any form of theater is encountered passively).[23] The stated perception of open-air theater as dissociated from the *air* is riddled with anthropocentric oversights pertaining to how practitioners imagine their work affecting theatergoers and how it actually affects them, missing the possibility of exploring the intersubjective relationship between theater, audience, air-deemed-open, and everything living in it, swirling through it. This book attempts to think carefully about the ideological and ethical-ecological work that open-air Shakespeares do with respect to the weather. Beyond the UK context, it speculates about what this thinking might mean for artistic works and cultural practices explicitly attempting to engage with ecology.

Shakespeare in the Weather

Theater scholarship already holds a mnemonic repository of the affective capacities of Shakespeare in the weather. Julie Sanders opens *The Cambridge Introduction to Early Modern Drama* (2014) with thunder and lightning at *Richard III*.[24] Gwilym Jones begins *Shakespeare's Storms* (2015) at a wet *King Lear*.[25] Helen Nicholson introduces *The Ecologies of Amateur Theatre* (2018) with soft rain at *Twelfth Night*.[26] Stephen Purcell ends *Popular Shakespeare* (2009) on a chilly starlit evening at *The Tempest*.[27] Within these memories of weather and Shakespearean theatergoing, perceived convergences between real-world atmosphere and dramatic performance are later deemed worthy bookends. The weather profoundly affects these professional theater spectators and seeps into their work.

Thinking specifically about contemporary performances at Shakespeare's Globe, Tim Carroll, Stephen Purcell, and Penelope Woods all point out how in-text references to weather, when either confirmed or contradicted by the actual

---

[23] Jacques Rancière, *The Emancipated Spectator* (London and New York: Verso, 2009).
[24] Julie Sanders, *The Cambridge Introduction to Early Modern Drama, 1576–1642* (Cambridge: Cambridge University Press, 2014), 21.
[25] Gwilym Jones, *Shakespeare's Storms* (Manchester: Manchester University Press, 2015), 2.
[26] Helen Nicholson, with Nadine Holdsworth and Jane Milling, *The Ecologies of Amateur Theatre* (London: Palgrave, 2018), 1.
[27] Stephen Purcell, *Popular Shakespeare: Simulation and Subversion on the Modern Stage* (Basingstoke: Palgrave, 2009), 222.

weather, tend to prompt laughter.[28] Carroll's reflection arises from thoughts on directing *The Tempest*, suggesting that there are two ways in which audiences can encounter the text—and that both are funny.

> When Trinculo talked about "yond black cloud, yond huge one" (*The Tempest* 2.2.20), we found, strangely, that it worked just as well whether there was such a cloud or whether the sky was completely blue; two different jokes, two different *kinds* of joke, both delightful.[29]

Gwilym Jones, however, conceives of multiple possibilities for "environmental irony" written into Shakespeare's dramatic texts performed in the weather and argues that "differentiated levels of weather can be stratified beyond a simple real/theatrical binary."[30] To extend Jones's historical work to the contemporary moment and spaces beyond the Globe (either in its early modern guise or one of its later reconstructions), consider an imaginary, indicative outdoor production of *A Midsummer Night's Dream*. This play, Sophie Chiari points out, "repeatedly depicts poor meteorological conditions."[31] She hypothesizes that in its early modern context "persisting rain or cool temperatures that were likely to attend its performances certainly contributed to arouse, among the audience, real feelings of empathy with the plight of the young lovers plodding along in the damp Athenian night."[32] But how might the possibilities for Jones's environmental irony play out today? Imagine that the performers race through the play's exposition and Egeus, an angry Athenian father, storms off stage having demanded his choice of suitor, a convent, or death for his daughter Hermia. Left alone, Hermia's preferred husband Lysander asks, "why is your cheek so pale? / How chance the roses there do fade so fast?" (*A Midsummer Night's Dream* 1.1.128–129). "Belike for want of rain," she replies, "which I could well beteem them from the tempest of mine eyes" (*Dream* 1.1.130–131). It is raining, so the line about the rain triggers laughter from the audience, signaling the moment where actors and audience relax into the Elizabethan play within the wider context of the twenty-first-century

---

[28] Tim Carroll, "Practising Behaviour to His Own Shadow," in *Shakespeare's Globe: A Theatrical Experiment*, eds. Christie Carson and Farah Karim-Cooper (Cambridge, Delhi and New York: Cambridge University Press, 2008), 39; Purcell, *Popular Shakespeare*, 45; Woods, "Globe Audiences: Spectatorship and Reconstruction at Shakespeare's Globe" (PhD thesis, Queen Mary University of London, 2012), 249.
[29] Carroll, "Practising Behaviour," 39 [original emphasis].
[30] Jones, 9 and 13.
[31] Sophie Chiari, *Shakespeare's Representation of Weather, Climate and Environment: The Early Modern "Fated Sky"* (Edinburgh: Edinburgh University Press, 2018), 39.
[32] Ibid.

theatrical event. Laughter arises because there is no want of rain. A performer's looking toward the sky, pulling a face, or wiping rain from their body performs disjuncture between the immediately lived weather conditions and Hermia's predicament, expressed in familiar terms amid unfamiliar, historical language. The laughter denotes the beginnings of temporary fellowship—or at least imagined temporary fellowship[33]—between the audience and the actors, and amongst audience members, that lasts for the play's duration.

Consider the same scene played in fair weather. "Belike for want of rain" passes without significant response (unless the actor chooses to step out of character to gesture towards the pleasant conditions). Theatergoers can invest in the fiction without a need to respond to the immediate weather. If the weather is acknowledged at all, it is with quiet contentment that there is no rain presently, or a quiet desire for rain if there has been drought. Neither of these responses is likely to be communicated at volume or with hearty laughter.

A further rainy iteration of the same scene might see soaking actors ignoring the weather and delivering the lines seriously, as if real rain underscores human pain. Such a version would also ignore the audience's being rained on, establishing an imaginary fourth wall between the play and those watching it.

The point is that there are strata here, as Jones observes, and these strata contain new possibilities in the contemporary moment, extending beyond a real/imaginary weather binary. Thinking through the implications of his historicist work for presentist ecocriticism Jones hypothesizes that "Any encounter with environmental irony, whether storms by Shakespeare, or, say, silence by John Cage, makes us briefly uncannily aware of our latent environmental attitudes."[34] In partnering Shakespeare as theater and Cage's performance art in the same thought about weather in reception as revealing "latent environmental attitudes," Jones touches polar edges of the contested patches to which I have alluded above. I trudge through them next.

What Open-Air Shakespeare Is Not

Shakespeare's plays were—we were told for a long time—written for early modern theater conventions, located in spoken references to geography, time, and weather that indicate where, when, and in what conditions scenes

---

[33] Sally Mackey and Sarah Cole, "Cuckoos in the Nest: Performing Place, Artists and Excess," *Applied Theatre Research* 1, no. 1 (2013): 52. Mackey and Cole cite Zygmunt Bauman *Community: Seeking Safety in an Insecure World* (Cambridge: Polity Press, 2001) on perfunctory "carnival bonds" that last only the length of the performance.

[34] Jones, *Shakespeare's Storms*, 21.

happen.[35] Bert States describes the Elizabethan stage as a "tabula rasa whereupon the actor could draw the ever-shifting pictures of the text."[36] Philip Schwyzer considers Rudyard Kipling's *Puck of Pook's Hill* (1906), where schoolchildren summon the spirit of Shakespeare's Puck with an outdoor re-enactment of *A Midsummer Night's Dream*, going as far as to suggest that "in the light of actual Elizabethan staging practices, the notion of Shakespeare writing *Dream* for outdoor performance in a Fairy Ring—or even imagining such a performance—can only seem absurd."[37] Responding to the spatial turn of the 1960s and 1970s, Peter Brook's famous declaration that "I can take any empty space and call it a bare stage"[38] was held up as an example of the erroneous, anthropocentric assumption that space can ever be "empty."[39] In direct contrast to States' early modern stage as a "tabula rasa," Miwon Kwon argues that as the term "site-specific" proliferated to describe a set of twentieth-century art practices, "the space of art was no longer perceived as a blank slate, a tabula rasa, but a real place."[40] The origins of contemporary site-specific performance traced through the late twentieth-century "happenings," the practices of the Situationists, and the work of the Land Artists all represent projects motivated by different political objectives to open-air Shakespeares.[41]

But if opposing conceptions of performance space as or not as a "tabula rasa" might appear to offer one easy way of distinguishing the respective spatial

---

[35] Alan Dessen, *Elizabethan Stage Conventions and Modern Interpreters* (Cambridge and New York: Cambridge University Press, 1984), 84–104; Darlene Farabee, *Shakespeare's Staged Spaces and Playgoers' Perceptions* (Basingstoke: Palgrave Macmillan, 2014), 93; Pauline Kiernan, *Staging Shakespeare at the Globe* (London: Macmillan Press, 1999), 71; Andrew Gurr in J. R. Mulryne and Margaret Shewring, *Shakespeare's Globe Rebuilt* (Cambridge: Cambridge University Press, 1997), 167; J. L. Styan, *Shakespeare's Stagecraft* (London and New York: Cambridge University Press, 1967), 44–7.

[36] Bert O. States, *Great Reckonings in Little Rooms: On the Phenomenology of Theater* (London and California: University of California Press, 1981), 56.

[37] Philip Schwyzer, "Shakespeare's Arts of Reenactment: Henry at Blackfriars, Richard at Rougemont," in *The Arts of Remembrance in Early Modern England: Memorial Cultures of the Post Reformation*, eds. Andrew Gordon and Thomas Rist (Farnham and Burlington: Ashgate, 2013), 179.

[38] Peter Brook, *The Empty Space* (London: McGibbon and Kee, 1968), 11.

[39] For examples of resistance to Brook, see Marvin Carlson, *The Haunted Stage: Theatre as a Memory Machine* (Michigan: University of Michigan Press, 2001), 132; Gay McAuley, *Space in Performance: Meaning Making in the Theatre* (Ann Arbor, MI: University of Michigan Press, 2000), 2; Purcell, *Popular Shakespeare*, 174.

[40] Miwon Kwon, *One Place after Another: Site-specific Art and Locational Identity* (Cambridge, MA: MIT Press, 2004), 11; Fiona Wilkie clarifies that "site does not operate simply as a synonym for place or space. Rather it is an idea that is often produced as a result of the performative framing of more than one place" in "The Production of 'Site': Site-Specific Theatre," in *A Concise Companion to Contemporary British and Irish Drama*, eds. Nadine Holdsworth and Mary Luckhurst (Oxford: Blackwell, 2008), 100.

[41] Stephen Hodge and Cathy Turner, "Site: Between Ground and Groundlessness," in *Histories and Practices of Live Art*, eds. Deirdre Heddon and Jennie Klein (Basingstoke: Palgrave Macmillan, 2012), 95.

aesthetics of early modern theater and contemporary site-specific performance, early modernists problematize any tempting simplicity by challenging the widely held belief that the Elizabethan stage was bare as "one of the biggest misapprehensions of early modern theatre criticism."[42] Spectacular stage effects, including changes to the material atmospheric composition of a theater—using smoke, gunpowder, fireworks, perfumes, incense, and herbs—mean that the Elizabethan theater space wasn't empty either.[43]

For these reasons, a striking number of influential theater scholars since the 1980s have utilized open-air Shakespeares to define what their work is not. It is worth hearing some of these clarifications at length, not to undertake a pedantic kind of "form-policing," but because scholarly views of creative practices that are constructed in opposition to open-air Shakespeares overlook the weather's affective contribution to how these (and therefore other) cultural works are received and the environmental attitudes that are revealed, rehearsed, and potentially challenged, in these encounters. Proposing a spatially experimental theater that he calls "environmental scenography" ("environment" referring to spatial configuration rather than then emergent "environmentalism"), Arnold Aronson argues that "most open-air theatres, the Shakespeare-in-the-park theatres [...] are *nothing more* than frontal stages moved outside."[44] My suggestion is simply that the act of "moving outside" into the weather fundamentally changes the experience of what is on the frontal stage. Bim Mason, writing on street theater and outdoor performance, differentiates from open-air Shakespeares in a similar vein, affording the audience-stage spatial configuration the prominent affective role:

> In London's Regent's Park every summer, plays by Shakespeare are performed at night with lights, on a stage, with a backdrop, wings and a seated audience. Although this is undeniably theatre outdoors and very professional, it is *not substantially different* from indoor theatre.[45]

Again, my proposition is that these performances are different in substance from indoor theater, for reasons that pertain to the framing of weather as theater in the context of the experience of the weather. More recently, Phil Smith

---

[42] Jenny Sager, *The Aesthetics of Spectacle in Early Modern Drama and Modern Cinema: Robert Greene's Theatre of Attractions* (Basingstoke: Palgrave, 2013), 1.

[43] Chloe Preedy, *Theatres of the Air: Representing Aerial Environments on the Early Modern Stage, 1576–1609* (Forthcoming).

[44] Arnold Aronson, *The History and Theory of Environmental Scenography* (Ann Arbor, Michigan: UMI Research Press, 1981), 3 (emphasis added).

[45] Bim Mason, *Street Theatre and Other Outdoor Performance* (London and New York: Routledge, 1992), 6–7 (emphasis added).

argues that the term site-specific "is now regularly *purloined* for 'Shakespeare in the Park,'"⁴⁶ apparently aggrieved. My thought is that the theft to which he alludes is more than the clumsy appropriation of the latest fashionable or avant-garde term, but a desire to account for how much weather and place affect the experience of Shakespeare "in the park." Rosemary Gaby notes Bridget Escolme's remark that "Shakespeare outside of the theatre might rather recall relentlessly cheerful summer productions, set against lovely, verdant or historical backdrops but in no way infected or inflected by 'site', except insofar as the actors are required to shout beyond their capacity."⁴⁷ With Gaby's counter to Escolme, I would agree that all outdoor Shakespeares are "inevitably infected and inflected by site"⁴⁸ and go further to argue that these inflections reveal how practitioners have historically conceived of their relationship with the environment, performing anthropocentricism in aesthetic approaches to representing nonhuman nature.

Theater and performance scholarship that addresses the current environmental crisis continues to bear out the same tendency. Downing Cless, who "eco-directs" canonical plays to accentuate their environmental themes, distances his work from outdoor Shakespeares by positing that "be it Shakespeare 'in the park' and 'under the stars' or massive reinventions of Eden on indoor stages [...] modern theater tends to romanticize nature in the few instances when it is not erased within domestic realism."⁴⁹ Twenty years after her 1994 landmark article first called for an "ecological theater," Una Chaudhuri expresses concerns that her prior "injunction to deal with 'nature itself' frequently led to the practice of site-specificity, or at least of outdoor theatre. Going to the park—if not to the forest—felt somehow more 'ecological' than staying cooped up in the black box of the theatre."⁵⁰ With the playwright Shonni Enelow, Chaudhuri clarifies that:

> The impulse to displace eco-performance from the cultural space of theatre into the supposedly natural space of a park reproduced a discourse that has come, eventually, to be recognized as one of the very sources of our current ecological crisis: the sentimental discourse of a romanticized nature, "capital N-nature", constructed as the pristine opposite of culture.⁵¹

---

⁴⁶ Phil Smith, "Turning Tourists into Performers: Revaluing Agency, Action and Space in Sites of Heritage Tourism," *Performance Research* 18, no. 2 (2010): 113 (emphasis added).
⁴⁷ Rosemary Gaby, *Open-Air Shakespeare: Under Australian Skies* (Basingstoke: Palgrave, 2014), 11.
⁴⁸ Gaby, *Open-Air Shakespeare*, 11.
⁴⁹ Cless, *Ecology and Environment in European Drama*, 6.
⁵⁰ Una Chaudhuri and Shonni Enelow, *Research Theatre, Climate Change, and The Ecocide Project* (Palgrave Macmillan: New York 2014), 29.
⁵¹ Chaudhuri and Enelow, *Research Theatre*, 29.

Using the same criticisms that have been levelled at outdoor Shakespeares—namely, the anthropocentric conception of space as a theatrical backdrop—Steve Bottoms, Aaron Franks, and Paula Kramer argue, "Environmental theatre and site-based performance practices have sometimes framed their given surroundings as the scenic backdrop to an anthropocentric drama."[52] Whether or not Bottoms, Franks, and Kramer are right to tarnish environmental theater and site-based performance with this resourcist brush in seeking to encourage new forms of relational, intersubjective "ecological" practices, it is interesting to note their sense that in 2012 theater had yet to engage successfully with ecology in outdoor settings. Most recently, Carl Lavery's cynicism about "claims for theatre's capacity to bring about behavior change, more often than not, through some ecstatic or enchanted immersion in 'environment' or 'nature'"[53]—and his skepticism of phenomenological suppositions that "the experience of the real is a kind of embodied lodestar, a way of dwelling that affirms the weather existing beyond the boundaries of a distorting theatricality that would deny the vitality of authentic, platial experience"[54]—boldly sets aside both site-specific works *and* representational theater, presenting a philosophical and aesthetic preference for postdramatic theater as climate. If doubt remained, Lavery's assertions seem to be the nail in the coffin for open-air Shakespeares.

In important respects, distancing creative works that seek explicitly to address environmental concerns from any uncritical advocacy for the in-situ experience of nonhuman nature makes sense, especially in light of legitimate criticisms of a perceived conservatism in both Shakespeare and open-air theater, and the extractavism of any practice that romantically, sentimentally utilizes landscape as picturesque theatrical scenery. In concert with these warnings, this book unpacks the damaging discourse of a romanticized nature in both historical and contemporary performances of Shakespeare's plays in the open-air. I share the suspicion of simplistic approaches to theater, imagined as a tool for behavior change, and also have misgivings about uncritical assumptions that "authentic" nature experiences outdoors are automatically in some way "ecological." I am likewise apprehensive of instrumental approaches to reception that seek to utilize "findings" to manipulate future hypothetical audiences. Cumulatively, however, this collection of dismissals contributes to building a homogenous category

---

[52] Steve Bottoms, Aaron Franks, and Paula Kramer, "Editorial: On Ecology," *Performance Research* 17, no. 4 (2012): 1.

[53] Carl Lavery, "Introduction," in *Performance and Ecology: What Can Theatre Do?* ed. Carl Lavery (London and New York: Routledge, 2018), 1.

[54] Carl Lavery, "From Weather to Climate: A Note," *Performance Research* 23, no. 4–5 (2018): 7.

of open-air theater as epitomizing opposition to consciously progressive or environmentally engaged arts practices, which diminishes an acknowledgment of just how much and in what ways the weather influences reception at open-air Shakespeares and, beyond them, at all kinds of performance in the weather. While I am sympathetic to the arguments that are outlined above, I worry that they run the risk of inscribing an indoor/outdoor binary even in their rejection of the nature/culture split. My aspiration is to advocate for more care in advancing *any* form as more environmentally "efficacious" than another.[55] There is considerable work still to be done in unpacking the ecological affects of all kinds of theater and performance—including outdoor, site-specific, immersive, *and* varied representational practices undertaken inside theaters (none of which are discrete, generalizable categories anyway).

One way to begin to contest these histories might be to think about works as united by their happening in weather, encountered through the frame of the theatrical event, prior to classifying them by other spatial configurations or aesthetic arrangements. David Williams's entry on "Weather" for the journal *Performance Research* usefully remarks that:

> all outdoor site work necessarily engages with the unpredictabilities of weather, either opening itself to the generative possibilities of weather's creative agency within the work—weather as co-author of events in contexts where site is conceived as active medium—or (fruitlessly) trying to deny it entry to the site as "container"/backdrop.[56]

Rather than thinking in terms of indoor or outdoor performance, classifying theater and performance by its deliberate positioning "in the weather" might offer a more generative starting place for considering its affects. Going further than Williams's comment, Martin Welton ventures that the weather conditions in which a performance is encountered extend to climate and have a bearing on "*aisthesis*—what Jacques Rancière calls 'the sensible fabric of experience in which [works of art] are produced,'" and, Welton adds, the conditions by which they are "experienced or received."[57] Thinking about Rancière's "sensible fabric of experience" in relation to a contemporary open-air dance piece, Welton finds "no

---

[55] Chaudhuri and Enelow, *Research Theatre*, 29, explain their approach to producing *Carla and Lewis* in a black-box theatre studio: "rather than simply refusing the difference between inside and outside and collapsing the two, we wanted to preserve that difference but treat it as a point of departure for a dynamically interpenetrating world in which the matter inside the black-box of theatre is as alive, as lively (or as "vibrant," to invoke Jane Bennett's important theory) as the matter in a forest or a field."

[56] David Williams, "Weather," *Performance Research* 11, no. 3 (2006): 142.

[57] Martin Welton, "Making Sense of Air: Choreography and Climate in *Calling Tree*," *Performance Research* 23, no. 3 (2018): 80–90, 84.

necessary cause and effect relationship between being in weather and one's state of mind or feelings" but argues that "such feelings are as recognizably climatic as subjective."[58] It is to the sensible part of this fabric of human experience, perceptible in performances of weathering, that I turn next.

Performing Weathering

Human critters—to disperse Donna Haraway's levelling term—are mostly muddling along in the weather as the earth's climate changes.[59] Richard Mabey refers to our muddled adaptations to a changing climate as "a tragicomic street theatre of daily coping," noticing the performative nature of weathering as a quotidian practice.[60] Weathering refers to survival as much as to bodies and objects altered by meteorological forces. To weather something can mean to be reduced and to exhibit negative traces of the atmospheric wearing down that causes this change. To weather something also means to make it through—maybe changed, but through: if you weather the storm, you're still there when the storm is over (and weathering continues in the aftermath, until you're worn away). Weathering can be generative: it is the process through which soils are made. In geography, Eliza de Vet calls for more methodological variety, specificity, and care in researching what she calls "weather-ways"—physical and discursive practices of responding to the weather in everyday life.[61] This book proposes weathering as a way of thinking about "audiencing" at outdoor Shakespeares. Weathering cuts across the chapters, thematically, across time, space, and weather, and irrespective of approaches to staging or actors' performance choices. Theatrical productions instigate performances of weathering as a set of physical and discursive practice from theatergoers, who enact heightened quotidian performances of weathering with spoken utterances and physical gestures. While the performances of weathering identified in this book emerge thematically as an activity in their own right from ethnographic research amongst theatergoers for open-air

---

[58] Welton, "Making Sense of Air," 84.
[59] Donna Haraway, *Staying with the Trouble: Making Kin in the Chthulucene* (Durham and London: Duke University Press, 2016), 169, for critters as an "everyday idiom for varmints of all sorts. Scientists talk about their 'critters' all the time; and so do ordinary people all over the U.S., but perhaps especially in the South. The taint of 'creatures' and 'creation' does not stick to 'critters'; if you see such a semiotic barnacle, scrape it off."
[60] Richard Mabey, *Turned Out Nice Again: On Living with the Weather* (London: Profile Books, 2013), 90.
[61] Eliza de Vet, "Exploring Weather-Related Experiences and Practices: Examining Methodological Approaches," *Area* 45, no. 2 (2013): 198–206; "Weather-Ways: Experiencing and Responding to Everyday Weather" (PhD Thesis, University of Wollongong, 2014).

Shakespeares, they share concerns with philosophical approaches to theorizing the weather as ways to understand climate through the body.

For Astrida Neimanis and Rachel Loewen-Walker, weathering is ontological.[62] The feminist new materialist origins of their argument for weathering extend Stacy Alaimo's "transcorporeality,"[63] which develops Karen Barad's "intra-action,"[64] to think of weathering as ongoing process of becoming that traverses bodies, human and nonhuman: "We are not the masters of climate, nor are we just spatially 'in' it," Neimanis and Loewen-Walker provoke, "As weather-bodies, we are thick with climatic intra-actions."[65] Together, they propose that weathering offers one way to "reduce the distance between the enormity of climate change and the immediacy of our flesh."[66] Taken on these terms, worlding as weathering goes further than phenomenological arguments for bodies being *in* weather—such as Tim Ingold's thinking in terms of "immersion" or "inhabitation"[67]—because Neimanis and Loewen-Walker offer that all becomings are intra-actions with weather. Morgan Vanek maintains that the politics of the weather comes from how humans are differently exposed to it.[68] "We're" all in different storms with and without access to different kinds of metaphorical boats. Accordingly, in Neimanis's later work on weathering with Jennifer Hamilton, weathering becomes "a practice and a tactic: to weather means to pay attention to how bodies and places respond to weather-worlds which they are also making; to weather responsively means to consider how we might weather differently—better—and act in ways that can move towards such change."[69] While an intentional practice such as Neimanis and Hamilton envisage is beyond the findings of this book, theirs is a good reminder that access to shelter is a primary requirement for the act of naming any kind of activity—theater or otherwise—"open-air."

Social sciences research suggests that people in industrialized countries tend to spend at least 93 percent of their time indoors.[70] Studies also variously

---

[62] Astrida Neimanis and Rachel Loewen-Walker, "*Weathering*: Climate Change and the 'Thick Time' of Transcorporeality," *Hypatia* 29, no. 3 (2014): 558–75.
[63] Stacy Alaimo, *Bodily Natures: Science, Environment, and the Material Self* (Bloomington: Indiana University Press 2010).
[64] Karen Barad, *Meeting the University Halfway: Quantum Physics and the Entanglement of Matter and Meaning* (Durham and London: Duke University Press, 2007).
[65] Neimanis and Loewen-Walker, "*Weathering*," 558.
[66] Neimanis and Loewen-Walker, 562.
[67] Tim Ingold, *Being Alive: Essays on Movement, Knowledge and Description* (Oxon and New York: Routledge, 2011).
[68] Morgan Vanek, "Where the Weather Comes From," *The Goose Journal* 17, no. 1, 46 (2018), 1–13.
[69] Astrida Neimanis and Jennifer Mae Hamilton, "Open Space Weathering," *Feminist Review* 118, no. 1 (2018), 80–4, 81.
[70] Matthew C. Keller et al., "A Warm Heart and a Clear Head. The Contingent Effects of Weather on Mood and Cognition," *Psychological Science* 16, no. 9 (2005): 724–31, 725.

demonstrate how the weather influences human behaviors, emotions, financial markets, productivity, mood, physical and mental health, emotional vulnerability, self-control, risk perception, the way media cover the news, tipping in restaurants, dating, flirting, hitchhikers' successes, aggression in sports, how we measure life satisfaction, and whether we show up to vote or respond to surveys—to name just some of its affects.[71] Without making too great a generalization, it is fair to venture that many of the people in theater audiences for open-air Shakespeares in the UK spend significant proportions of a day otherwise indoors. In trying to acknowledge how the weather inflects experiences, I hope to complicate the invigorating, masculine "outdoorsy" activities, of which Timothy Morton is rightly wary; fearful of "the injunction to turn on, tune in, shut up, go outdoors and breathe Nature?"[72] How to be simultaneously sensitive to experiential, embodied responses and alert to the cultural constructions of "being outdoors" that correspond with oppressive forms of masculinity, nationalism, ableism, and resourcism? Extending Tim Ingold's argument that "it is one thing to think *about* land and weather and another to think *in* them," I advocate for thinking about performances that are consciously placed in the weather—holding onto the problems and contradictions outlined above.[73] *Weathering Shakespeare* interrogates the attempted—sometimes successful, sometimes unsuccessful—appropriation of the weather for Shakespearean performance. It also looks at productions of plays by Shakespeare that imagine the weather, in Williams' words, as "co-author of events."[74] Together, this set of productions shares the fact of happening in weather. I think of weathering as their common denominator prior to classifying

---

[71] Anna Bassi, "Weather, Mood, and Voting: An Experimental Analysis of the Effect of Weather beyond Turnout," (2013); Anna Bassi, Riccardo Colacito and Paolo Fulghieri, "'O Sole Mio: An Experimental Analysis of Weather and Risk Attitudes in Financial Decisions," *The Review of Financial Studies* 26, no. 7 (2013): 1824–52; Alexander Cohen, "Sweating the Vote: Heat and Abstention in the US House of Representatives," *Political Science and Politics* 45, no. 1 (2012): 74–7; Marie Connolly, "Some Like It Mild and Not Too Wet: The Influence of Weather on Subjective Well-Being," *Journal of Happiness Studies* 14 (2013): 457–73; Curtis Craig et al., "A Relationship between Temperature and Aggression in NFL Football Penalties," *Journal of Sport and Health Science* 5 (2016): 205–10; Sean Masaki Flynn and Adam Eric Greenburg, "Does Weather Actually Affect Tipping? An Empirical Analysis of Time-Series Data," *Journal of Applied Psychology* 42, no. 3 (2012): 702–16; Nicolas Guéguen, "Weather and Courtship Behavior: A Quasi-Experiment with the Flirty Sunshine," *Social Influence* 8, no. 4 (2013): 312–19; Nicolas Guéguen and Jordy Stefa, "Hitchhiking and the 'Sunshine Driver': Further Effects of Weather Conditions of Helping Behavior," *Psychological Reports: Sociocultural Issues in Psychology* 113, no. 3 (2013): 994–1000; Sylvia Kämpfer and Michael Mutz, "On the Sunny Side of Life: Sunshine Effects on Life Satisfaction," *Social Indicators Research* 110 (2013): 579–95; Claudia Schmiedeberg and Jette Schröder, "Does Weather Really Influence the Measurement of Life Satisfaction?" *Social Indicators Research* 117 (2014): 387–99; Bu Zhong and Yong Zhou, "'Under the Weather': The Weather Effects on U.S. Newspaper Coverage of the 2008 Beijing Olympics," *Mass Communication and Society* 15, no. 4 (2012): 559–77.
[72] Timothy Morton, *The Ecological Thought* (Cambridge and London: Harvard University Press, 2010), 16.
[73] Ingold, "Earth, Sky, Wind, and Weather," 29 [original emphasis].
[74] Williams, "Weather," 142.

them by other spatial configurations or aesthetic arrangements, and observe how practitioners' use of space in conjunction with their treatment of early modern plays instigates performances of weathering from audiences in attendance.

In thinking of reiterated cultural behavior by theater audiences as performance, my work has affinities with Caroline Heim's extensive argument for the "audience as performer."[75] Heim draws on Erving Goffman's work on "social performance" and asks her reader "to gaze not at the stage, but at the audience."[76] She argues for the performing audience with "its own idiosyncrasies, prescribed gestures and spontaneous expressions."[77] Performances of weathering at open-air Shakespeares are undertaken for the benefit of the individual self, for others within an audience, and also for the actors, as a demonstration of commitment to the event. Physical responses to the weather form a "repertoire" of movement, to think with Diana Taylor's compelling argument for how "expressive behaviour (performance) transmit[s] cultural memory and identity,"[78] underscoring spoken conversations. Amongst themselves, theatergoers glance, grimace, and giggle at one another; wriggle restlessly in the heat; fan themselves with theater programs; ostentatiously wipe moisture; brace bodies against the wind; compare sodden clothes; and silently share pleasure, discomfort, and strategies for staying dry—all while attempting not to disrupt the actors. Spoken conversations about the plays all arise from within a movement vocabulary of performed weathering. These performances of weathering comprise lived practices enacted by real bodies in a world and are more material than metaphor.[79]

Where daily coping is performative, performances of weathering represent affective encounters with climate. Philip Smith and Nicolas Howe make a case for "climate change within the public sphere [taking] the form of a social drama."[80] They appeal to an Aristotelian model of *drama*, however, and pursue

---

[75] Caroline Heim, *Audience as Performer: The Changing Role of Theatre Audiences in the Twenty-First Century*. (London and New York: Routledge, 2016), 1–2.
[76] Heim, *Audience as Performer*, 1.
[77] Heim, 2.
[78] Diana Taylor, *The Archive and the Repertoire: Performing Cultural Memory in the Americas* (Durham and London: Duke University Press, 2003), 16–33 and xvi.
[79] Stacy Alaimo, *Exposed: Environmental Politics and Pleasures in Posthuman Times* (Minneapolis and London: University of Minnesota Press, 2016), 5, argues for "Performing exposure as an ethical and political act means to reckon with—rather than disavow—such horrific events and to grapple with the particular entanglements of vulnerability and complicity that radiate from disasters and their terribly disjunctive connection to everyday life in the industrialized world." Performing weathering in this book is not the same as "performing exposure" as Alaimo conceives of it. This book's performances of weathering are neither intentionally ethical nor political acts, although they have ethical and political implications.
[80] Philip Smith and Nicolas Howe, *Climate Change as Social Drama: Global Warming in the Public Sphere* (New York: Cambridge University Press, 2015), 6.

a Geertzian anthropology of "thick description" that reads culture as text.[81] As such, theorizing climate change as a social drama gets only part way toward identifying the insights that performance studies might offer when it comes to climate and weather. *Weathering Shakespeare* attempts to think with Dwight Conquergood's work on performance and ethnography instead, rejecting the ethnocentrism of culture as something that can be translated into words by observers and advocating instead for a decolonized "view [of performance] from ground level, in the thick of things," circulating "within a community of memory and practice."[82] Crucially, Conquergood is not "replacing, the romance of performance for the authority of the text," but "embracing both written scholarship and creative work, papers and performances."[83] In the ethnographies encouraged by Conquergood, performances of weathering might be conscious of and attentive to what Neimanis and Loewen-Walker call "the spatial overlap of human bodies and weathery nature."[84]

I hesitate to invoke Diana Taylor's archive and repertoire because her context is marginalized communities in the Americas, from whose experience the audiences in this book are far. Attending an open-air Shakespeare is obviously a low-risk, low-stakes, and time-limited leisure activity. Theater audiences include people many of whom will be the last to feel the worst effects of a changing climate. That said, a repertoire can sustain the status quo as well as enact subversive or survival tactics, and the cultural construction of climate transmitted through performance at these theatrical events bears thinking through with reference to history, the weather, and national identity.[85]

Climate, Weather, and National Character

Lucian Boia points out that the weather "is probably the most common dialogue between human beings."[86] This is partly because weather-talk, as Jan Golinski explains, is an example of "'phatic' communication, in which the primary

---

[81] Clifford Geertz, *The Interpretation of Cultures* (New York: Basic Books, 1973), 33.
[82] Dwight Conquergood, "Performance Studies: Interventions and Radical Research," *The Drama Review* 46, no. 2 (2002): 146.
[83] Conquergood, "Performance Studies," 151.
[84] Neimanis and Loewen-Walker, "*Weathering*," 560.
[85] Claire Cochrane, *Twentieth-Century British Theatre: Industry, Art and Empire* (Cambridge: Cambridge University Press, 2011), 5, argues with Edward Said's recommendation for contrapuntal reading of the cultural archive, proposing that "not all 'other' histories are constructed in direct opposition to the dominant discourse, some actually co-operate with it."
[86] Lucian Boia, *The Weather in the Imagination* (London: Reaktion Books, 2005), 10.

meaning lies not in what is referred to but in the social bonds strengthened by the exchange."[87] Mike Hulme argues that the weather is the human body's sensory encounter with climate and he therefore proposes that "climate—as it is imagined, studied and acted upon—needs to be understood, first and foremost, culturally."[88] It is not just humans and nonhumans who are weathered, Hulme maintains, but cultures too, which "bear the imprint of the weather in which they exist and to which they respond."[89] Wolfgang Behringer's *A Cultural History of Climate* (2010) takes a similar view, maintaining that how humans react to climate change is a "cultural question."[90] Golinski proceeds to argue that "the cultural significance of our weather worries" today stems from "prevailing concerns about modern life itself, which is thought to have exposed us to new hazards by trespassing upon the natural environment."[91] As Amitav Ghosh puts it, "There was never a time [...] when the forces of weather did *not* have a bearing on our lives—but neither has there ever been a time when they have pressed themselves on us with such relentless directness."[92]

In *The Weather in the Imagination* (2005), Boia provides an overview of centuries of damaging philosophical arguments for environmental determinism, spanning antiquity to the present, that have deployed climate as the shaper of national character under the umbrella premise that "Human beings are different because they live under different skies."[93] In one early rejoinder to environmental determinism, the Scottish enlightenment philosopher David Hume advances social and moral causes instead, disavowing any "static or definitive 'national character' in the first place."[94] Today, however, Boia continues, anthropogenic climate change connects horrific acts carried out by certain groups of humans to other humans under the banner of environmental determinism *and* horrific

---

[87] Jan Golinski, "Time, Talk, and the Weather in Eighteenth-Century Britain," in *Weather, Climate, Culture*, eds. Sarah Strauss and Ben Orlove (Oxford and New York: Berg, 2003), 29.
[88] Mike Hulme, *Weathered: Cultures of Climate* (Los Angeles and London: Sage, 2017), xii.
[89] Hulme, *Weathered*, xv.
[90] Wolfgang Behringer, *A Cultural History of Climate*, trans. Patrick Camiller (Cambridge and Malden: Polity Press, 2010), 217; John E. Thornes, "Cultural Climatology and the Representation of Sky, Atmosphere, Weather and Climate in Selected Art Works of Constable, Monet and Eliasson," *Geoforum* 39 (2008): 571, advances a new field of "cultural climatology" as "climatology and geography that is attempting to work across the divide between the social and physical sciences [...] currently populated by both human and physical geographers, especially those working on the impacts of climate on culture and culture on climate."
[91] Jan Golinski, *British Weather and the Climate of Enlightenment* (The University of Chicago Press: Chicago and London, 2007). See also James Rodger Fleming, Vladimir Jankovic, and Deborah R. Cohen, eds., *Intimate Universality: Local and Global Themes in the History of Weather and Climate* (Science History Publications: Sagamore Beach, 2006).
[92] Ghosh, *The Great Derangement*, 62.
[93] Boia, *The Weather in the Imagination*, 11.
[94] Boia, 53.

acts carried out by (many of the same) groups of humans to the nonhuman environment, highlighting the existential dangers of both environmental determinism *and* any absolute denial of climate's "undeniable presence."[95] Simply, powerful people have killed, enslaved, and impoverished others bolstered by environmentally determinist philosophies. At the same time, anthropocentric responses that reject the shaping forces of climate and environment—such as Hume's—have contributed to the catastrophic failure to acknowledge the climate's impact upon the capacity for life on earth, ironically exacerbating the damage to both human and nonhuman life that environmental determinism empowered.

Golinski finds that English "relations between climate and national character were first articulated during the eighteenth-century Enlightenment."[96] He expands that at this time:

> The weather was also thought to have shaped the character of the people, their temperament having been hardened by a climate that was often bracing but rarely harsh. It was believed that the national character benefited from the stimulus of frequent atmospheric change.[97]

Pertinent to open-air Shakespeares as I find them, one of the illustrative examples upon which Golinski alights is the eighteenth-century historian John Campbell, who posits that "the beneficial consequences of the British climate were to be found in the character of its people—in their energetic initiative, their willingness to explore other parts of the world, their resistance to political tyranny, and their ample share of creative genius."[98] Golinski builds a compelling argument for the weather as having "always escaped comprehension within systems of enlightenment rationality."[99] Weather evaded capture by culture, even at the time when science, rationality, and human exceptionalism were most triumphantly celebrated. Bruno Latour's provocation that "we have never been modern" gains traction in Golinski's research, which not only uncovers the ideological work to which the weather has been put but simultaneously evidences how weather-anxieties persist in part today from the niggle that, despite best efforts, the weather always gave the enlightenment the slip.[100]

---

[95] Boia, 54.
[96] Golinski, "Time, Talk, and the Weather," 18.
[97] Golinski, *British Weather*, 58.
[98] Golinski, 60–1.
[99] Golinski, "Time, Talk, and the Weather," 19.
[100] Bruno Latour, *We Have Never Been Modern*, trans. Catherine Porter (Cambridge, MA: Harvard University Press, 1993).

Even after the Second World War (a time now associated with "The Great Acceleration"), Nikolaus Pevsner still exemplifies a typically dangerously determinist approach to art criticism in proposing that certain English "national traits" can be found by looking at "race and climate": race, he wavers, is "a dangerous tool" but with climate "one is on safe ground,"[101] confident of stability and regularity. He pronounces a "moderate" climate whose qualities are "immediately reflected" in English art exemplifying "moderation, reasonableness, rationalism, observation and conservatism" in conjunction with just the appropriate—of "imagination, fantasy and irrationalism."[102] Historical intersections between race and climate explain the lingering whiteness of many open-air Shakespeares—a legacy of British Imperialism and the demographic make-up of rural populations, sustained by performances of nation and enabled by culture and the weather. The claim that a national climate determines national character persists and needs to be viewed in conjunction with the residue of British Imperialism—acquired with the assistance of environmentally determinist philosophies.

This book attends, then, to the cultural particularity of performances of weathering in response to open-air Shakespeares, noting the composition of climate and nation performed in concert with the weather. Theatergoers perform banal acts of weathering in support of Hulme's proposition that "although the English might not mention climate explicitly in their weather-talk, one can see how the idea of an expected English climate is the shared tacit framework which brings intelligibility, order and meaning into their social interactions."[103] Hulme's specifying "English" rather than "British" climates extends Pyrs Gruffudd's observation that during the Second World War, whilst rhetoric frequently appealed to "'Britishness,' the myths and landscapes presented were generally those of England."[104] When Hulme identifies "English" weather-talk, he extends these myths and landscapes to the present.

In performances of weathering at open-air Shakespeares, the myths and landscapes of Englishness continue to infuse "imagined communities"[105] that are "creatively produced or staged."[106] Michael Billig argues that the weather continues to be "routinely nationalised" in the UK as a form of "banal

---

[101] Nikolaus Pevsner, *The Englishness of English Art* (The Architectural Press, London, 1955), 184–6.
[102] Pevsner, *The Englishness of English Art*, 184–6.
[103] Hulme, *Weathered*, 5 [original emphasis]).
[104] Pyrs Gruffudd, "Reach for the Sky: The Air and English Cultural Nationalism," *Landscape Research* 16, no. 2 (1991): 19 and 23.
[105] Benedict Anderson, *Imagined Communities: Reflections on the Origin and Spread of Nationalism*, revised edition (London and New York: Verso, 2016).
[106] Jen Harvie, *Staging the UK* (Manchester and New York: Manchester University Press, 2005), 5.

nationalism."[107] Deictic references to "the weather" in UK reports, for instance, that speak of rain across "the country" without mentioning England by name, quietly contribute to practices of homeland making. A "sizzling-heat" news headline obviously refers to a hot UK day as "Hot weather abroad would not be newsworthy."[108] Billig expands:

> A homeland making move transforms meteorology into *the* weather. […] "The weather" appears as an objective, physical category, yet it is contained within national boundaries. At the same time it is known that the universe of weather is larger than the nation. There is "abroad"; there is "around the world." These are elsewhere beyond "our" elsewhere. […] All this is reproduced in the newspapers; and all this, in its small way, helps to reproduce the homeland as the place in which "we" are at home, "here" at the habitual centre of "our" daily universe.[109]

Building on Billig, Michael Skey's 2011 research into national identity in everyday life continues to find the weather "routinely perceived and articulated in national terms."[110] Shakespeare, we know, has been used to do similar nationalist work, devastatingly across what was the British Empire. Throughout this book, a banal nationalism is "flagged"[111]—to continue using Billig's terms—in performances of weathering that respond to Shakespeare.

A self-consciously abashed insider pride in English weather-talk endures despite Timothy Morton's assertion that "reassuringly trivial conversation about the weather" is no longer possible because it now "either trails off into a disturbingly meaningful silence, or someone mentions global warning."[112] Contra Morton, Kate Fox's *Watching the English* (2004) continues to insist on weather-talk as a pretext for social exchanges. Moreover, Fox ventures that "the weather may be one of the few things about which the English are still unselfconsciously and unashamedly patriotic."[113] Sue Clifford, of the English environmental charity Common Ground, maintains that "The national stereotype is well founded and,

---

[107] Michael Billig, *Banal Nationalism* (Los Angeles and London Sage, 1995), 174.
[108] Billig, *Banal Nationalism*, 116.
[109] Billig, 117.
[110] Michael Skey, *National Belonging and Everyday Life: The Significance of Nationhood in an Uncertain World* (Basingstoke: Palgrave Macmillan, 2011), 42.
[111] Billig, *Banal Nationalism*, 93.
[112] Timothy Morton, *The Ecological Thought*, 28, uses theatrical metaphors when he argues that "The weather no longer exists as a neutral-seeming background against which events take place. When weather becomes climate—when it enters the realms of science and history—it can no longer be a stage set."
[113] Kate Fox, *Watching the English: The Hidden Rules of English Behaviour* (Hodder and Stoughton: London, 2004), 33.

given our quixotic weather, why not?"[114] Popular nonfiction titles, including *And Now the Weather: A Celebration of Our National Obsession* (2017), published by the BBC, *The MET Office Book of the British Weather: UK Weather Month by Month* (2010), and *The Story of the British and Their Weather* (2015), reinforce the insider genre in a similar manner.[115] *Weathering Shakespeare* is concerned with the construction of an English climate present in responses to the weather at open-air theater, situating cultural performances—social and theatrical—as globally affective and attempting to bring together the cultural and experiential aspects of weathering as performance in response to Shakespeare in the open-air.

Shakespearean Ecocriticism and Ecotheater

Wide-ranging literary ecocritical research concerned with Shakespeare and his early modern contemporaries is now variously attentive to subjects vast as weather and climate, pastoral, landscapes, seascapes and oceans, migration and displacement, trees, plants, animals, soil, environmental degradation, fossil fuels, atmospheric pollution, gendered and queer naturecultures, rural and urban spaces, and waste, to identify just some of the subjects amongst mushrooming ecological concerns.[116] This book does not analyze performance as an instrument for conveying literary-ecocritical messages.

---

[114] Sue Clifford and Angela King with Gail Vines, Darren Giddings, and Kate O'Farrell for Common Ground, *England in Particular: A Celebration of the Commonplace, the Local, Vernacular and the Distinctive* (London: Hodder & Stoughton, 2006), 435.

[115] Patrick Nobbs, *The Story of the British and Their Weather: From Frost Fairs to Indian Summers* (Gloucestershire: Amberley 2015); Alison Maloney, *And Now the Weather: A Celebration of Our National Obsession* (London: Penguin, 2017).

[116] Lynne Bruckner and Dan Brayton, eds., *Ecocritical Shakespeare* (Farnham and Burlington: Ashgate, 2011); Todd Borlik, *Ecocriticism and Early Modern English literature: Green Pastures* (London: Routledge, 2011); Dan Brayton, *Shakespeare's Ocean: An Ecocritical Exploration* (Charlottesville: University of Virginia Press, 2012); Sophie Chiari, *Shakespeare's Representation of Weather, Climate and Environment: The Early Modern "Fated Sky"* (Edinburgh: Edinburgh University Press, 2018); Craig Dionne and Lowell Duckert, "Introduction: Shake—Scene," *Early Modern Culture* 13, no. 5 (2018): 72–8; Gabriel Egan, *Green Shakespeare: From Ecopolitics to Ecocriticism* (Oxon and New York: Routledge, 2006) and *Shakespeare and Ecocritical Theory* (London: Bloomsbury, 2015); Simon C. Estok, *Ecocriticism and Shakespeare: Reading Ecophobia* (New York: Palgrave Macmillan, 2011); Jennifer Mae Hamilton, *This Contentious Storm: An Ecocritical and Performance History of King Lear* (London: Bloomsbury, 2017); Andreas Höfele, *Stage, Stake and Scaffold: Humans and Animals in Shakespeare's Theatre* (Oxford: Oxford University Press, 2011), Gwilym Jones, *Shakespeare's Storms*. Manchester: Manchester University Press, 2015); Randall Martin, *Shakespeare & Ecology* (Oxford: Oxford University Press, 2015); Steve Mentz, *At the Bottom of Shakespeare's Ocean* (London and New York: Continuum, 2009); Jennifer Munroe and Rebecca Laroche, *Shakespeare and Ecofeminist Theory* (London: Bloomsbury, 2017); Vin Nardizzi, *Wooden Os: Shakespeare's Theatres and England's Trees* (Toronto, Buffalo and London: University of Toronto Press, 2013); Robert N. Watson, *Back to Nature: The Green and the Real in the Late Renaissance* (Philadelphia: University of Pennsylvania Press, 2006). This is an indicative and not an exhaustive list of work in a rapidly expanding field.

Historicist studies of early modern literature and theater offer subterranean water for the work. They bubble up from time to time, but the reader will find less of an exploration of ecocritical readings of early modern drama translated into performance than an attempt to present open-air Shakespeares in their performance contexts in their own right. In these regards, *Weathering Shakespeare* rides the "whirl" of presentism clinging to historical context.[117] Shakespeare's words—and the words of his collaborators on plays given his name—occasionally find their way into the analysis, but they are less the focus than the performances in their own historical moments, viewed from today.

Until recently, eco-critics largely re-read early modern drama as literature or considered the works in their original performance context rather than analyzing the plays in subsequent performances.[118] Although Randall Martin proposes in *Shakespeare & Ecology* (2016) that "Shakespeare's greatest possibilities for becoming our eco-contemporary lie not in academic discourse but in performance,"[119] Gwilym Jones still remarks in a 2017 survey of Renaissance ecocriticism that few ecocritics have considered performance, while noting budding presentist and historicist work.[120] As Jennifer Hamilton's vibrant and insightful "big" performance history of *King Lear* since demonstrates, theater history and ecocriticism will benefit from keeping more company in the future.[121] The 2018 Special Issue of *Shakespeare Bulletin* on "Shakespeare and Ecology in Performance"—which Randall Martin and I edited, and to which Hamilton also contributes[122]—further contains articles on open-air productions in different climates: Gretchen Minton dramaturgs *Macbeth* in wildfire smoke,[123] Rebecca Salazar analyzes *Hamlet* after hurricanes,[124] Rob Conkie worries about the lack of storms for *King Lear*,[125] and I remember a blustery encounter with

---

[117] Cohen and Duckert, *Veer Ecology*, 3.
[118] Cless, *Ecology and Environment in European Drama*, 91–118, includes a chapter on "ecodirecting" *A Midsummer Night's Dream* and *The Tempest*, although Cless's use of his own productions as case studies limits the scope of his study; David Hartwig, "The Place of Shakespeare: Performing *King Lear* and *The Tempest* in an Endangered World" (PhD thesis, University of Warwick, 2010) is another exception.
[119] Martin, *Shakespeare & Ecology*, 167.
[120] Gwilym Jones, "Environmental Renaissance Studies," *Literature Compass* 14, no. 10 (2017): 14.
[121] Hamilton, *This Contentious Storm*.
[122] Randall Martin and Evelyn O'Malley, "Introduction: Eco-Shakespeare in Performance," *Shakespeare Bulletin* 36, no. 3 (2018): 377–90.
[123] Rob Conkie, "Nature's Above Art (An Illustrated Guide)," *Shakespeare Bulletin* 36, no. 3 (2018): 391–408.
[124] Gretchen E. Minton, "'… The Season of All Natures': Montana Shakespeare in the Parks' Global Warming *Macbeth*," *Shakespeare Bulletin* 36, no. 3 (2018): 429–48.
[125] Rebecca Salazar, "A Rogue and Pleasant Stage: Performing Ecology in Outdoor Shakespeares," *Shakespeare Bulletin* 36, no. 3 (2018): 449–66.

All's Well That Ends Well.[126] Katherine Steele Brokaw and Paul Prescott's ongoing work with Shakespeare in Yosemite, begun in 2017, develops applied theatre approaches to ecology and outdoor performance, "leveraging Shakespeare's cultural currency" alongside the words of the environmentalist John Muir.[127] Packed conference seminars and panels on ecological topics and early modern drama suggest the continued flourishing of these fields.

If the context of an endangered planet was reportedly slow to reach drama, theater, and performance studies—as it was to reach Shakespeare—it has mycelium roots now. Parallel to the above work in literary and early modern ecocriticism, and likewise parallel to growing public awareness of anthropogenic global warming beyond the scientific community, a rapidly growing array of scholarship now addresses diverse environmental concerns. Despite calls from Una Chaudhuri and Erika Munk for theater to engage seriously with ecology in 1994, in 2007 Baz Kershaw still finds the field to be "ambivalent."[128] In 2012, Wendy Arons and Theresa J. May's note in *Readings in Performance and Ecology* that "critical and theoretical intersections between literary ecocriticism and theatre/performance studies […] have been slowly but increasingly articulated over the past two decades."[129] In this collection, Arons and May call for "ecodramaturgy"—a term originally coined by May—as "theatre and performance making that puts ecological reciprocity and community at the centre of its theatrical and thematic intent."[130] More recently, May revises ecodramaturgy to designate performance that confronts "environmental justice, sustainability and democracy" explicitly.[131] But although Arons and May have reasonable grounds to argue that in 2012 "as a scholarly and artistic community we have largely failed to rise to Una Chaudhuri's [1994] challenge,"[132] and Stephen Bottoms has cause to lament the lack of interest from the discipline of drama and theater studies more broadly in 2013,[133] these cries were answered by more theoretical sophistication, proliferating publications, complex performance

---

[126] Evelyn O'Malley, "'To Weather a Play': Audiences, Outdoor Shakespeares, and Avant-Garde Nostalgia at The Willow Globe," *Shakespeare Bulletin* 36, no. 3 (2018): 409–27.
[127] Katherine Steele Brokow and Paul Prescott, "Shakespeare in Yosemite: Applied Theatre in a National Park," *Critical Survey* 31, no. 4 (2019): 15–28.
[128] Kershaw, *Theatre Ecology*, 10.
[129] Arons and May, *Readings in Performance and Ecology*, 3.
[130] Arons and May, 3.
[131] Theresa J. May, "Tú eres mi otro yo-Staying with the Trouble: Ecodramaturgy & the AnthropoScene," *The Journal of American Drama and Theatre* 29, no. 2 (2017): 1.
[132] Arons and May, *Readings in Performance and Ecology*, 2.
[133] Lisa Woynarski, "A Brief Introduction to the Field of Performance and Ecology," March 10, 2015 https://performanceandecology.wordpress.com/2015/03/10/a-brief-introduction-to-the-field-of-performance-and-ecology/

work, themed conferences, and interdisciplinary research projects.[134] It is sobering to remember that even if every theater and literary scholar turned their best urgent efforts to the environment with immediate effect, we couldn't "fix" climate change—or even work out what that would mean—let alone document, record, or "bear witness" to the extent of its attendant damages.[135]

What exactly ecodramaturgical theater and performance "can do"—as Carl Lavery provokes—(or, indeed, what it has done) is the subject of dispute.[136] As Lavery argues, rather than "hubristic and misguided thinking that would purport to save the planet through performance," theater's role is not to "produce the real" but to "make the world problematic, multiple and complex."[137] Timothy Morton, however, ventures that "The time should come when we want to ask of any text, 'What does this say about the environment?'"[138] The performances discussed in this book frame ecological relations as theater—intentionally or not—and conversations amongst audiences of various guises reveal clues about how we have arrived, at, perpetuated, and worsened environmental concerns, as well as pointing to possibilities for how we might begin to ameliorate some of them; to chip into the moldy plaster from ecocritical and ecodramaturgical sides of a wall that won't be up much longer.

Ethnography and Audience Research

Concurrent with the simultaneous surges of interest in ecocritical re-readings of Shakespeare's plays, and in theater/performance and ecology, audience researchers have been calling for more direct consultation with "real" audiences. Until relatively recently, the lived experience of theatergoers was considered

---

[134] Wallace Heim, "Epilogue," in *Readings in Performance and Ecology*, eds. Wendy Arons and Theresa J. May (Basingstoke and New York: Palgrave Macmillan, 2012), 211–12, suggests that the collection to which she contributes contains responses that are "redeeming," "pathological," and "quick." She anticipates further "theorizing that not only makes explicit how performance and theater create particular modes of ecological knowledge and what this knowledge means, but that activates the interchange of this knowledge across disciplines and practices." See also Vicki Angelacki, *Theatre & Environment* (Basingstoke: Macmillan, 2019); Chaudhuri and Enelow, *Research Theater*; Birgit Däwes and Marc Maufort, eds. *Enacting Nature: Ecocritical Perspectives on Indigenous Performance* (Brussels: P.I.E. Lang 2014); Deirdre Heddon and Sally Mackey, "Environmentalism, Performance and Applications: Uncertainties and Emancipations," *Research in Drama Education* 17, no. 2 (2012): 163–92; Rachel Fensham, Eddie Paterson, and Paul Rae, eds., "On Climates," *Performance Research* 23, no. 3 (2018): 1–5; Lisa Woynarski, *Ecodramaturgies: Theatre, Performance, and Climate Change* (Basingstoke and New York, Palgrave: 2020). This is an indicative and not exhaustive list of a quickly growing and increasingly theoretically sophisticated field, as Heim anticipates.
[135] Kirsten E. Shepherd-Barr, *Modern Drama: A Very Short Introduction* (Oxford: Oxford University Press, 2016), 102.
[136] Lavery, *Performance and Ecology*, 1–8.
[137] Lavery, 5.
[138] Morton, *Ecology without Nature*, 5.

too difficult to capture, too time-consuming, and costly for theater scholars to undertake. Of the audience research that existed, much was quantitative, reporting on demographics for arts funders, participation data, and marketing strategies.[139] In 2015, however, Matthew Reason and Kirsty Sedgman hope their themed section on theater audiences in *Participations Journal of Audience & Reception Studies* "might mark the point within theater studies when we can stop bemoaning the absence of audiences as a topic of empirical research."[140] Indeed, Stephen Purcell sketches out theater studies' "long, if undervalued, history of empirical audience research,"[141] summarizing multiple and multifarious approaches derived from semiotics, cultural studies, and phenomenology, and noting "renewed drive in the discipline to investigate the responses of actual audiences rather than speculate on their behalf."[142] There is now no dearth of audience research, or interest in methodologies.[143] Sedgman, in fact, finds herself pushing back against critiques of "empirical" audience research in a riposte to anxieties sometimes framed in terms of a neat opposition between positivist, qualitative, and objective empiricism on the one hand and reclaiming the authority of the expert, professional spectator on the other.[144]

Weathering Shakespeare combines historiographical audience research with present-day ethnography. It seeks to enable others to account for their own encounters with Shakespeare in the open-air, despite the author's role in crafting the chapters and the acknowledgment that experience cannot be captured and served up as writing. Part One asks how we might learn

---

[139] Susan Bennett, *Theatre Audiences: A Theory of Production and Reception* (London and New York: Routledge, 1997). Bennett's theoretical study of reception remains a key reference point for scholarship on theater audiences.

[140] Matthew Reason and Kirsty Sedgman, "Editors' Introduction: Themed Section on Theatre Audiences," *Participations* 12, no. 1 (2015): 117.

[141] Stephen Purcell, *Shakespeare and Audience in Practice* (Basingstoke: Palgrave Macmillan, 2013), 55.

[142] Purcell, *Shakespeare and Audience in Practice*, 60.

[143] For examples, see Caroline Heim, *Audience as Performer: The Changing Role of Theatre Audiences in the Twenty-First Century* (London and New York, Routledge 2016); Jennifer Radbourne, Hilary Glow, and Katya Johanson, eds., *The Audience Experience: A Critical Analysis of Audiences in the Performing Arts* (Bristol: Intellect, 2013); Kirsty Sedgman, "Audience Experience in an Anti-Expert Age: A Survey of Theatre Audience Research," *Theatre Research International* 42, no. 3 (2017): 307–22; and Sedgman, *Locating the Audience: How People Found Value in National Theatre Wales* (Bristol: Intellect, 2016); Matthew Reason and Anja Molle Lindelof, eds., *Experiencing Liveness in Contemporary Performance: Interdisciplinary Perspectives* (London, Routledge, 2016); Matthew Reason, "Asking the Audience: Audience Research and the Experience of Theatre," *About Performance* 10 (2010); Janelle Reinelt, "What UK Spectators Know: Understanding How We Come to Value Theatre," *Theatre Journal* 66, no. 3 (2014): 337–61; Ben Walmsley, *Audience Engagement in the Performing Arts: A Critical Analysis* (Basingstoke and New York: Palgrave Macmillan, 2019).

[144] Kirsty Sedgman, "We Need to Talk About (How We Talk About) Audiences," Interventions, *Contemporary Theater Review* (October 2019) https://www.contemporarytheatrereview.org/2019/we-need-to-talk-about-how-we-talk-about-audiences/. See also, Kirsty Sedgman, "On Rigour in Theatre Audience Research," *Contemporary Theatre Review* 29, no. 4 (2019): 462–79.

about the present-day ecologies of open-air performance by thinking with and about historical audiences, by drawing on archived newspaper reviews and press releases, recognizing that these records offer only partial accounts of performance response from certain groups of employed individuals.[145] Reviews tend to cover the first night of a show and so can miss the changes that occur over the course of a run. While this limitation poses a challenge for inquiries into past performance, it is especially vexing when it comes to the weather, which significantly alters the encounter with open-air theater—aesthetically and affectively. In alighting upon particular theatrical events, I build on Jim Davis and Victor Emeljanow's extensive study of London theater audiences between 1840 and 1880, which finds that "there was no such thing as a Victorian audience, but rather a variety of audiences, embodying a wide range of perspectives."[146] The presentist view of historical works in Chapters 1 and 2 doesn't "judge" these works by today's criteria but rather thinks about what they were doing environmentally then with what we know about the environment now, helping to reveal historical attitudes toward the weather and nonhuman nature that are complicit in today's environmental crisis.[147]

Part Two goes on to undertake ethnographic fieldwork at contemporary performances, in conversation with "ordinary" audiences in the weather.[148] Developing methodologies first explored by Penelope Woods at Shakespeare's Globe, I make direct social contact with audience members, observing and interacting with multiple groups of individuals and analyzing these encounters.[149] My work with audiences diverges from other ethnographies in that the nature of researching audiences does not allow for a sustained observation of any one group of people. Theater's "transitive" nature, Peter Eversmann notices, limits the conclusions a researcher can draw from audience research.[150] You can't sit in

---

[145] Willmar Sauter, "The Audience," in *The Cambridge Companion to Theatre History*, eds. David Wiles and Christine Dymkowski (Cambridge: Cambridge University Press, 2013), 181. Sauter draws on nineteenth-century theater reviews to propose that, in light of the references to the rest of the audience that reviewers tend to make at this time, despite a few anomalies, "it is a reasonable assumption that critics shared their broad value judgement with the rest of the audience."

[146] Jim Davis and Victor Emeljanow, *Reflecting the Audience: London Theatregoing, 1840–1880* (Hatfield: University of Hertfordshire Press, 2001), 229.

[147] See J. Donald Hughes, *What Is Environmental History?* (London: Polity Press, 2006), 98–101, for a summary overview of resistance to environmental history's "presentism" and "declensionist narratives."

[148] Heim, *Audience as Performer*, 4. I share Heim's dissatisfaction with the term "ordinary" for audience members, distinguishing them from professionals such as reviewers, and use the term with hesitance.

[149] Penelope Woods's qualitative audience research at Shakespeare's Globe was a valuable starting point for my methodology, as was Woods herself in offering generous assistance early on in the project.

[150] Peter Eversmann, "The Experience of the Theatrical Event," in *Theatrical* Events. *Borders-Dynamics-Frames*, eds. Vicky Ann Cremona et al. (Amsterdam and New York: Rodopi, 2004), 141.

the same audience twice.¹⁵¹ Although *all* live theater happens in circumstances that are "for one night only," at these performances, there is a palpable sense that the composite of live performance, landscape, and weather could not be replicated. The transitory nature of theater events taking place in unrepeatable weather circumstances makes their reception all the more seeming-ephemeral, intensifying the desire to hold onto what happens by chance and what is soon gone. If my time in the actual field comprised short bursts of activity, my engagement with the field was of much longer duration; I sustained contact by sustaining engagement with audiences. If the audience gatherings were as short-lived as an encounter with a performance—no performance lasts more than a few hours, meaning that the window of opportunity for speaking to people was smaller still—my time among audiences has been lengthier, extending over successive years.

Although James Clifford once suggested that ethnographies were "partial truths" or "fictions,"¹⁵² post-positivist approaches to new ethnography now maintain that the world is not considered objectively knowable and the truth of direct experience was never obtainable. D. Soyini Madison describes the tenets of a post- or non-positivist approach as "the recognition and contemplation of subjective human experience, contingencies of truth claims, value-laden inquiry, and local knowledge and vernacular expressions."¹⁵³ My work accords with criticisms of Clifford Geertz's "thick description"¹⁵⁴ that find culture irreducible to text. A verbal account of a performance experience—even when recorded immediately after the event—provides no more access to "truth" than other forms of reflection. How likely is any audience member to reveal personal responses to a stranger as part of an unexpected encounter? Even if someone were so inclined to share freely, to what extent could they actually articulate their experience of performance? What kind of account of experience might speaking about experience actually bring about? And how does that story change over time? In his foundational work on nonrepresentational theory, Nigel Thrift proposes that "there is no stable 'human' experience because the human sensorium is constantly being

---

[151] Shaun Moores, *Interpreting Audiences: The Ethnography of Media Consumption* (London: Sage, 1993), 4, argues that "reception studies can still properly be called ethnographies," making the important distinction between a qualitative researcher in the social sciences attempting to identify recurring patterns from recorded interviews and the physical presence of the ethnographer in the field.

[152] James Clifford and George E. Marcus, eds., *Writing Culture: The Poetics and Politics of Ethnography* (Los Angeles and London: University of California Press, 1986), 6.

[153] D Soyini Madison, *Critical Ethnography: Method, Ethics, and Performance* (Thousand Oaks, London, and New Delhi: Sage, 2005), 12.

[154] Geertz, *The Interpretation of Cultures*, 33.

re-invented as the body continually adds parts in to itself; therefore how and what is experienced as experience is itself variable."[155]

Throughout the book, I seek to write in a way that encourages people to speak for themselves, after Tim Cresswell's argument for ethnographic participants as "everyday theorists who bring their own ideas of place to bear on the place they live in."[156] The book therefore meanders in a careful sense of that riverine verb—"veering" into new, vibrantly, and culturally materialist, historicist, ecofeminist, and ecophenomenological approaches.[157] I welcome the discomfort that arises between sometimes bristly companions, embracing the "creative tensions and cross-pollination"[158] in attempting to create a dialogue between "ordinary" conversations and capital "T" Theory. Theory helps to negotiate aspects of this work and is good to "think with."[159] In no way does it fix responses or have the last word. This theoretical meandering is slow and sensitive—but not sentimental—work, open to changing course with a wide and winding arc.

In this spirit, I embrace tentative qualifiers like "perhaps," "maybe," "might," "a sense of," "a kind of," "tends to"—hesitancies often excised from academic writing: a bit of *un*couraging, cherishing more maybes, perhapses, and mights, as a small political effort that is neither relativist nor denialist, but a commitment to reclaiming the uncertainty so forcefully rejected in (often unsuccessful) attempts to counter climate denial. Where scientists found out the hard way that uncertainty was weakness, and that chinks in the consensus enabled skepticism, the attempt to counter skeptics with confidence hasn't worked either. For similar reasons, audience researchers—myself included—can be reluctant to share findings that critique theater-making at a time when the arts are under subsidized and under regarded by state and education bodies, and especially when our hearts are captivated by the material. Those seeking chinks seem to be smashing through them anyway, despite best efforts to maintain a united front. If art is one way in which the world is deemed complex again, in concert with that complexity, *Weathering Shakespeare* commits to slow meandering. Writing on his own site-specific performance practices, Mike Pearson embraces

---

[155] Nigel Thrift, *Non-representational Theory: Space|Politics|Affect* (Oxon and New York: Routledge, 2008), 2.

[156] Tim Cresswell, *Place: A Short Introduction* (Oxford: Blackwell, 2004), 79; Moores, *Interpreting Audiences*, 5, calls for a kind of audience ethnography that is "not afraid to interrogate and situate their spoken accounts."

[157] Duckert and Cohen, *Veer Ecology*, 3.

[158] João Biehl, "Ethnography in the Way of Theory," *Cultural Anthropology* 28, no. 4 (2013): 573–97, 575.

[159] Haraway, *Staying with the Trouble*, 12, after Marilyn Strathern, proposes that "It matters what matters we use to think other matters with."

"the impossibility of any final account of things."[160] Tim Ingold proposes life, as "a movement of opening, not of closure."[161] Navigating performance through language offers one way in to a context.

Lastly, a brief word on the groups of people who gathered together for the performances. Jill Dolan captures the ephemerality of a theater audience when she refers to "a group of people who have elected to spend an evening or an afternoon not only with a set of performers enacting a story, but with a group of other people, sometimes familiar, sometimes strange."[162] Shakespeare studies houses well-rehearsed debates about whether early modern gatherings were audiences, visiting playhouses to hear a play, or spectators, who went to see a performance.[163] While audiences as early-modern hearers, Evelyn Tribble argues, have been overemphasized in historicizing early modern performance as auditory rather than visual, "audience" continues to be the preferred term.[164] Any choice of term is complicated by ethnographic encounters where people referred to themselves as "audience members," "spectators," "theatergoers," and occasionally "participants." I shift between audiences and theatergoers, aware of the sensory exclusivity of most of the terms. When I use "audience," it is to speak of the group as a collective, even whilst trying to avoid the "tendency to confuse individual and group response," against which Helen Freshwater warns, arguing that "each audience is made up of individuals who bring their own cultural reference points, political beliefs, sexual preferences, personal histories and immediate preoccupations to their interpretation of a production."[165] Eversmann balances that "while the emotional and perceptual dimensions are experienced individually, the cognitive analysis of a production is to a large extent a collective phenomenon, which may enhance the spectator's insight in a performance through communication with other audience members."[166] I pursue answers from individuals rather than utilizing the kinds of cognitive

---

[160] Mike Pearson, *In Comes I: Performance, Memory and Landscape* (Exeter: University of Exeter Press, 2006), 27.
[161] Ingold, *Being Alive*, 3–4.
[162] Jill Dolan, *Utopia in Performance: Finding Hope at the Theater* (Ann Arbor: University of Michigan Press, 2005), 10.
[163] Andrew Gurr and Mariko Ichikawa, *Staging in Shakespeare's Theatres* (Oxford: Oxford University Press, 2000), 18.
[164] Evelyn Tribble, *Cognition in the Globe: Attention and Memory in Shakespeare's Theatre* (Basingstoke: Palgrave Macmillan, 2013), 240.
[165] Helen Freshwater, *Theatre & Audience* (Basingstoke: Palgrave Macmillan, 2009), 5–6.
[166] Eversmann, "The Experience of the Theatrical Event," 171.

science methodologies that argue for general commonalities across audience experience.[167] As Haraway argues, "We become-with each other or not at all."[168] Putting multiple individual voices into a collective conversation at best reveals cooperation and at worst reveals a lack of sympathy for others, but the weathering is always together: a becoming-with.

Nature, Culture, Environment

Nature continues to be adopted uncritically as a term outside of the humanities. In the social sciences, studies are persistently less preoccupied with troubling what nature *is* and more interested in what nature *does* for physical, mental, and emotional health and wellbeing.[169] Similarly, attempts at nature conservation attend less to what makes nature nature than they do to recording, measuring, and protecting it. In these contexts, nature is presented unapologetically with its own materiality, distinct from culture: nature affects us and is something that—circumstances depending—we might love, fear, harm, protect, or need more or less. I mention these simplistic contexts for nature because in many respects they have an affinity with how the theatergoers to whom I spoke use and conceptualize it. There is a tangibly more-than-human capital "N" Nature in the responses of theatergoers too. Most typify Kate Soper's "nature endorsing" rather than "nature sceptical" perspectives, which appeal to nature "in validation of that which we would either seek to preserve or seek to instigate in place of existing actuality" and which "take either conservative or progressive forms."[170] Entangled with the physical experience of being outdoors are imagined constructions of theatrical scenery, the picturesque, the sublime, landscape painting, romanticized versions of English pastoral, and cultivated natures that are palpably cultural.

---

[167] See Bruce A. McConachie, *Engaging Audiences: A Cognitive Approach to Spectating in the Theatre* (Basingstoke: Palgrave Macmillan, 2008).
[168] Haraway, *Staying with the Trouble*, 4.
[169] Judith Chen-Hsuan Cheng and Martha C. Monroe, "Connection to Nature: Children's Affective Attitude Toward Nature," *Environment and Behavior* 44, no. 1 (2010): 31–49; F. Stephan Mayer and Cynthia McPherson Frantz, "The Connectedness to Nature Scale: A Measure of Individuals' Feeling in Community with Nature," *Journal of Environmental Psychology* 24, no. 4 (2004): 434–40; Richard M. Ryan et al., "Vitalizing Effects of Being Outdoors and in Nature," *Journal of Environmental Psychology* 30, no. 2 (2010): 159–68; Jo Thompson Coon et al., "Does Participating in Physical Activity in Outdoor Natural Environments Have a Greater Effect on Physical and Mental Wellbeing Than Physical Activity Indoors? A Systematic Review," *Environmental Science & Technology* 45, no. 5 (2011): 1761–72.
[170] Kate Soper, *What Is Nature?* (Oxford and MA: Blackwell, 1994), 34.

Shakespeare in this book likewise traverses multiple ideas of culture: as the subject of cultural studies approaches, a readily recognizable performance of a play, and a way of thinking about planned parks, umbrellas, and picnics. The cultural event is the lens through which nature is perceived, evoking ornamental landscapes—variously conceived of as theatrical scenery, fairy tales, romantic picturesque, as Shakespeare's pastorals and green worlds of Arden, Athens, and Bohemia, as island fantasy, and as nostalgia. Nature by way of return, variously makes culture seem any combination of out of place, at home, a friend, an enemy, synthetic, organic, artificial, and irrelevant. While Shakespeare and theater equate to a very narrow sense of culture, in keeping with Raymond Williams definition of "the works and practices of intellectual and especially artistic activity" this broadly reflects theatergoers' modes of expression.[171]

Entangled with the obliteration of a nature/culture binary is the complexity of the high/popular culture arguments within which Shakespeare is historically aligned. In 1869, one hundred years after David Garrick's infamously rained-off Shakespeare Jubilee parade in Stratford-upon-Avon conferred on Shakespeare the status of the National Poet,[172] Matthew Arnold infamously proclaimed "high culture" as "the best which has been thought and said in the world."[173] No figure more than Shakespeare has been used to exemplify high culture since. For Martin Ryle and Kate Soper, Arnold's *Culture and Anarchy* (1869) "marks the moment where 'culture' comes to denominate not just an inherited tradition of texts and an associated ideal of self-development, but the endeavor to make these current through education beyond a restricted leisure-class audience."[174] High culture and Shakespeare became associated with self-improvement that reinforces classed boundaries. The presumed acquisition of Pierre Bourdieu's "cultural capital" can be reasonably carried over into this context of Shakespeares in the open-air.[175]

Such claims that Shakespeare cultures whosoever encounters his work have been rightly criticized within cultural materialist frameworks.[176] Alan Sinfield

---

[171] Raymond Williams, *Keywords: A Vocabulary of Culture and Society* (London: Fontana Press, 1976), 90.
[172] Michael Dobson, *The Making of the National Poet: Shakespeare, Adaptation, and Authorship, 1660-1769* (Oxford: Oxford University Press, 1992).
[173] Matthew Arnold, *Culture and Anarchy*, ed. Jane Garnett (Oxford: Oxford University Press, 2006), 5.
[174] Martin Ryle and Kate Soper, *To Relish the Sublime?* (London and New York: Verso Books, 2002), 4.
[175] Pierre Bourdieu, *Distinction: A Social Critique of the Judgement of Taste*, trans. Richard Nice (London: Routledge, 2010).
[176] Jonathan Dollimore and Alan Sinfield, eds., *Political Shakespeare*, 2nd ed. (Ithaca and London: Manchester University Press, 1994), 260.

describes a time when the "canon was assumed to be more or less right; the task was to make it more widely accessible" within the British education system.[177] The structure of feeling derives from Arnoldian assumptions that education in high culture facilitates social good (Shakespeare for all!). Sinfield then observes a shift from seeking to make Shakespeare widely available, to proactively exposing Shakespeare's complicity in and with systems of oppression (Shakespeare the misogynist/racist/homophobe/ableist/extractivist!). Life, of course, does not reflect scholarship so neatly, and this book identifies elements of the first phase—of making Shakespeare widely accessible—as celebrated, fluctuating between residual, dominant, and emergent cultural processes.[178] The strength of pro-Shakespeare feeling, of support for a transcendental genius and the elitist object of high culture, is variously complicated by the practitioners' stated objectives and by the environments in which they work.

The culture that open-air Shakespeares represent is further complicated by their relatively low-status as "popular" entertainment within academic research. For Stephen Purcell, popular Shakespeares—a category into which he fits outdoor performances—offer "Not just a radical alternative to high-culture Shakespeare [but] an interrelated assortment of shifts, in what the name 'Shakespeare' means to us today."[179] A couple of attempts to recuperate community Shakespeares offer some assistance here. Jeremy Lopez looks to "bad" acting and "banal" performances at the Edinburgh Fringe in 2004, which, he argues, evince occasional glimpses of "greatness."[180] Dan Kulmala responds to Lopez in writing on American Shakespeare Festivals, suggesting "that academic discourse had not come to terms with 'bad' Shakespeare because it's too closed-minded and wrapped up in maintaining its own elite status to explore options in the cultural value of alternative and community-based productions of Shakespeare."[181] If we stop looking for Shakespeare, Kulmala proposes, we might find a kind of cultural value that can better be understood within anthropological terms. In this vein, Rebecca Scollen asks, "Does the Shakespeare in the Shakespeare in the Park matter?" Drawing on audience research undertaken at the University of Southern Queensland's Shakespeare in the Park Festival, she finds that

---

[177] Dollimore and Sinfield, *Political* Shakespeare, 255.
[178] Raymond Williams, *Marxism and Literature* (Oxford and New York: Oxford University Press, 1977), 121–7.
[179] Purcell, *Popular Shakespeare*, 5.
[180] Jeremy Lopez, "Small-Time Shakespeare: The Edinburgh Festival Fringe, 2003," *Shakespeare Quarterly* 55, no. 2 (2004): 207.
[181] Dan Kulmala, "'Is All Our Company Here?' Shakespeare Festivals as Fields of Cultural Production," *English Language and Literature Studies* 5, no. 1 (2015): 10.

Shakespeare is incidental to at least two-thirds of the people surveyed who are present because of the location.[182]

Lastly, the term "environment" also remains prolific in everyday language. Richard Schechner, who led the environmental theater movement with Arnold Aronson in the 1960s and 1970s, proposed two different ways of understanding environment from the perspective of performance-makers: "First, there is what one can do with and in a space; secondly, there is the acceptance of a given space. In the first case, one creates an environment by transforming a space; in the second case, one negotiates with an environment, engaging in a scenic dialogue with a space."[183] Schechner here encapsulates the anthropocentricism for which the term "environment" has lately been deemed dangerous. George Lakoff, for instance, from the field of cognitive science, dislikes the linguistic "environment frame"—that is, "the environment as separate from, and around us"—for the very premises articulated in Schechner's work: because they perpetuate the notion of humans and human performance at the center of a swirling world.[184] Epitomizing the difficulties of "environment" as an entrenched term, then, audience members frequently referred to "the environment" as what surrounded them, as did I in conversation with them. This environment remains, as Ingold proposes, "a world we live in and not a world we look at."[185]

Chapter Outline

Weathering Shakespeare is separated into three parts, each containing a pair of companion chapters that undertake a particular environmental inquiry. The ways that weathering is performed by audiences historically and in response to particular theater architecture, community settings, or staging decisions reveal shifting attitudes toward nonhuman nature, climate, and culture, which run through the book. Part One looks at historical moments, tracing audience performances of weathering across reviews and archives. Part Two presents ethnographic work amongst audiences undertaken at present-day outdoor Shakespeares. Local and temporally specific case studies resist the desire to

---

[182] Rebecca Scollen, "Does the 'Shakespeare' in Shakespeare-in-the-Park Matter? An Investigation of Attendances at and Attitudes to the University of Southern Queensland Shakespeare in the Park Festival," *Applied Theatre Researcher/IDEA Journal* 12, no. 6 (2011): 1–16.

[183] Schechner, "6 Axioms," 50.

[184] George Lakoff, "Why It Matters How We Frame the Environment," *Environmental Communication: A Journal of Nature and Culture* 4, no. 1 (2010): 76.

[185] Ingold, *Being Alive*, 95.

make larger generalizations but offer critical reflections on environmental issues in light of our urgent need to understand how weather is made culture in the anthropocene. Part Three gathers overarching concerns from across the contemporary productions and concludes the book by looking to Shakespeares created in response to climate change.

Chapter 1 identifies, as others have done, *As You Like It* at Coombe Woods, Surrey, in 1884 and 1885 as the beginnings of the kinds of open-air Shakespeares found across the UK today. I depart from previous analyses of this work by recuperating the collaboration between Lady Archibald Campbell and the American actress Eleanor Calhoun in the creation of Arden at Coombe. I propose that any gendered oversights in the ways that these influential performances are remembered carry ecological implications for understanding how their audiences conceived of the in-situ relationship between nature and Shakespeare. A performance of pastoral by audiences in 1884 begins to transition to a performance of weathering by 1885. The chapter therefore disturbs even as it supports received notions of Romantic pastoral in the late Victorian period. These women together set a precedent for others to come who continue to find breathing space for their creative work by exposing audiences to the weather.

The late nineteenth century is my starting point for a number of reasons. In theater history, this is where the performances that anticipate the kinds of open-air performances we see today emerge. Moreover, it coincides with the period in which Amitav Ghosh suggests the earth came to be regarded as moderate and orderly; the sublime disappears with the first performances and instead nature is seem as a tamable, beautiful plaything.[186] Today's performances are, in Marvin Carlson's words, "haunted" by the performances of the past, whether or not theatergoers and theater-makers are themselves aware of the hauntings.[187] Inherited historical narratives in fragments infiltrate contemporary atmospheric experiences, producing complex, plural, and messily contradictorily responses to performance and nonhuman natures.

Chapter 2 stops in 1933 and 1934, at Max Reinhardt's series of productions of *A Midsummer Night's Dream* outdoors and at the opening of the Regent's Park Open Air Theatre in London. It identifies the cultural construction of an English climate by way of references to the weather and national identity in response to staging. The chapter pivots around Reinhardt's Oxfordian *Dream* and analyzes an escalating fashion for lavish, extractivist, and wasteful spectacle

---

[186] Ghosh, *The Great Derangement*, 56.
[187] Carlson, *The Haunted Stage*.

utilizing huge quantities of electric lighting, uprooting and importing trees for vast audiences: itself a defiant and grandiose, but nevertheless flailing, response to political volatility.

Part Two departs from the historical sources of the first two chapters and draws on ethnographic fieldwork undertaken amongst twenty-first-century theatergoers between 2012 and 2019. Chapter 3 is an account of audiences for two nature-theaters created for Shakespeare in the Welsh and Cornish landscapes. It examines the storm scene from *The Tempest* at Minack and the enchantment of Falstaff at Herne's Oak in *The Merry Wives of Windsor* at the Willow Globe in performance at these theaters. Chapter 4 explores responses to three different "site-specific" Shakespeares outdoors. Each of the works takes its audience on a walk around a park, thinking of a few trees as woods. The focus on small-scale productions largely set apart from the mainstream British theater scene in this part of the book acknowledges Claire Cochrane's observation that "despite the huge population of London, the majority of the British people do not live there, although inevitably every aspect of their lives, including the theater they are able to access, is affected by the power that emanates from the center."[188] At the end of the twentieth century, multiculturalism as "the human legacy of empire" had visibly changed the "face of British theatre," Cochrane argues, "while any unified concept of what it means to be culturally British was coming under even greater challenge."[189] This altered, contested Britishness co-exists with the residual cultural imperialism advanced by open-air Shakespeares that are structurally English and historically, racially white. In the contemporary productions that follow, the actors, often hailing from London and other major cities—and, to a lesser extent, rural and tourist audiences—are more representative of this altered sense of multicultural Britishness than their predecessors in Chapters 1 and 2.

Part Three remains in the present, first identifying generalizable themes that appear across the contemporary ethnographic work, drawing on ideas that appear across locations, times, and weather, thinking of their ecopolitics. In seeking to learn about the affective and meteorological collisions in atmosphere, Chapter 5 considers what Raymond Williams identifies as a "green language" as it appears across all of the performances in Part Two: weather, and also wildlife, light, and landscape.[190] Chapter 6 concludes the book by asking if productions designed

---

[188] Cochrane, Claire. *Twentieth-Century British Theatre: Industry, Art and Empire* (Cambridge: Cambridge University Press, 2011), 2.
[189] Cochrane, *Twentieth-Century British Theatre: Industry, Art and Empire*, 4.
[190] Raymond Williams, *The Country and the City* (London: Hogarth, 1985), 133.

to address the anthropocene are any more capable of taking it on. I look at an all-female *As You Like It* by The HandleBards, a cycling, touring small-scale Shakespeare company, BP or not BP's Mischief Festival staged outside the Royal Shakespeare Theatre, seeking (successfully, as part of a sustained campaign) to get the RSC to relinquish oil sponsorship, and the environmental resonances evoked by Max Webster's waste-themed *As You Like It* at the Regent's Park Open Air Theatre.

Weathering a Play

In her keynote for the Art and the Anthropocene conference held at Trinity College Dublin in 2019, Una Chaudhuri argued that moving beyond "urgent consciousness-raising,"[191] theater's function has become about learning ways to "stay with the trouble" and practice "arts of living on a damaged planet."[192] At the beginning of the twentieth century, the theater director Edward Gordon Craig urged that we "not rush into the open-air and begin to wave our arms, and quote Shakespeare, and think we have achieved something by doing so."[193] Craig lists "enthusiasts" who think they have solved the "problem of theatre." Fittingly, one of his enthusiasts is passionate about open-air performance. A few caveats are usefully restated at this juncture, however banal they seem. It should go without saying that without actually undertaking research, we cannot speak for the immediate or longer-term affects a production may have. In overlooking responses to creative works, we lose the potential to learn a little about how we might communicate better. And we lose some of a sense of the complexity of the problems too. Responses may or may not accord with what performance-makers think they are doing. There are likely to be divergent responses to the same piece of work, even where some responses appear to reflect a community of feeling. Performance can too easily be construed as activism but does not work like a blunt instrument for effecting determinable and quantifiable changes in theatergoers.[194] Furthermore, the scale of climate change obliterates the size

---

[191] Una Chaudhuri, "'There Must Be a Lot of Fish in That Lake': Toward an Ecological Theater," *Theater* 25, no. 1 (1994): 23–31, 25.
[192] Donna J. Haraway, *Staying with the Trouble*; Anna Tsing, Heather Swanson, Elaine Gan, and Nils Bubandt, eds., *Arts of Living on a Damaged Planet* (Minneapolis and London: University of Minnesota Press, 2017); Una Chaudhuri, "AnthropoScenes: Enduring Performance" (Art in the Anthropocene conference. Beckett Theatre, Trinity College Dublin, June 8, 2019).
[193] Edward Gordon Craig, *Craig on Theatre*, ed. J Michael Walton (London: Methuen, [1910] 1999), 40.
[194] See Simon Estok, "Afterword: Ecocriticism on the Lip of a Lion," on ecocritical Shakespeare's "potential for activist comment," in *Ecocritical Shakespeare*, eds. Lynne Bruckner and Dan Brayton (Farnham: Ashgate, 2011), 246.

of theater audiences: they're only a pebble when it comes to thinking about cultural production—let alone anthroposcenes.[195] Whilst performance may reach a greater number of a different demographic than textual ecocriticism, these audiences pale in comparison with the reach of other media. I also urge attachment to *any* form of human culture as a way through the mess, only when it also makes a concerted effort to enter into a conversation with those who make and respond to the work. In spite of these caveats, the various productions of this study stir self-reflection and environmentally inflected conversations that are well worth the effort and the hearing. The people who attend the productions ponder the human experience of the (real and fictitious) weather and ruminate on the ways in which (real and fictitious) people are compelled to perform with it. David Abram suggests that talking about the weather is "an ever-present reminder that the reality we inhabit is ultimately beyond our human control."[196] Venturing into the weather for a play signals a conscious choice to spend a few hours exposed to an uncontrollable climate in the hope of a particular kind of aesthetic encounter: a humbling and hopeful desire to meet nature in culture, culture in nature and to sit in the reminder that they have always been the same.

I rehearse a memory, which corrects my posture, shoulders widening and ribcage expanding for a breath as my back recalls early spring sunshine entering the Willow Globe. Sitting in the blustery theater for All's Well That Ends Well, *as Helena offered the dying King her help—"my art is not past power nor you past cure" (2.1.157)—this audience member wholeheartedly allowed herself to hear what she wanted in the Shakespeare: that Helena could be speaking to us and offering a magical fix; that for a few breaths in a living theater in Wales, we could inhabit a future as well as a past, that the seasons had not yet altered beyond repair, that summer was still on its way, that words might still have power and we might still be cured.*

---

[195] Gaby, *Open-Air Shakespeare*, 3 and 109.
[196] David Abram, *Becoming Animal: An Earthly Cosmology* (New York: Vintage Books, 2010), 141.

Part One

1

Performing Pastoral: A New Form of Poetic Representation

In an environmentally attentive review of Sir Herbert Beerbohm Tree's production of *A Midsummer Night's Dream* at Her Majesty's Theatre, London, in 1900, the commentator discussed Hawes Craven's spectacular scenography, praising lifelike representations of Shakespeare's woods outside Athens, before going on to caveat his approval with a memory of another *Dream* seen years previously, in a garden. The commentator felt that it would be unfair to make a comparison between Tree's production and a *Dream* performed at the Villa once owned by Alexander Pope in Twickenham in 1887, presented by the retired actress Henrietta Labouchere, née Hodson (recently returned from America where she had helped to launch the actress Lillie Langtry's career)[1]:

> I can never be got to say that I ever saw a production of *A Midsummer Night's Dream* as wondrous as that which Mrs. Labouchere gave at Pope's Villa, Twickenham; but then she had spreading trees, and a beautiful garden, and night under the open sky, and in midsummer, to assist her. But without betraying my allegiance to that memorable representation, I am compelled to say that Mr. Tree's production is the best I have ever seen on the stage.[2]

However good Tree's *Dream*, the real experience of nature outdoors on a warm evening had created a superior memory for the reviewer: under a clear night sky in the west of London, summer weather, landscaped gardens, and mature trees represented the latest innovation in picturesque theatrical scenery for Shakespeare's plays.

On the cast list for Labouchere's *Dream* at the Pope's Villa is a Lady Archibald Campbell playing Oberon, directly connecting this *Dream* to the open-air

---

[1] Hodson was married to the M.P. Henry Du Pré Labouchere, whose infamous Labouchere Criminal Law amendment was later used to convict Oscar Wilde for gross indecency.
[2] "A Midsummer Night's Dream," *Mainly about People in the Green Room*. Week ending January 27, 1900, 80.

performances *As You Like It* that had taken place just a few years earlier at Coombe Woods, Surrey.³ Campbell—known as "Lady Archie" and regarded "one of the most important women in the aesthetic movement"⁴—was jointly responsible, with the American actress Eleanor Calhoun, for the first woodland staging of *As You Like It* at Coombe in July 1884, where Campbell had played Orlando and Calhoun Rosalind. Although the designer and architect Edward Godwin, introduced to the women by the artist James Whistler, gets much of the credit for producing *As You Like It* at Coombe, Godwin was only brought on board toward the end of what Calhoun qualifies as "a year's happy cooperation by Lady Archibald and myself."⁵ Michael Dobson's history of amateur Shakespeare in the open-air begins with *As You Like It* at Coombe in 1884 and The Pastoral Players (the company that Campbell and Godwin formed in 1885) before departing toward work by Sir Philip Barling Ben Greet—who was, Dobson argues, the "single most important popularizer of outdoor Shakespeare"⁶—in the decades that followed. To my knowledge, however, in existing accounts of open-air theater (and in performance histories of *A Midsummer Night's Dream*), Labouchere's production does not appear at all—notwithstanding glancing references to fashionable amateur and charity theatricals in aristocratic circles—despite her *Dream*'s nature aesthetic haunting encounters with Beerbohm Tree's landmark *Dream* years later.⁷ Nevertheless, the reception of nature in the twenty-first-century performances of chapters to come is as much indebted to Labouchere, who is entirely beholden to Campbell, Calhoun, and the Pastoral Players, as it is to Greet. Furthermore, this chapter proposes that any gendered oversights in the ways that these influential performances have been remembered carry ecological implications for the ways we conceive of the in-situ reception of Shakespeare in nature at this time.

My intention is to recuperate these women's creative and intellectual labor in an effort to enrich the ways we think about audiences for pastoral Shakespeare in the weather. What follows demonstrates how *As You Like It* at Coombe in the warm, dry summer of 1884 instigated a performance of pastoral in theatergoing

---

³ The casting of Oberon with a female actress continued the tradition that began with Madame Lucia Vestris, who played this part in 1840.
⁴ Susan Weber, *E. W. Godwin: Aesthetic Movement Architect and Designer* (New Haven: Yale University Press, 1999), 36.
⁵ Eleanor Calhoun, "Pastoral Shakespeare: Princess Lazarovich Tells of the Earliest Productions in England," *New York Times*, March 18, 1916.
⁶ Michael Dobson, *Shakespeare and Amateur Performance: A Cultural History* (Cambridge: Cambridge University Press, 2011), 172.
⁷ For an account of actresses and charity work, garden parties, and theatricals in this period, see Catherine Hindson, *London's West End Actresses and the Origins of Celebrity Charity, 1880–1920* (Iowa City: University of Iowa Press, 2016).

practices: audiences "performed" the play's pastoral trope—physically and discursively—in their retreat to rurality before returning to city life, imaginably renewed by the experience of Shakespeare's poetry. The weather-narratives surrounding these outdoor productions feed the book's overarching argument for social performances of weathering undertaken by theater audiences as they encounter staged performances of Shakespeare's plays in the open-air. As I will show, performing pastoral in response to a sentimental nature at the Coombe *As You Like It* in 1884 acts as a precursor to performances of weathering undertaken by theatergoers at the wetter and colder 1885 revival. These performances of weathering go on to inflect the written reception of Labouchere's *Dream* in 1887. By beginning with Beerbohm Tree's *Dream*, an iconic moment in theater history, and reaching back via Labouchere's production to linger at *As You Like It* at Coombe, I hope to highlight the environmental significance of the Victorian open-air Shakespeare aesthetic established by Campbell and Calhoun that later endures in the consciousness of audiences attending London's indoor theaters. Remnants of this aesthetic persist today, with legacy implications for how people encounter and conceptualize nature. Together, these women set a precedent for others to come—also excluded from prominent roles in mainstream theaters—who continue to find breathing space for their creative work by exposing their audiences to the weather.

The Pastoral as a Retreat from London

Summarizing contemporary ecocritical resistance to literary pastorals, Greg Garrard argues that the presumption of a "stable, enduring" Nature evoked by the literary form of the pastoral was always untenable, linked to "outmoded and poorly understood scientific models" of equilibrium and harmony.[8] Sentimental, regressive nostalgia for Theocritus's Sicilian shepherds' idyll, Virgil's mythical Arcadia, and subsequent diverse, wide-ranging literary iterations of Golden Ages, sunsets, and green pastures all variously espouse the delusion of stable ecosystems that has been shattered by "post-equilibrium" ecologies, as Steve Mentz points out (think *King Lear* not *As You Like It*).[9] But as Lawrence Buell—whose *The Environmental Imagination* (1995) Garrard builds upon—observes, pastoral's "ideological valence" cannot be reduced to

---

[8] Greg Garrard, *Ecocriticism* (London and New York: Routledge, 2012), 63.
[9] Steve Mentz, "Strange Weather in *King Lear*," *Shakespeare*, 6, no. 2 (2010): 139–52.

progressive/regressive or left/right politics and is only comprehensible within its "contextual frame."[10] The historical, geographical, cultural, and aesthetic "frame" in which these—social and staged—performances take place supports Buell's observation of "the tendency to identify nation with countryside promoted by the English squirearchy" (undertaken by actors, reviewers, and audiences in this chapter), whilst also supporting Garrard's setting-aside of the pastoral as an environmental impasse from a distance.[11] Campbell, Calhoun, and Labouchere alight upon the potential for a "more densely imaged, environmentally responsive art," such as Buell proposes might coexist with the damaging work of "reducing the land to a highly selective ideological construct," which their work also does.[12] The "internal contradictions" of these historical performances disclose their simultaneous but unbalanced environmentally "constructive" and "compromised" potential.[13]

Terry Gifford identifies three (overlapping) categories that help to disentangle the cultural work of these theatrical productions and their relationship to the pastoral: the classical pastoral as literary conventions referencing shepherds' lives; pastoral as a more general context for literature and culture that invoke a retreat from the city to the country, often in response to industrialization and its associated waste and displeasures; and pastoral used pejoratively, obfuscating violence, exploitation, and hardship in the landscape, promulgating regressive values and ideology.[14] *As You Like It* at Coombe in 1884 and 1885 and *A Midsummer Night's Dream* at the Pope's Villa in 1887 intersect all three categories. First, they present the classical pastoral textual tropes explored by Shakespeare in both plays for a learned, upper-class theater audience, extending the "playful artifice" already inherent in the literary pastoral form with theatrical staging.[15] Second, the productions provide the context for a rural retreat, performed by theatergoers who escape London's civilization and politics for the supposed simplicity of the unspoilt (landscaped) English countryside before returning to the city. Third, pejorative presentist critiques of the pastoral enable us to historicize the aestheticization of beautiful landscapes coded as theater, facilitated by private land ownership and the expansion of empire, in whose mesh these performances are both caught and culpable.

---

[10] Lawrence Buell, *The Environmental Imagination: Thoreau, Nature Writing, and the Formation of American Culture* (Cambridge, MA and London: Harvard University Press, 1995), 49.
[11] Buell, *The Environmental Imagination*, 32.
[12] Buell, 32.
[13] Buell, 32.
[14] Terry Gifford, *Pastoral* (London and New York: Routledge, 1999), 1–2.
[15] Buell, *The Environmental Imagination*, 32.

Permeating the aesthetic of these pastoral Shakespeares was the material atmosphere in which they were performed. Late nineteenth-century environmental conditions in England had been transformed by capitalism, driven by imperial and colonial projects. The country's transition to a fully industrial and fossil fuel based economy was almost complete. Although population growth continued as it had throughout the century, rural depopulation and poverty accelerated as people left the country for fast-growing towns and cities. Environmental historian Ian Simmons notes of this period that although most "city people were moved away from the close interaction that farmers experience [...] they were not immune to weather, nor to a particle-laden atmosphere nor to contaminated groundwater."[16] Atmospheric pollution—comprising smoke from burning domestic and industrial coal, organic matter, hydrochloric acid, and hydrogen sulphide for alkalis manufacturing—was at its worst in London where air quality was seriously detrimental to human and animal health. Expanding cities contributed to nostalgia for rural life, which in turn contributed to a flight to the suburbs where air quality was markedly better. Amid a period of sustained climatic warming (between 1850 and 1950, temperatures rose by 1 degree centigrade), high rainfall in 1879 and 1880 devastated English agriculture.[17] Between 1881 and 1885—the years leading up to and surrounding the first pastoral performances at Coombe (and the first years for which such records exist)—London saw significantly less sunshine than country towns as a result of atmospheric pollution. Visibility was worst in the city in winter but poor visibility seeped into the summer months.[18] *As You Like It* at Coombe in 1884 followed three summers of relatively good weather at a time when the desire to leave London's polluted atmosphere for fresh air and clear skies was keenly felt. As I will show, the pastoral retreat became as much a performative exercise for the leisure classes as a literary trope which they had previously consumed as its intended readers.

The primary sources cited profusely in this chapter include selected extracts from Campbell's 1887 article "The Woodland Gods" for *The Woman's World* (containing critical reflections on The Pastoral Players and a eulogy for Godwin, who died in 1886), Calhoun's extensive account of *As You Like It* at Coombe in her 1915 memoir, over one hundred reports and reviews from newspaper

---

[16] Ian G. Simmons, *An Environmental History of Great Britain: From 10,000 Years Ago to the Present* (Edinburgh: Edinburgh University Press, 2001), 149.
[17] Simmons, *An Environmental History*, 152.
[18] Brian W. Clapp, *An Environmental History of Britain since the Industrial Revolution* (London and New York: Longman, 1994), 14.

publications and periodicals. Cumulatively these documents offer an alternative to the language of emerging weather forecasts and empirical reports of the period, as a cultural record of environmental conditions and narrated encounters with the weather, integrated into written commentaries that speak of attending Shakespeare's plays.

As You Like It at Coombe Woods, 1884 and 1885

Lady Archibald Campbell was born Janey Sevilla Callander in Scotland in 1846 and became a ward of the Duke of Argyll when her father died. Upon marrying Lord Archibald Campbell, second son of the Duke of Argyll, in 1868, she moved south to England, eventually arriving at Coombe in Surrey. There, the Campbell family had an entrance key, which granted them access to the private crown woods, affording Campbell the opportunity to stroll alone with her American actress friend, Eleanor Calhoun.

Calhoun also wandered the English woods at Coombe with something of an outsider's perspective. She had arrived in London from California with her own ecologically and economically charged backstory. Her early American education was sponsored by a Phoebe Hearst, married to the silver-ore mining millionaire George Hearst, but when the Hearst's son (William Randolph) and Calhoun declared their intention to get married, the actress was hastily dispatched to England to pursue her career there: thus a fortune made from natural resource extraction both subsidized Calhoun's education and propelled her across the Atlantic Ocean. Remembering walks in the woods with Campbell, Calhoun writes in her memoir, "Not a soul did we ever meet there [, for] only once or so a year did the royal ranger ever come to disturb its solitudes by a few hours of shooting."[19]

To set the scene for what unfolded in the woods, here is Calhoun's memory of spring at Coombe at length, prompted by the experience of successive springs elsewhere:[20]

> When spring appears, and the tender young grass unheaves the moist sod, left all fresh by melted snows and winter rains; when bright flowers once more break through and flutter their perfumes to the air, dancing in happy praise of the god

---

[19] Princess Lazarovich-Hrebelianovich (Eleanor Hulda Calhoun), *Pleasures and Palaces; the Memoirs of Princess Lazarovich-Hrebelianovich, Illustrated with Drawings by John Wolcott Adams and with Photographs* (New York: The Century company, 1915), 70–1.

[20] After her work with The Pastoral Players, Calhoun continued her acting career in Paris, eventually meeting and marrying the Prince of Serbia and becoming the Princess Lazarovich-Hrebelianovich.

Hyacinth's return and of nature new-create, I see again the blue hyacinths of England massed by the million under the grand old oaks and pines of Coombe Wood. In my mind I stroll again with a rare and noble friend amid the tall green bracken by those purple pools of blossom, whose scent mingles with the faint, fine smell of the yellow primroses stuck thickly and closely to the earth at every path-edge and tree-root cranny and beside every clod.[21]

Calhoun's memory of spring's return to a winter-weathered landscape in Surrey, of animate flora's colors and smells, exemplifies what Timothy Morton calls "ecomimesis," where the more earnest her attempt to capture the world in writing the more distant the materiality of that world becomes.[22] The more faithfully Calhoun attends to remembering the detail the more of a page and the less of a world she has. The care with which she turns plants and weather to text evokes a nostalgic landscape such as George Levine describes as an English Victorian pastoral, which imbued quotidian and human-sculpted nature—rather than the awesome mountains of Scotland or wilderness of Californian terrain with which Campbell and Calhoun respectively self-identify—with a mundane version of a "sublime" experience.[23]

The pastoral that Calhoun remembers idealizes the warming woodlands at Coombe, where hyacinths, ferns, and primroses ushered in the spring. Out walking in this arboreal playground, Calhoun often dressed in the Ganymede costume made for her London debut as Rosalind in *As You Like It* at the Imperial Theatre in 1882. She writes, "I sometimes used to have the costume with me at Coombe from Saturday to Monday, high leather boots at all, and wore it under a long ulster during the rambles that Lady Archibald and I used to enjoy in the glorious warren."[24] Having felt a "new joy of going along free, like treading the air" upon first stepping onto the indoor stage costumed in Ganymede's britches, the sensory experience of wearing the costume outdoors in the weather and in sight of no audience but her friend was enhanced for Calhoun.[25] So, it was costumed for the stage as Ganymede that Calhoun imagined herself really Rosalind in English woods on an unusually sunny day and was inspired to

---

[21] Lazarovich-Hrebelianovich, *Pleasures and Palaces*, 59.
[22] Timothy Morton, *Ecology without Nature: Rethinking Environmental Aesthetics* (Cambridge, MA: Harvard University Press, 2007).
[23] George Levine, "High and Low: Ruskin and the Novelists," in *Nature and the Victorian Imagination*, eds. U. C. Knoepflmacher and G. B. Tennyson (London and Los Angeles: University of California Press, 1977), 149. Amitav Ghosh, *The Great Derangement*, 56, argues that "for poets and writers, it was not until the late nineteenth century that Nature lost the power to evoke that form of terror and awe that was associated with the 'sublime.'"
[24] Lazarovich-Hrebelianovich, *Pleasures and Palaces*, 69.
[25] Lazarovich-Hrebelianovich, 70.

suggest the woodland performances of *As You Like It*. Her written recollection—brimming with weather references—conjures a mundanely sublime pastoral as the location for the first open-air Shakespeare performance that had less to do with early modern theater conventions than with the Victorian theater's painted pictorial scenography. The weather evoked by Calhoun is active—a powerful sun deigns, splashes, flames, and vivifies—and into this picturesque weather-world she inserts herself as a Shakespearean actress:

> One summer day when the sun, a somewhat exclusive god in England, deigned to show forth in full power, and splash the forest with splendor, flaming on the trees and between their dark velvety masses of shadow, making more vivid still the crimsons and purples and rose-colours of the stretches of rhododendrons, it seemed to me that in such an English forest must the vision of *Rosalind* have first come to Shakespeare. In an impulse at the thought, I threw off my wrap and began to speak *Rosalind's* words.[26]

In such a wood, of course, Shakespeare did not first imagine Rosalind. Rhododendrons were only introduced to England in the late eighteenth century to decorate landscaped gardens and provide ground cover for hunting game birds, which the Duke of Cambridge occasionally came to shoot at Coombe.[27] Certainly, Shakespeare never saw a rhododendron in England. But, in such a (private) wood (planted with ostentatious, invasive shrubs imported to facilitate virile pastimes), Calhoun imagined Shakespeare imagining Rosalind disguised as Ganymede. As Robert Watson argues, *As You Like It* is preoccupied with "likenesses," and Calhoun's inference that Coombe was "like" Arden extends the "representational anxieties" that permeate the play in its early modern context to its staging here.[28]

Calhoun's account also appears to record the first woodland performance of Shakespeare's pastoral play invigorated by a romantic self-conscious awareness of being in the weather.[29] The actress's utterance of Shakespeare's lines instigated another kind of performance from her friend who was watching: "Lady

---

[26] Lazarovich-Hrebelianovich, 71.
[27] Richard I. Milne and Richard J. Abbott, "Origin and Evolution of Invasive Naturalized Material of *Rhododendron ponticum* L. in the British Isles," *Molecular Ecology* 9 (2000): 541–56, 542.
[28] Robert N. Watson, *Back to Nature: The Green and the Real in the Late Renaissance* (Philadelphia, PA: University of Pennsylvania Press, 2006), 100.
[29] Conflicting accounts of the origin of *As You Like It* at Coombe cite Campbell's painting a portrait of Calhoun dressed as Rosalind in the woods and scenes from *Romeo and Juliet* apparently performed in the open-air in Cornwall in 1880. All accounts may contain some truth, but airing Calhoun's here is undertaken in a feminist spirit, thinking with the theater historian Jacky Bratton's argument for anecdote as history and the "world of historical meaning in what they [performers] say about themselves, whether or not we have tangible proof of its truth" in *New Readings in Theatre History* (Cambridge: Cambridge University Press, 2003), 131.

Archibald stood far back as an audience while I acted through the scenes."[30] In response to Calhoun's impromptu offer of Rosalind-disguised-as-Ganymede, Campbell was compelled to perform the role of an audience member. Just as spontaneously as Calhoun became Rosalind as Ganymede, Campbell stepped back to watch, improvising in the space to create a theatrical frame for the scene. This first documented audience member for the outdoor Shakespeares synonymous with English summers today was conscious of herself weathering Calhoun's performance only inasmuch as she performed pleasure in the sunshine to encourage her friend.[31]

If Calhoun remembers inspiration for the outdoor performances at Coombe swelling up from the thawing earth, Campbell attributes "the love of the beautiful" to her role in the work.[32] Campbell's approach to nature as culture was derived from her involvement with the aesthetic movement and commitment to the sanctity of "art for art's sake" rather than for the fulfilment of any social or moral purpose. While she plays an enthusiast for Calhoun's impulsive Rosalind in the woods, Campbell therefore recalls detractors amongst her potential audience, alluding to concerns around upholding art/nature distinctions within her social circle:

> When I first thought of open-air plays it was repeatedly said to me that art and Nature could not be brought into contact without destroying dramatic effect: but I considered that there were certain plays, of which the chief elements and surroundings were so eminently natural, that open-air representation not only would not weaken, but would rather strengthen, their dramatic effect.[33]

As far as Campbell was concerned, *As You Like It*'s pastoral content made it an apposite choice for woodland performance. She argued that each character in the play was "illustrative of the different moods of Nature."[34] To perform *As You Like It* outdoors in the woods, following Campbell's logic, was simply to stage the play

---

[30] Lazarovich-Hrebelianovich, *Pleasures and Palaces*, 71.
[31] Some way into the rehearsal process, Campbell, who had no acting experience, took on the role of Orlando. It is plausible to imagine that during this instigatory impromptu performance in the woods, Calhoun addressed Ganymede's lines to Campbell, as the only other person present. The subsequent same-sex casting for Rosalind and Orlando at Coombe (and Campbell's later appearance as Oberon in Labouchere's *Dream* at the Pope's Villa in 1887) continued the established practice of women playing young men's parts. Campbell and Calhoun's performances of Rosalind and Orlando ultimately practice femininity in a way that rehearses and upholds heterosexual marriage, even as they perform the play's homoerotically charged gender-swapping. See Sharon Marcus, *Between Women: Friendship, Desire, and Marriage in Victorian England* (Princeton and Oxford: Princeton University Press, 2007).
[32] Janey Sevilla Campbell, "The Woodland Gods," in *The Woman's World*. 2 vols., ed. Oscar Wilde (London: Cassell & Company, 1887), 5.
[33] Campbell, "The Woodland Gods," 1.
[34] Campbell, 2.

so that Shakespeare's Arden accorded with nature's already-(put)there (by human landscape-gardeners): "Can we be wrong, then, in utilizing Nature to illustrate herself?" she mused, pursuing harmony between performance and environment.[35]

Although Calhoun imagined Shakespeare's inspiration springing from a landscape he never encountered, and although Campbell anticipated the tarnished sentimentality we have come to associate with twenty-first-century eco-critiques of pastoral conventions, neither woman was entirely at home in the English wood. Calhoun argued that Campbell "dwelt with the fairies in the green hills of Scotland," alluding to a romantic sensibility derived from a more rugged mountainous (awesome not mundane sublime—Celtic) landscape.[36] Similarly, Calhoun brought the Californian climate with her to Coombe. She self-proclaimed an ability to recuperate a wilder, more "authentic" Shakespeare than that contemporaneously dwelling inside Victorian theaters, to which she attributed to her dirt-floor upbringing. Her suggestion was that the American desert was closer to Shakespeare's imagination than any nineteenth-century English theater building: "The earth of my California Mountains still clung to my shoes," Calhoun wrote, "and it was more natural for my motions to run free in a wild grove than to remember theater exigencies and restrict the realization of the poet's imaginings within the means of the footlights."[37] Shakespeare's natural origins, she romanticized, were lost inside the Victorian theater and rediscovered at Coombe by female friends who identified with wilderness. In a reversal of perennial claims for Shakespeare's universality, Calhoun maintained, "However universal Shakespeare is, his genius is essentially English."[38] So too was the nature they encountered and curated for *As You Like It* "essentially English." Irrespective of the extent to which the women perceived indoor theaters failing Shakespeare, they steadfastly conceived of themselves restoring Shakespeare to England with *As You Like It*. Both contributed to creating the Victorian pastoral aesthetic that continues to color the lenses through which audiences view open-air Shakespeares, as later chapters will argue.

But as Calhoun described rehearsals for a pastoral fantasy within an artificial but animate landscape, she also observed acquisitions from British colonies abroad, disrupting her evocation of a pure English nature. Whilst preparing the performance, the women encountered an "Australian ostrich"—presumably an emu—brought to the woods; abalone shells were acquired to decorate Campbell's

---

[35] Campbell, 2.
[36] Lazarovich-Hrebelianovich, *Pleasures and Palaces*, 64.
[37] Lazarovich-Hrebelianovich, 75.
[38] Lazarovich-Hrebelianovich, 192–3.

"Iris room" inside the house; and *As You Like It* was nearly cancelled when the mostly absent Duke returned unexpectedly to find a gardener arranging moss for the stage, stripped from the graves of his Crimean War-dead relatives, Calhoun writes.[39] The Victorian vision of an English pastoral Shakespeare was carried out within a material mesh of imperialism and plunder, private ownership, and landscape gardening, circulating within and amongst a living woodland of birds, plants, trees, and weather. To the landscape of *As You Like It* at Coombe, Campbell and Calhoun brought what we might today view as a naive resourcism, conceiving of nonhuman nature as raw material available for their purpose. Despite differences, their accounts primarily imagined the woods to be reflecting and refracting human emotions. They were nonetheless simultaneously attentive to the life of the landscape, even where their interest was predominantly aesthetic and characteristically sentimental. As Calhoun romanticized Shakespeare's nature, she was attentive to inward and outward flows through a place, beginning with her Californian self. Even as Campbell aestheticized harmony and beauty, she grasped a living more-than-human world—although what she grasped was a romantic nature with limited agency of its own. Both conceptualized an unchanging pastoral nature underscoring human passions and stories. The English Shakespeare they endorsed reinforced pastoral conventions, as the following reviews show, and theatergoers' performances of weathering propagated the staging and performance of an English climate.

Arden Itself

The 1884 performance of *As You Like It* at Coombe was an unabashedly elite event. Its audience of over five hundred people comprised royalty, aristocrats, statesmen, diplomats, writers, and artists of note, forming "a goodly company of fashionable folk," *The Stage* reported.[40] Audiences sat to watch the performance with their backs to the west so that afternoon sun lit the actors. Tiered seating was flanked by green walls to blinker the view and the landscape was framed by a curtain tethered between two trees, paralleling the painted scenery and lighting of a darkened nineteenth-century indoor theater auditorium. Calhoun remembers the audience as "peepers," outside the stage picture, "invisibly peering into that forest world of life and romance."[41]

[39] Lazarovich-Hrebelianovich, 80–2.
[40] Grimalkin, "Chit Chat," *Stage*, July 25, 1884, 12–13.
[41] Lazarovich-Hrebelianovich, *Pleasures and Palaces*, 85–6.

Robert Watson reads *As You Like It* as a play which "insistently tests the membrane separating the biological world from human artifice and illusion."[42] The pushed-at partition that Watson identifies in this play filtered into the ways in which reviewers attempted to make sense of their encounter with Arden, nonhuman nature, and theatrical representation at Coombe. Amongst the many existing reviews of these performances, multiple correspondents admired a sympathy between the play's pastoral ideas, the Coombe woodland landscape, and staging. *The Illustrated Sporting and Dramatic News* related that "the scenery blended in wonderful effect with the natural background of wood and foliage."[43] *The Graphic*'s reporter also compared the outdoor performance space with indoor theaters: most of the pastoral scene was received as already present, preexisting the theater in the landscape: "Except a felled trunk and a pile of faggots here and there, little was to be observed in the way of accessories which the natural resources of the spot had not furnished."[44] The pastoral poet Alfred Austin, who attended the performance, compared the living landscape with painted theatrical scenery in his account for *The National Review* (reflecting his own predilection for floral prose):

> One found oneself comfortably seated and shut in, with green leaves and blue sky for canopy, and in front of tall, straight-growing elms, whose lower trunks were hidden from view by a loosely-stretched curtain. Suddenly it fell, and you were in the Forest of Arden; not a painted semblance of the forest, not a dexterous picture befooling the eye for a moment, but Arden itself, with its sylvan occupants, its green glades, its cool glimpses, its grassy sward, its colouring bracken, its fallen boughs and branches, its fortuitous fagots [sic], its hind's shelter, its twitter of birds and glitter of butterflies, its flocks and distant bleating, all things native and natural, as to the manner born.[45]

The theater critic Clement Scott traced an indoor theater space onto the temporary outdoor set-up, drawing a stage-set over the landscape in his detailed review for *The Theatre*, and noting that the Arden upon which Austin alighted was not in fact "Arden itself," but more "like" Arden, carefully and masterfully curated by Campbell:

---

[42] Watson, *Back to Nature*, 96. Not coincidentally, Watson actually makes this observation in response to his daughter looking at the real/scenographic grass at an open-air production of *As You Like It*.
[43] "'As You Like It' at Coombe House," *Illustrated Sporting and Dramatic News*: London, England, August 2, 1884, 530.
[44] "A Play in the Open Air," *Graphic*; August 2, 1884, 108.
[45] Alfred Austin, "In the Forest of Arden," *National Review*, September 19, 1884, 128.

Many happy suggestions were made by Lady Archibald in the arrangement of the ground, such as the erection of a rustic shed attached to the tree around which the action of the play would centre. Faggots of wood were heaped up to cover the exits, and the construction of the auditorium, the falling curtain, and the fern-bank in lieu of foot-lights, were all planned and directed by the manager. The curtain was worked by means of guiding-cords and pulleys held in two pieces of wood attached to the two trees that formed the extreme ends of the proscenium.[46]

Across these reviews, desire shifted between suggestions that nature was already theatrical (like stage scenery) and that stage scenery was already like nature. Either way, an indoor/outdoor binary was blurred into a nature/culture that was all culture, and nonhuman nature was wholly captured by humans in the name of art and representation. Indeed, as open-air performances like Campbell and Calhoun's grew in popularity, designers for the indoor theaters developed their simulations of natural landscapes inside (most spectacularly in Hawes Craven's work for Beerbohm Tree's indoor *Dream* in 1900, with its "real" babbling brook and rabbits on stage). The "nature as a theater for human events," that Buell argues should be abandoned for more "ecocentric" pastorals today, was not metaphor but material fact at Coombe.[47]

The Coombe *As You Like It* in 1884 instigated an escapist performance of pastoral from its audiences—a performative doing necessitated by the material conditions of the production. The act of retreating to the country to attend a play literalized even as it idealized the pastoral landscape. In performing pastoral, the audience physically enacted the literary convention. Echoing *As You Like It*'s flight to Arden from the court, most of the audience at Coombe temporarily abandoned London's pollution and politics to see the play in the Surrey countryside before returning to the city, assumedly rejuvenated—if not enlightened or transformed—by their leisurely time in the English woods. *The Stage*'s commentator encapsulated this social performance of pastoral when he welcomed "the change from the oppressive atmosphere of a London theater to a bright and glorious landscape, away from the trouble and the turmoil of the busy city" that attending the production facilitated.[48] Paralleling the audience retreat was the Pastoral Players treatment of the text, which omitted *As You Like It*'s opening court scenes and began with Rosalind and Orlando's first meeting

---

[46] Clement Scott, ed., "Our Omnibus Box. The Theatre: A Monthly Review of the Drama, Music and the Fine Arts," September 4, 1884, 160.
[47] Buell, *The Environmental Imagination*, 52.
[48] Grimalkin, "Chit Chat," *Stage*, July 25, 1884, 12–13.

in Arden. Thus, the audiences' arrival at Coombe and the commencement of the production were also an arrival in Arden in terms of the scenes they witnessed and the words they heard.

Fine weather in 1884 meant that records of *As You Like It* at Coombe reported the play as picture-perfect. The audience delighted in their own performance of pastoral, giving shape to their responses, which were enchanted and untroubled by the novelty of being outdoors. Notably, there was little mention of the weather in the idyllic reviews of the 1884 performances, save occasional references to "blue sky" incorporated into accounts of a picturesque setting. One small hint of the shift to come appeared in Austin's account of his journey to attend the play. Setting-out from London, he observed with foreboding "a somewhat threatening heaven, which fortunately did not carry out its menace till too late to mar the enjoyment of the spectacle."[49]

Chiding Summer Winds

In the wake of overwhelmingly positive reception for the 1884 *As You Like It*, Campbell and Godwin founded The Pastoral Players, a dramatic company of professional and amateur performers, whose name now endorsed the form at the heart of their practice. The Pastoral Players repeated *As You Like It* in May and June of 1885. Reporting on the revival for *The Dramatic Review*, the aesthete Oscar Wilde mused on his own journey to see the play at Coombe with reference to the Greek home of poetry, venturing that "Few things are so pleasurable as to be able by an hour's drive to exchange Piccadilly for Parnassus."[50] Reviews of the revival, however, revealed a creeping awareness of the relationship between the meteorological and the pastoral, the demands of which were beginning to supersede the novelty of inhabiting the landscape. Whilst the second year's iteration of *As You Like It* solicited familiar effusive prose singing the praises of the picturesque setting at Coombe, reviews began to feature extensive passages on the weather, which was, on the whole, wetter and windier than it had been during the summer of 1884. Future performance dates were listed with the caveat, "if the present fair weather continue."[51] Steve Mentz argues that the "competing frames" of "static" and "dynamic" ecosystems require "shifting from a pastoral vision, in which nature resembles a pasture

---

[49] Alfred Austin, "In the Forest of Arden," *National Review*, September 19, 1884, 126.
[50] Oscar Wilde, "'As You Like It,' at Coombe House," *Dramatic Review*, June 6, 1885, 297.
[51] "Music and the Drama," *Glasgow Herald*, June 1, 1885.

or garden, to a meteorological one, in which nature changes constantly and challenges the body at its boundaries."[52] In presenting *As You Like It* in a new context, designed to pay homage to the pastoral, the meteorological pierced the membrane of the artifice (and the leak wasn't absorbed by the pastoral ideal or the bodies encountering it). Real weather unsettled the possibility of enacting the perfect pastoral, drawing attention to the theater-makers' inability to retain control of the imagery.

Into the texts produced in response to *As You Like It* at Coombe in 1885 crept an acknowledgment that the pleasures of pastoral performance were not without risk and contingent on a dry day. "Like" Arden was not and never had been "Arden itself." In accordance with Mike Hulme's proposition that climates are discursively constructed through weather-talk, from this moment onward, reviews of and responses to English open-air Shakespeares began to allude to the weather and its impact upon the comfort of the audience—often as much as they referred to a production or the play.[53] Weather appeared in conjunction with references to the landscape as a stage setting, actors' performances, and costumes, although theatrical foci received proportionally less weight as the weather gained importance.

The *Glasgow Herald*'s reviewer described "fairly fine weather" for the 1885 opening performance of *As You Like It*, mildly uneasy about the experience.[54] *The Times* deemed it necessary to inform readers that theatergoers' comforts "were interfered with by a sudden chill in the weather and by occasional drops of rain."[55] *The Morning Post* observed discrepancies between the play in performance and the weather conditions:

> In spite of Miss Calhoun's prettily-rendered invocation contained in the Cuckoo song, that bird of spring denied its presence at Coombe House on Saturday, when Lady Archibald Campbell's company repeated last year's experiment of playing the forest scenes from "As You Like It," with Nature's own scenery for background, the leafy trees overhead, the fern-strewn turf beneath their feet, the song of the bird, the tinkle of the sheep bell, and the distance-softened bleating of its wearers for accompaniment. [...] On Saturday, with one exception, nothing could have been more attractive than the aspect of the chosen site. The exception named above was the almost total absence of the sun.[56]

---

[52] Mentz, "Strange Weather in *King Lear*," 140.
[53] Mike Hulme, *Weathered: Cultures of Climate* (London: Sage, 2017), 5.
[54] "London Gossip," *Nottingham Evening Post*, June 1, 1885, 2.
[55] "The Pastoral Plays at Coombe House," *Manchester Guardian*, June 1, 1885.
[56] "The Pastoral Players," *Morning Post*, June 1, 1885.

The dull weather detracted from the pastoral illusion that the writer depicted vividly from desire, riffing off and rupturing literary conventions. *The Morning Post* likewise integrated remarks about how audience members responded to spots of rain into writing that exhibited the pastoral in the imagination and gentle disappointment with the actual experience.

> There were none of those exquisite pencils of light shining down through the leaves to fall like silver rain on fern, frond, and turf, and make each tree trunk a thing of beauty; the clouds threatened all through the afternoon, and once or twice the pattering of a few drops of rain caused umbrellas to be opened, while a stiff breeze acted upon the great dark green curtain, which, suspended between two elms, shut off the natural stage and filled it like some great sail.

So complimented for its charm the previous year, the trunk-tethered curtain billowed out of control. Performed in response to the weather and in front of the play, the physical act of opening umbrellas undertaken by theatergoers communicated the emergence of a repertoire of audience gestures. The reviewer continued to elaborate on comfort, alluding to theatergoers' "costumes"[57]: "This absence of the sun too, with the brisk breeze, made the park chilly enough for warm wraps to be a pleasant addition to the comfort of the audiences"—audiences who imaginarily pulled these wraps tighter to brace against the wind.[58] The performance of pastoral began to look a bit like a performance of weathering, building a movement vocabulary for open-air audiences that was enacted in the presence of the theatrical performance.

Playfully integrating Shakespearean allusions into their weathered review-writing, further commentators amended Duke Senior's reference to the "churlish chiding of the winter wind" (*As You Like It* 2.1.7) to fit the blustery May afternoon:

> It must be admitted that on Saturday "the churlish chiding of the summer wind" now and then tended to make the dialogue inaudible, but the pictures presented were always pretty, and on a less windy day even the acoustic properties of the sylvan theatre would be perfect.[59]

The writer for the *Pall Mall Gazette* seized upon the same phrase, building on Shakespeare's anthropomorphized weather to characterize the already bad-tempered wind as morally repugnant. However bad the wind, it proved better for audiences than the rain it blew in another direction:

---

[57] Aoife Monks, *The Actor in Costume* (Basingstoke and New York: Palgrave, 2013), considers what audiences wear to the theater in terms of costume.
[58] "The Pastoral Players," *Morning Post*, June 1, 1885.
[59] "The Pastoral Plays at Coombe House," *Manchester Guardian*, June 1, 1885, 5.

> The only thing that in any way marred the performance of the "Pastoral Players" at Coombe House on Saturday was "the churlish chiding of the summer wind." It not only kept up a rustling in the leafy canopy, but penetrated, a chartered libertine, behind the scenes, and rendered flowing draperies somewhat unmanageable. However, we have no doubt to thank it for keeping off the rain which threatened more than once. With a little more stillness and sunshine the performance would have been altogether delightful.[60]

Compounding the intertextual Shakespearean insertions into newspaper reviews was a sense that Shakespeare's was an "English" climate. *The Observer*, for instance, framed its writing in terms of unreliable weather, musing that "Garden theatricals must necessarily be dependent upon the weather, and the weather in England is dependent upon we know not what."[61] Demonstrating the eccentricity historically associated with English people in the weather —what Michael Billig refers to as "one of the stories England has been telling itself about itself for a long time"[62]—*The Observer* commented that given the risks of outdoor performance, "No sane manager, [...] would commit himself to such an undertaking as a matter of business, even though he were granted a pitch in Hyde Park for nothing."[63] Here were both the equation of The Pastoral Players as characteristically eccentric and a slur on the women's theatrical efforts as devoid of business savvy. *The Illustrated Police News* also personified the weather within the context of an unpredictable English summer:

> For the purpose of such *al fresco* entertainments as that at Coombe House the English climate is, to say the least of it, unsympathetic. The barometer behaved well on Saturday, but up to the last moment many an anxious eye must have looked at the clouds overhead which threatened a deluge that would speedily have driving the exiles of the Forest of Arden to seek more friendly, if less romantic shelter.[64]

The paternalistic and patronizing language of "good behaviour" here faintly echoes colonial and classed attempts to uphold hierarchies and control subordinate subjects: literary expertise, in the form of pastoral and Shakespearean allusions, compensated for what was ultimately a lack of control over the unpredictable subject. Making further textual allusions to *As You Like It*, *The Observer*'s commentator suggested that "the summer day-dream of the

---

[60] "Occasional Notes," *The Pall Mall Gazette*, June 1, 1885.
[61] "Garden Theatricals at Coombe House," *Observer*, May 31, 1885, 3.
[62] Michael Billig, *Banal Nationalism* (Los Angeles and London: Sage, 1995), 70.
[63] "Garden Theatricals at Coombe House," *Observer*, May 31, 1885, 3.
[64] *The Illustrated Police News*, 6 June, 1885.

poet was realized, and it only needed a few more days of sunshine and a few less gusts of wind to transport us to that 'golden world' where 'they fleet the time carelessly.'"[65] The capable audience could have upped and left, opted not to endure the performances—or simply not have come in the first place—had the rain been heavier. A lived experience of the pastoral idyll was still the desired outcome for those who came to Coombe, but literal rather than literary skies were less confidently pronounced.

In addition to providing an alternative cultural record of the weather to that which can be found in meteorological reports and forecasts, theater reviewers disclosed contradictions between the kinds of responses to nature that the theater-makers hoped their work would elicit amongst their audiences and what the work actually accomplished for those in attendance. In Calhoun's memory, for instance, *As You Like It* transported Coombe to Arden, to Arcadia, when nature and Shakespeare appeared entirely in harmony, moving the otherwise rational audience to tears. She remembered watching the audiences' responses to the play from her on-stage vantage point as Rosalind, citing the seventeenth-century poet John Milton as a touchstone for the collective feeling she imagined herself witnessing:

> "As You Like It" pulses in such unison with nature that its world of creatures and the forest, being brought together in our interpretation of it, glowed with intermingled and intenser life, forming a harmony of beauty to "dissolve the soul in ecstasy." Those words of Milton do not overreach expressions used that day by onlookers, men and women of discretion and intellect, not usually given to extravagance. The intensity of the spell was such that when, during a scene, a young bird floundered and fell from its twig to the ground, and was picked up by an actor and tenderly tossed up to its nest among the branches, tears started to the eyes of persons present.[66]

The Nottingham Evening Post remembered a similar accident differently. The reporter recounted that "There was a real jackdaw's nest just over the stage, but at a critical moment the old bird inopportunely dropped one of its brood on to the heads of the players."[67] In this second memory, the falling bird was "inopportune" and caused an awkward hiatus for the viewer. No further elaboration in this review suggested anything like the extravagant tears Calhoun remembers. The attention drawn to "real" nature, however (whatever the bird might have made of the play happening in its habitat), revealed a little about ecologically

---

[65] "Garden Theatricals at Coombe House," *Observer*, May 31, 1885, 3.
[66] Lazarovich-Hrebelianovich, *Pleasures and Palaces*, 91.
[67] "London Gossip," *Nottingham Evening Post*, Nottingham, England, June 2, 1885, 2.

attentive response to theater in the open-air. Simply, this reported failure of the production to harmonize with its living surroundings drew attention to the life of the bird as independent to theater and not subsumed into it. We might note, in this case, that rupture rather than harmony drew attention to ecology (although attention didn't shift as far as the life of the bird, but to the limits of representation).

Campbell, however, like Calhoun, insisted that spectators were moved to tears by the production. She too integrated her literary competence into her memory of audience response, citing the nineteenth-century American writer Edgar Allan Poe in her account:

> Players and spectators alike cannot but be carried into a realization of actual pastoral life while Nature's vibrating accompaniment speaks to them in the lisp of leaves and "the murmur that springs from the growing of grass," in the song of birds, and in the many outward symbols of her ceaselessly pulsating life. In effect, it is through the feelings she inspires, under certain conditions of harmony, that the sensitive spectator is moved to a delight which finds its expression in tears. Nature is then as the voice of the beloved, singing to one alone."[68]

Campbell's "Mother Nature"—the historically acquired role of the "mother" for nature upholding nineteenth century romantic conceptions of "nature as a [female] person writ large," identified by Carolyn Merchant[69]—addressed the individual as "one alone" within the audience, rather than an interdependent collective of theatergoers. Campbell felt that the performance in the woods offered its audience a sense of "actual pastoral life," as though pastoral life was an obtainable, lived experience rather than a literary convention (which, for her audiences, it was). Nature addressed the individual in the crowd, and individuals responded by weeping at the beauty of the English countryside (personified as a musical lover). Shakespeare's play arrived home at Coombe whilst the peeping audience remained outside looking on, incongruous in the landscape:

> The fact that many among the more observant spectators confessed to finding themselves the only notes out of tune with the natural surroundings, is perhaps the best proof that a union of art with Nature was then and there consummated. The audience really became the only external conventionality which appeared out of place, because Nature had not absorbed them, as it were, and made them her own.[70]

---

[68] Campbell, "The Woodland Gods," 4.
[69] Carolyn Merchant, *Reinventing Eden: The Fate of Nature in Western Culture* (New York: Routledge, 2004), 136.
[70] Campbell, 5.

Campbell's vision of the union of nature and art excluded its audience, some of whom saw themselves as out of place, blotting an otherwise perfect pastoral landscape (in fact, disjuncture between the audience and the world of the play was anticipated by Godwin, who dressed as a friar—casting himself as the "wise man" who returns Rosalind at the end of *As You Like It*—for the duration of the in-situ rehearsal process. Godwin aimed to better blend with the surroundings by dressing in costume during rehearsals.) Despite their co-presence with the production of *As You Like It* in shared daylight, the audience was outside the imaginary proscenium looking on, neither participant nor implicated in the theatrical world.

Watson draws attention to *As You Like It*'s editors, disunited over whether the Duke Senior declares that he and his exiles feel "*not* the penalty of Adam" or "*but* the penalty of Adam" in the Forest of Arden.[71] At stake in this small word is the extent to which the Duke and his followers are unaffected by the hardships of forest life ("not"), or invigorated by "good, honest, primal, outdoorsy pain" ("but").[72] Overwhelmingly present in the reception of this 1885 revival of *As You Like It* was a sense that the performance of pastoral—so willingly undertaken as a lighthearted exercise in 1884 ("like the exiles, we do not feel Adam's penalty")—gave way to a growing recognition of the event's contingency upon the weather ("we feel *but* Adam's penalty, and it is just about worth it for the proximity to the Arden it affords us; although it reinforces the unobtainability of Arden in the 'real' world"). Like Shakespeare's shepherd Corin, who Watson identifies as the play's empiricist, audiences at Coombe became bodily aware that rain's "property" is to "wet".[73] As *The Nottingham Evening Post* bluntly put it, "People are, however, sadly wearying of "As You Like It," with guinea tickets, a twenty mile drive, and the chance of a wetting."[74] Interwoven with a tenacious inscription of indoor theatrical space onto the landscape and the social performances of weathering instigated by the theatrical events, disequilibrium between the pastoral idyll and the lived experience made an easy target for commentators who alighted upon the theater makers' powerless desire to fall in with the weather (if not to control it) and audiences' desire to control (if not the weather) at least the extent of their exposure. Some self-awareness in the reviews attracted by The Pastoral Players seemed archly awake to the limits of desire but satisfied with knowing the literary and aesthetic possibilities of pastoral (from a position of shelter).

---

[71] Watson, *Back to Nature,* 80.
[72] Watson, *Back to Nature,* 80.
[73] Watson, *Back to Nature,* 91.
[74] "London Gossip," *The Nottingham Evening Post*, Nottingham, England, June 2, 1885, 2.

John Lucas argues that by the end of the nineteenth century, poets either "clung to a pastoral vision of England" or "committed themselves to that vision of primitivism which emerged in the later years of the century as a regenerative alternative to the decadence of the society of the city."[75] The Pastoral Players, equated with summer leisure activities for the erudite exiles, absolutely evinced the former. Theatrical performances of Shakespeare and social performances of weathering from their audiences all performed Englishness, where England was equated with a (managed) rural arcadia, visited by the best of the aristocracy (who, in addition to inherited wealth, were the recipients of income from farming, mining, manufacturing, and the exploitation of natural resources stretching across the empire), who reaffirmed a conviction that Englishness meant cultured pastoral and unpredictable weather, whilst keeping the environmental realities of city life "invisible."[76]

Henrietta Labouchere's *A Midsummer Night's Dream*, 1887

I would like to return to Henrietta Labouchere's "sylvan scenes" from *A Midsummer Night's Dream*, featuring Campbell as Oberon at Pope's Villa—the scenes with which I started—before drawing this chapter to a close. Labouchere's *Dream* was so well received in July 1887 that it was repeated in August for a garden party in aid of the Charing Cross hospital. Although it is nowhere mentioned in the commentary on the play, it is pleasing to fancy that for some of those in the audience, the spatial "palimpsest" of Alexander Pope's gardens as "host" for Labouchere's *Dream* may have been "ghosted" by Pope's own historical relationship to the literary pastoral—not least his scathing critique of the poet Ambrose Philips's *Pastorals* in a 1713 *Guardian* article laced with ironic praise—and inflected by Pope's famous landscaping interventions at the Villa (which featured a subterranean tunnel from the house into the gardens and a grotto, originally intended by Pope to look "natural" but later transformed to resemble a diamond mine).[77] Responses to Labouchere's *Dream* continued to devote considerable portions of their word-count to describing landscape and weather. The first night was remembered as "warm, fair and starry" with a

---

[75] John Lucas, *England and Englishness* (London: The Hogarth Press, 1990), 9.
[76] Lucas, *England and Englishness*, 9.
[77] The notion of a "host" site, "ghosted" by site-specific performance is put forward by Pearson and Shanks, after Cliff McLucas, in *Theatre/Archaeology*, 37.

"harvest moon."[78] The grounds offered "an undulating auditorium, the rolling sward into a most picturesque arena, and the noble beeches furnished a sylvan background to as true a piece of poetic action as ever fascinated the eyes of fair women and brave men."[79] As at Coombe, the fair and brave cohort for whom Labouchere's Shakespeare was performed comprised high-profile "gay and gallant gentlefolk […] famous and expert in literature, society, and the arts."[80] One guest commended the attire of those in attendance, suggesting that—also as at Coombe—the audience occupied a space outside the pastoral picture. Far from seeking to blend with their pastoral surroundings, over four hundred theatergoers aspired to stand apart from the contrivances of the *Dream*'s nature aesthetic as cultured individuals: "arrayed in every variety of costume from Mr. Hermann Vezin in boating flannels to Mr. Hamilton Aidé in full ball costume. The sage of Northampton was himself clothed in a post hat and a Norfolk jacket, which set off his figure to perfection."[81]

Although some sheltered seating was provided, of Labouchere's guests, including the actress Ellen Terry (once married to Godwin of The Pastoral Players), "over 100 visitors sat in the open outside, these having, perhaps, the most enjoyable positions, owing to the perfect weather and the serenity of the atmosphere."[82] To be exposed to the elements was to have the best position for weathering the play, thanks to the serene atmosphere, which contrasted with the noisy breezes remembered at Coombe. The Pastoral Players' *As You Like It* took place during the afternoon in natural daylight but Labouchere presented her *Dream* at dusk, which the *Morning Post* compared favorably with the Coombe matinees:

> There [at Coombe] the garish light of day had beaten somewhat too fiercely upon the actors' paint and tinsel. Something, too, there was of erudity in the juxtaposition of the conventional personages and the real *mise-en-scene*. […] Here on Saturday the harmony between the poem and its setting was complete. Not a breath was stirring to intercept the players' lines or the undercurrent of Mendelssohn's music. The bright moonshine streaming through the boughs of the tall wych-elms shamed the rough substitute imagined by the clowns in the play.[83]

---

[78] "Latest London News." *Aberdeen Journal*, August 8, 1887, 5.
[79] "'A Midsummer Night's Dream' at Pope's Villa," *Exeter and Plymouth Gazette*, August 8, 1887, 3.
[80] "Shakespeare and Twickenham," *Pall Mall Gazette*, July 26, 1887.
[81] "Shakespeare and Twickenham," *Pall Mall Gazette*, July 26, 1887.
[82] "'A Midsummer Night's Dream' at Pope's Villa," *Exeter and Plymouth Gazette*, August 8, 1887, 3.
[83] "'A Midsummer Night's Dream' at Pope's Villa," *Morning Post*, August 8, 1887, 3.

Memories of The Pastoral Players' *As You Like It* were still fresh enough to feature as recent comparators but the retrospective critique invited by a few years' distance indicated that the harmony that Campbell envisaged at Coombe hadn't been unanimously felt at the time. Labouchere's *Dream* began at half-past eight, requiring electric lighting to illuminate the pastoral escape into the woods outside Athens. Many reviewers commented on the fading daylight as the performance began: "the attendant gloom cast by the shadow of the great trees was dispersed by the glow cast by the electric light, and Theseus with his courtiers was seen approaching."[84] In the gardens at Pope's Villa:

> Every leaf in the foliage seemed separately illuminated, the tree trunks appeared as though iridescent in the light, and the ferns and harebells on the sward waved to and fro in the shifting air as though really growing in the forest where the action of the play is supposed to take place.[85]

Of course the plants were "really growing" in the gardens but it is worth noting that the commentator thought of them as living in Shakespeare's imaginary woods outside Athens as though Shakespeare's woods were at Pope's Villa. The effects of electric lighting on trees in the darkness were uniquely noted as a positive formal development, made possible by the later starting time (they also anticipate Max Reinhardt's aesthetic proclivity for lighting "real" trees in the twentieth century, discussed in the next chapter).

By the time of Labouchere's *Dream*, pleasure was routinely documented in responsive writing that integrated references to the outdoor setting, weather, and audience. Reviewers were alert to the possibility that the embodied encounter with the dramatic performance had the potential to chafe with the environmental conditions as much as it could be enhanced by them. Expressions of desire for the perfect pastoral, for optimum weather and harmony between play, production, and place, continued to characterize responses to the theatrical events. Spectatorship—when the pastoral picture didn't quite work out—was self-reflexively attentive to inconvenience, highlighting the dream of what the pastoral could be and the luxury of a choice to practice leisure where and when it suits.

It is Labouchere's *Dream* that the reviewer of Herbert Beerbohm Tree's production can't forget. And with Campbell playing Oberon at the Pope's Villa and Campbell's retrospective writing on The Pastoral Players and eulogy for Godwin published in "The Woodland Gods" (also 1886), it is reasonable to assume that

---

[84] "'A Midsummer Night's Dream' at Pope's Villa," *Exeter and Plymouth Gazette*, August 8, 1887, 3.
[85] "'A Midsummer Night's Dream' at Pope's Villa," 3.

her philosophies of pastoral performance continued to circulate at Twickenham too. Loitering in these gardens and drawing an arc between Campbell, Calhoun, and Labouchere help us to observe intersubjective performances of weathering that reflect overlapping visions of pastoral: as a classical literary convention (present in the performance of Shakespeare's texts); as a cultural context for a retreat from the urban into nature (enacted in the theatrical performances and the practices undertaken by audiences in attending the productions); and (retrospectively) as the works' complicity in historic environmental damage, ideologically and materially construed.

Had the second performance of Labouchere's *Dream* been scheduled to take place one week later, it would have been rained off. The season's weather report documented: "The fine dry weather which characterized the summer of 1887 continued until the middle of August, when a decided change took place, the remainder of the season being cold, showery, and thundery."[86]

The Very First Forest Production of Any Play

The desire to commune with "Mother Nature" pursued by Campbell and Calhoun ran distinct from Ben Greet's "copycat"[87] work with The Woodland Players in the years that followed, continuing into and through the twentieth-century productions in the next chapter (Greet was motivated by a different set of impulses—God and business mostly). Michael Dobson argues that "whether or not Greet saw the Aesthetes *As You Like It* at Coombe, he certainly heard about it and recognized its commercial potential."[88] Greet himself downplayed The Pastoral Players' innovations when publicizing his own work:

> The fact is, we used to give out-of-door performances at school, and when I first went on the stage, the idea of open-air entertainment went with me. Lady Campbell revived the old notion, and knowing she would never want to take out a professional company I thought I would, and, as you know, I did, and very successful and encouraging the out-of-door performances have been.[89]

Calhoun refuted Greet's dismissal in a letter to the *New York Times* in 1916:

---

[86] "Monthly Weather Report, June 1885," 59–61.
[87] Dobson, *Shakespeare and Amateur Performance*, 173.
[88] Dobson, 173.
[89] "A Chat with Ben Greet," *Era*. December 2, 1899, 15.

Mr Greet was not the originator nor the initiator of the pastoral production of plays. The summer representation, in the early eighties, of "As You Like It," in Coombe Grove, Surrey, England, imagined first by me, and in which I acted Rosalind, while the Hon. Lady Archibald Campbell of Argyll, took the part of Orlando, was the very first forest production of any play, and was hailed in England and on the Continent as the initiation of a new form of poetic representation arousing a new aesthetic emotion.[90]

In his work on Victorian women in the theater, Kerry Powell argues for the "revolutionary aspects" of *As You Like It* at Coombe, noting the feminist significance of Calhoun and Campbell's collaboration and arguing that "in moving the production out-doors they were introducing a drama beyond the reach of male actor-managers and the theaters that they ruled."[91] By making their work outdoors, Powell contends, Campbell and Calhoun evaded the patriarchal structures of the indoor theaters of the time. Together with Labouchere, their pastoral Shakespeares in gardens on the edges of London evidence gendered slippages between professional and amateur theater-makers that continue to persist in this form. Moreover, they instigate a particular kind of spectatorship from audiences for outdoor Shakespeares—who performed pastoral first as novelty and began to perform weathering as a temporary but fruitful inconvenience in the years that followed.

Environmentally, what is lost by emphasizing Godwin and Greet instead of Campbell, Calhoun, and Labouchere, is what these women's work reveals about the reception of Victorian pastorals in the weather. Theirs are the first of now-pervasive form of performance framed by nature, and different entirely to the Shakespeares that seek to emulate early modern performance conditions, such as those Elizabethan revivals later undertaken by William Poel and the Elizabethan Stage Society (from 1895). Their pastoral performances of *As You Like It* and *A Midsummer Night's Dream*—and the audience performances of weathering that they bring about—persist in complex ways in the reception of nonhuman nature at open-air Shakespeares today.

Writing in a contemporary anthropocene context, Terry Gifford proposes that thinking of pastoral as a "cultural function" rather than a "genre" or "discourse"

---

[90] "Pastoral Shakespeare: Princess Lazarovich Tells of the Earliest Productions in England," *New York Times*. March 18, 1916. In a letter to Godwin dated May 20, 1885, Wilde apologized to Godwin for not having praised him in his May 1885 write-up on "Shakespeare and Stage Costume" for the *Nineteenth Century* magazine: "Thanks for your praise of my article. The reason I spoke of 'Lady Archie's' production was this. I had spoken before of you in *Claudian*, and was afraid that a second mention would look as if you had put me up to praise you. But everyone knows you did it all. The glory is yours entirely."

[91] Kerry Powell, *Acting Wilde: Victorian Sexuality, Theatre, and Oscar Wilde* (Cambridge: Cambridge University Press, 2009), 154.

might pave the way for the utility of a less ecologically defunct "post-pastoral."[92] He proposes that it might be possible to "bypass[...] the British critical dead end for pastoral by identifying a version of continuity that is itself aware of the dangers of idealized escapism while seeking some form of accommodation between humans and nature."[93] Within their arboreal prosceniums, Campbell, Calhoun, and Labouchere demonstrate no awareness of the dangers (to others—human and nonhuman—in their time) of a romanticized escapism lurking in pastorals, nor could we expect them to. On the contrary, they epitomize them. Their work revels in what are today the most worrisome versions of pastoral. *As You Like It* at Coombe and *A Midsummer Night's Dream* at the Pope's Villa might seem to seek some form of accommodation between humans and nonhuman nature, but the desire for accommodation stems from seeking to harness nature for the realization of a literary trope. Indeed, in Campbell's version of the pastoral stage, a nature/culture binary subsumes nature into art, imagining the harmonious possibilities of the human-made pastoral trope as the pre-existing conditions for rural life, whilst enabling the audience to imagine themselves outside (not implicated in) this idealized world.

The Greeks enjoyed halcyon days for winter performances. Once early modern performers moved from the open-roofed playhouses to indoor theaters, there was no nostalgia for the discomfort of the former amphitheater spaces.[94] Unlike the exposed playhouses of Shakespeare's day, open-air performances at Coombe and Twickenham were exposed to the weather as an aesthetic maneuver. Shakespeare subsumed nature into his pastorals, and Shakespeare was regarded as subsumed into nature in these productions—inasmuch as the text was sympathetically trimmed, costumed, and staged to fit the natural environment. Furthermore, these productions required their audiences to undertake a performance of pastoral, temporarily leaving city dwellings and politics for the fresh air and aesthetic beauty of cultured suburban gardens and managed countryside. As coming chapters show, theater audiences continue to perform weathering in response to Shakespeares outdoors into and through the twentieth century, to the present day. When the next chapter thinks of weathering Shakespeare in the 1930s, it remembers Calhoun, Campbell, and Labouchere, whose audiences undertook embodied, imagined, and narrated practices in response to a leisure activity tethered to high literary and aesthetic culture.

---

[92] Terry Gifford, "Pastoral, Anti-Pastoral, and Post-Pastoral," in *The Cambridge Companion to Literature and Environment* (Cambridge: Cambridge University Press, 2014), 26.
[93] Gifford, "Pastoral, Anti-Pastoral, and Post-Pastoral," 26.
[94] Gabriel Egan, *Green Shakespeare: From Ecopolitics to Ecocriticism* (Oxon and New York: Routledge, 2006), 47.

2

"Light them at the fiery glow-worm's eyes": Max Reinhardt's *A Midsummer Night's Dream* and the Regent's Park Open Air Theatre

Most of the fireflies that shone so brightly in the warm Italian air, decorating Max Reinhardt's production of *A Midsummer Night's Dream* at the Boboli Gardens, Florence in May 1933, perished en route to Oxford.¹ Both sexes of adult *luciola italica* or *luciola lusitanica* fly on summer evenings and were the likely conscripted performers in their starlit Florentine habitat.² But unless larvae were also shipped to Oxford and provided with suitable nourishment as they hatched mid-journey, any captured originals would have reached the end of their short life cycles within a week. Accustomed as they are to Mediterranean climates, the fireflies would never have settled in England anyway. By the time Reinhardt's production of Shakespeare's *Dream* transferred to the Hollywood Bowl in California in September 1934, it featured thousands of electric fireflies, creating the imagery now synonymous with his 1935 film.³

Better disposed to interclimatic travel was Catharine Sibley, a 25-year-old aspiring theater-maker originally from Montana, USA. In 1932, Sibley travelled from her

---

¹ Richard Kerridge, "An Ecocritic's Macbeth," in *Ecocritical Shakespeare*, eds. Lynne Bruckner and Dan Brayton (Farnham and Burlington: Ashgate, 2011), 193–210, notes inaccuracies found by Edward A. Armstrong (1946) in Shakespeare's representations of the natural world, one of which was that "If he [Shakespeare] had picked up a glow-worm he might easily have ascertained that the fairies could not light their tapers at its eyes—for the luminescence is in its tail."
² Frederick Tollini, *The Shakespeare Productions of Max Reinhardt* (Lewiston, Queenston and Lampeter: The Edwin Mellon Press, 2004), 196. Although I have been unable to identify this surviving pair, Michael Geiser, coleopteran curator at London's Natural History Museum, offers that the species of fireflies likely to have been incorporated into the Florence *Dream* can be narrowed down to these two possibilities.
³ Leonard M. Fiedler, "Reinhardt, Shakespeare, and the 'Dreams,'" in *Max Reinhardt: The Oxford Symposium*, eds. Margaret Jacobs and John Warren (Oxford: Oxford Polytechnic, 1986), 79, argues that Reinhardt's 1905 production of *A Midsummer Night's Dream* attracted crowds no longer interested in seeing "Shakespeare's play, but Reinhardt's *Dream*; a development which sanctioned the rise of the director and directing as a new artistic medium and as an art in its own right."

then home in California to Salzburg, Austria, where she encountered Reinhardt's *Dream* in rehearsal for the first time. Her journal entry for August 10 reads:

> Was it all only a midsummer night's dream—there in the garden of that charming little old Castle Klessheim, a short hour's ride from the Baroque-towered town of Salzburg? A full moon was overhead, a breathless stillness in the air, an excited expectancy as we took our seats on the benches improvised for the occasion. […] I have at last been in the midst of something that is alive. The theatre breathed tonight and pulsed its throbbing vitality through my whole being![4]

Sibley remembers that Reinhardt's promenade production brought its audience on a journey through the castle grounds, pausing in different locations to witness scenes from the play.[5] Audiences began the evening event in the gardens, moved to an area "dominated by a tall tree" for the *Dream*'s forest scenes, and concluded in one of the castle's grand reception rooms.[6] Entirely entranced by Reinhardt's approach to directing Shakespeare and the reception his work received from audiences, Sibley went on to work as his general assistant on the series of outdoor *Dream*s that followed: first at Mussolini's invitation to the Florence May Festival in 1933 (where she would have brushed air with the native fireflies); then at the Headington Gardens in Oxford, also in 1933 (where the poor fireflies failed to fly); and finally in California in 1934 (amongst flickering firefly substitutes).

In Florence's Boboli Gardens, Sibley photographed the Danish performer Nini Theilade rehearsing the first fairy dances on the garden steps leading away from the Pitti Palace and toward the Abbondanza statue, framed by four giant holm oak trees. Danced to Mendelssohn's Nocturne, Theilade's solo famously concluded with a male actor carrying her away into the darkness on his back, in a moment of staging that Gary Jay Williams reads as the darkness of twentieth-century troubles in Europe infiltrating Reinhardt's neoromantic aesthetic.[7] The light given by the fireflies would have offered some continuity between the stage area in which Theilade performed and the dark night air into which he carried her and in which audiences sat, piercing gradations of darkness with flashes of their living presence. Theilade then accompanied the *Dream* from Florence to Oxford where she reprised her first fairy dances (without the *corps de luciola*). She remained in England to perform the fairy dances in the *Dream* at the newly opened Regent's Park Open Air Theatre in London that same summer, before

---

[4] Catharine Sibley, "The Magic of Max Reinhardt," *California Monthly*. June, 1934, 9.
[5] Reinhardt was taking Shakespeare for a walk in the park long before the idea of promenade theatre became common and then passé.
[6] Sibley, "The Magic of Max Reinhardt," 10.
[7] Gary Jay Williams, *Our Moonlight Revels*: A Midsummer Night's Dream *in the Theatre* (Iowa: University of Iowa Press, 1997), 176.

following Reinhardt's *Dream* to the Hollywood Bowl in California and ultimately into immortality in his film.

The fireflies, Sibley, and Theilade are of interest ecologically for intersecting reasons that color the performances of weathering enacted by audiences in response to this chapter's open-air Shakespeares. First, the ill-fated *luciola* exemplify the environmental resourcism of Shakespeare production at this time, concerned with harnessing natural resources and making them appear spectacularly cultural in performance—at once proclaiming and discrediting man's desires to manipulate nonhuman life to satisfy aesthetic ambition. Second, Sibley is herself a uniquely placed spectator of Reinhardt's *Dream* for this succession of open-air performances, having traveled between countries and climates with the production, documenting the work as she went. Third, Theilade danced for Reinhardt's *Dream* in its various locations and at the Regent's Park Open Air Theatre. In each location, the reception of her fairy performance encapsulates a fetishizing of "little" and pretty dancers as (super)natural others, reflecting perceptions of an ethereal femininity, cast as closer to nature than man, nature's sculptor.[8] Together, the fireflies, Sibley, and Theilade reflect familiar hierarchical, unjust and untenable ecological relations: where bodies gendered as female watch or support male genius at work in nature, when they are not gazed upon *in* it or essentialized as closer *to* it. And when glowing insects are unable to meet the joint demands of art and climate, they are simply replaceable with innovative technologies.

The historiographical approach to storytelling utilized in this chapter continues my attempt to study reception retrospectively in the first part of this book, drawing on the words of (a limited group of) participants, theater reviewers, and critics, to demonstrate the ideological work of weathering performed as a cultural practice in response to Shakespeare in the open-air. I draw on Sibley's archive, press releases, newspapers, and periodicals that respond to Reinhardt's *Dream*, alongside reviews and production notes for the parallel productions and performances at the Open Air Theatre in Regent's Park. The two years with which this chapter is primarily concerned—1933 and 1934—do not attempt to represent chronological progress from the Pastoral Players at Coombe Woods in 1884 and 1885, as though such a trajectory were possible or desirable anyway. I hope that stopping here nevertheless illuminates continuities and contrasts in the environmental, material, sociocultural, and historical conditions for performances of weathering as they can be (re)constructed from documents generated in reception. If the Pastoral Players at Coombe disclose a sentimental pastoral disrupted in the previous chapter,

---

[8] George W. Bishop, "The Ideal Open Air Play," *Daily Telegraph*, June 20, 1934, 8. Across the reviews of the *Dream* in all locations, there are multiple references to the ballets and dancers, Theilade in particular, as "little" and "exquisite."

Reinhardt's *A Midsummer Night's Dream* and Regent's Park's open-air Shakespeares adopt grandiose and controlling approaches to the nonhuman environment.⁹ Propagating the notion of not just an economic but an aesthetic "resourcism" in environmental discourse in the 1980s, Neil Evernden draws on the metaphor of "casting," conflating allusions to the processes of metal and plasterwork and the theater industry's process of selecting actors for a role: "resourcism," Evernden writes, "is a kind of modern religion which casts all of creation into categories of utility."¹⁰ Of course, the resourcist nature of Reinhardt's work happens before anthropogenic climate change is a known scientific fact, but a showy hubris goes hand in hand with environmental degradation in productions that are preoccupied with an abundant materiality, with the "stuff" of theater-making. Moreover, the productions take place in tandem with the rise of European nationalism alongside growing confidence in Man's ability to know and mitigate the weather. They also represent a denial of (or resistance to) the rise of Hitler and Nazi Germany. In some respects, then, Reinhardt resists one kind of mid-twentieth-century nationalism only to fuel another kind with his lavish productions in support of an English Shakespeare. Weathering Shakespeare in this chapter is therefore undertaken in conjunction with the endeavor to master all of the elements of outdoor production—from vulnerable nonhuman and human bodies to landscapes and atmosphere. Pursuing Reinhardt's *Dream* west to California discloses networks of gendered and politicized cultural production across climates that leave environmental devastation in their wake.¹¹

---

⁹ Stacy Alaimo, *Exposed: Environmental Politics and Pleasures in Posthuman Times* (Minneapolis and London: University of Minnesota Press, 2016), 94, argues for "carbon-heavy masculinities," identifying an "impenetrability and aggressive consumption" in post 9/11 American masculinity that revels in a blatant disregard for climate change, driving bigger vehicles, faster, and taking pleasure in burning fossil fuels and causing pollution. The behavior in this chapter is "carbon heavy" and in some senses "masculinist," although it is not brashly denialist in the same anthropocene context that Alaimo writes.

¹⁰ Neil Evernden, *The Natural Alien: Humankind and Environment*, 2nd ed. (Toronto: University of Toronto Press, 1993), 23.

¹¹ Academic accounts of Reinhardt's outdoor *A Midsummer Night's Dream* suggest the scope for an ecologically attentive reassessment of Reinhardt's shifting aesthetic within the varied climates. J.L. Styan, *Max Reinhardt* (Cambridge: Cambridge University Press 1982), 54–61, skips over Florence but offers an overall trajectory that starts with Reinhart's first indoor production at the Neues Playhouse in 1905. Styan provides the most extensive existing account of the Oxford production; Tollini, *The Shakespeare Productions of Max Reinhardt*, 195–205, follows the open-air *Dreams* from Florence and Oxford through to the California performances; Williams, *Our Moonlight Revels*, 174–8, takes a holistic look at Reinhardt's engagement with the play over a thirty-year period, also starting with the Neues Playhouse production in 1905 and including a quick trip through the "spectacular" outdoor performances; none of these accounts consider the aesthetic relationship to ecology and none isolate the outdoor series. That the outdoor performances come toward the end of a longer trajectory of *Dreams* is important nevertheless because it evidences Reinhardt's growing confidence in his ability to imagine and create landscapes. The transition to working outdoors was also a necessity, compounded by the loss of his own Schloss Leopoldskron under the Nazi regime.

A(nother) New Poetic Reality: Oxford, 1933

Immediately after the opening of the Florence *Dream* in the Boboli Gardens, on a night when "threatening clouds" gave way to "bright stars," Sibley accompanied Reinhardt from Italy to England.[12] There, keen actors from the Oxford University Dramatic Society eagerly anticipated his masterly direction. Audiences from across the country scrambled to secure tickets, reassured only by the news that there would be multiple opportunities to encounter the famed director's *Dream*.[13] Upon arrival at the performance site in Oxford, Sibley found the "open English meadow between occasional trees" on the South Bank in Headington Hill to be in "complete contrast" with the "scrambly" castle grounds in Salzburg or "regal" gardens of Florence.[14] In Oxford, Reinhardt was reported to be working on a scale of "not feet but acres."[15] The "new poetic reality," however, that Sibley declared he achieved at the intersection of town and countryside was only a partial fulfilment of the director's fantasy of an English Shakespeare.[16] For although Reinhardt cabled ahead from Florence requesting that the Oxford production take place on a hill, the University gardens are flat, and Felix Weissberger, Reinhardt's assistant director, in fact, chose the most appropriate site and began rehearsals in advance of his arrival.[17] Reinhardt therefore had limited time to interfere with the landscape in England, however much anecdotal accounts of his first visit reveal a desire to do so: upon seeing a distant village behind the chosen stage area, he is remembered as exclaiming "That town—it must go!" and demanding "80 extras and a lake" to complete the stage picture.[18]

E.S., writing for *The Saturday Review*, recorded benign weather for the opening performance of the *Dream* in Oxford, reporting that toward the end of the evening "two little hesitant stars came out high above" and "the breeze blew softly."[19] Documenting some of the visual stage pictures, Sibley photographed groups of actors in baroque costumes, shipped from Reinhardt's theater in Austria, and hunting dogs accompanying Theseus and Hippolyta—further nonhuman performers drafted for Shakespeare. Sibley also captured chiffon-clad

---

[12] "'A Midsummer Night's Dream' Herr Reinhardt's Open-Air Production," Milan, June 1. *Times*, 1933, 10.
[13] "Professor Max Reinhardt and Oxford," *Manchester Guardian*, April 28, 1933, 8. The cast comprised student members of the Oxford University Dramatic Society and professional actresses from London. The O.U.D.S. did not permit women to join the society until 1963. Reinhardt accepted no fee for the production and received an honorary degree while in Oxford.
[14] Sibley, "The Magic of Max Reinhardt," 9 and 10.
[15] "A Reinhardt Production." *Daily Telegraph*, June 16, 1933, 8.
[16] Sibley, "The Magic of Max Reinhardt," 9.
[17] Sibley, 11.
[18] Felix Felton, "Max Reinhardt in England," *Theatre Research* (1958), 134–42, 140.
[19] E. S., "A Dream of Beauty," *The Saturday Review*, June 24, 1933, 614.

Figure 2.1 Audience hats at Max Reinhardt's *A Midsummer Night's Dream* in Oxford, 1993. Photograph courtesy of the University of Binghamton.

fairies on camera, glimpsed from behind the tips of summer hats on audience members looking at the stage. Oxford's *Dream* environment was more arboreal than Florence's, with *The Times* noting "elm and beech and may" present in the meadow.[20] *The Sphere* observed "lighting effects making magical the leaves, and the scents and sounds of a summer evening intoxicating the senses."[21] Felix Felton, the actor who played Bottom, remembered the landscape as inanimate before human performance, writing that as Lords and Ladies stepped out from behind the trees to begin the play, the "whole landscape suddenly, effortlessly, alive."[22] A slightly less anthropocentric reading of the play in the landscape imagined it "alive" only when populated by fairies. For *The Manchester Guardian*, Reinhardt's production was "at its best towards the end of the evening," when the "shadowy background" was "alive and peopled with fairies."[23] Furthermore,

[20] "O.U.D.S. Midsummer Night's Dream," *Times*. June 16, 12.
[21] "A London News Letter," *The Old Stager. The Sphere*. June 24, 1993, 472.
[22] Felton, "Max Reinhardt in England," 141.
[23] "'A Midsummer Night's Dream' Reinhardt's Production for the O.U.D.S.," *Manchester Guardian*, June 17, 1933, 16.

the "natural surroundings" added "great beauty" to Theilade's already beautiful ballets.[24] The recurring suggestion from reviewers was that the landscape came to life when it was animated by humans, not that it was alive prior to their presence. Supernatural creatures—portrayed mostly by young female dancers dressed as fairies—appeared to live in closer proximity to nonhuman nature than the play's human characters. No longer "a story of mortals in this world behind whom an enchantment has arisen," *The Times* observed, Shakespeare's *Dream* became "a tale of sprites and goblins pursuing the natural life of their own dwelling-place, into which men and women have blindly wandered."[25] While widespread and unabashed anthropocentrism is a fairly banal observation to make of theater history, especially in light of the reviewers' task to critique the human activity of performing a play, the absence of weather-inflected commentaries in accounts of the first night of Reinhardt's Oxfordian *Dream* indicates that weather conditions did not interfere with the audience experience of the opening performance in any significant way.

In light of the relative absence of the weather in documents surviving the performance, then, it is all the more striking to hear Reinhardt's reflections on Oxford in an interview in *The Observer* in July 1933. That he first acknowledged himself impressed by the talent and commitment of the largely amateur actors is hardly surprising. Unprompted, however, were his comments about also being struck by the audience's determination to endure Shakespeare in performance whatever the weather: "What was equally remarkable was the enthusiasm of the public who sat through all weathers good and bad, in their eagerness for Shakespeare."[26] At no other location did Reinhardt specifically praise audiences' resolve for weathering Shakespeare. In this "enthusiasm" and "eagerness" that he observed amongst audience members, Reinhardt alighted upon the latest iteration of a performance of weathering, concerned with national identity and allied to notions of aspirational control. Although "different every night" is a favorite trope of advocates for live theater, the weather vastly intensifies nightly differences, especially from the perspective of a theatergoer. Fine weather for the opening performance of the *Dream* at Oxford jolts us to remember that reviews covering first performances and don't offer a good overview of what occurs over the duration of a run. Reinhardt's remarks commending the audiences he encountered during his time in England, sandwiched between his Salzburg,

---

[24] "'A Midsummer Night's Dream' Reinhardt's Production for the O.U.D.S.," *Manchester Guardian*, June 17, 1933, 16.
[25] "O.U.D.S. Midsummer Night's Dream," *Times*. June 16, 12.
[26] "Max Reinhardt's Plans: His Production of 'Faust' Salzburg Visit," *Observer*, July 2, 1933, 11.

Figure 2.2 *A Midsummer Night's Dream* at Oxford, 1933. Photograph courtesy of the University of Binghamton.

Florence, and California productions, gloss a growing national-cultural practice for reproducing climate as culture by performing weathering in response to Shakespeare in the open-air. More than the wistful desire for Shakespeare and weather to fall in harmony together at Coombe's *As You Like It*, this desire now began to be articulated with attendant, overt allusions to military practices, linked to imperialist impulses for mastery, as what follows at the Regent's Park's Open Air Theatre will show.

Art Superior to Park Nature: Regent's Park, London, 1933

Coincidentally on the same day that Sibley and Reinhardt arrived in England from Florence—June 5, 1933—*Twelfth Night* opened at the new open-air theater in Regent's Park, London. What we glimpse in Reinhardt's remarks about English weatherers in Oxford above is explicated more extensively—pre-empted and reinforced—by looking at the parallel work of the Regent's Park Open Air Theatre during the same summer. In anticipation of the theater's opening, the *Daily Mail*'s correspondent advised would-be theatergoers that a "big tent" outside the auditorium had been erected for a Lord Dunboyne, a popular weather-forecaster, "the first weather prophet ever engaged by a theatrical manager!"[27] Dunboyne's appearance was not insignificant to the performance of weathering as a national practice undertaken by audiences at the theater. If, as Jan Golinski argues, the "relations between climate and national character were first articulated" in England in the eighteenth century, by the 1930s they were increasingly made with reference to military practices.[28] Linguistically conflating religious and scientific hermeneutics, the "prophet's" tent was "equipped with a telephone" to "keep in touch with the Air Ministry."[29] As the UK Government Department with responsibility for weather forecasting between 1918 and 1963, the Air Ministry was tasked with providing weather data to the Royal Air Force for forecasting. Dunboyne had had a military career, during which he received one year's funding to study meteorology. His work never gained credibility in the sciences, but he wrote forecasts for the elite gentleman's magazine *The Field* and later for the *Daily Mail*, always refusing to disclose his secret methodologies. In the scientific journal *Nature* in 1927, prior to Dunboyne's appointment at Regent's Park, a Captain Charles Cave presented evidence to suggest that Dunboyne's accuracy was no "better than could be obtained by purely fortuitous predictions."[30] Although the written anticipation around Regent's Park alluded to military-grade forecasting, then, and although perceived advances in long-range weather forecasting rhetorically further aided performance forecasts, Dunboyne's employment revealed this as posturing and performance. It echoed the narrative that the best of British science could protect its citizens—and, by extension, its theater audiences—from the weather (and anthropogenic threats too). Certainly there was no communication between Dunboyne's tent and the Air Ministry, let alone a direct line, but the desire for control that underpins the combined providentialist—a weather "prophet"—and emergent empiricist narratives—a prophet who speaks not to god but to the Air Ministry—resides in ongoing attempts to know in advance what weather was coming, where and when, connecting Dunboyne's performance given in support of the theater to the authority of national institutions.

---

[27] "Rain Prophet for Open Air Theatre," *Daily Mail*, May 23, 1933, 5.
[28] Jan Golinski, "Time, Talk and the Weather in Eighteenth-Century Britain," in *Weather, Climate, Culture*, eds. Sarah Strauss and Ben Orlove (Oxford and New York: Berg, 2003), 18.
[29] "Rain Prophet for Open-Air Theatre," *Daily* Mail, May 23, 1933, 5.
[30] Charles Cave, "Popular Long-Range Weather Forecasts," *Nature*. January 8 (1927): 52–5. Dunboyne's brother Captain R. P. Butler refuted Cave's claims, differentiating between empirical forecasting for popular and scientific purposes and maintaining the necessity of methodological secrecy while Dunboyne's work was unsupported by government funding. The controversy was parked and there is no further mention of Dunboyne in subsequent histories of meteorology that I can find.

Also building anticipation for the theater's opening in Regent's Park, Margaret Lane shared that the auditorium resembled "a haven of cool greenness in the middle of a hot afternoon."[31] Reflecting the pastoral retreat of the Coombe performances in the previous chapter, Lane predicted that audiences would enjoy "the most cool, unusual, and romantic first night you could find in any hot and dusty city" at Regent's Park.[32] *Twelfth Night*, as it happened, opened in "broiling sun" and the envisioned escape from the London heat failed to materialize.[33] In a review of *Twelfth Night* that is chiefly concerned with the weather, F. G. Prince-White—also of the *Daily* Mail—lamented that:

> A primary reason for establishing this theatre is to make an escape from the summertime heat within walls. The audience at yesterday's matinee performance had a vague vision of an ironical joke in this, but was much—oh, *much* too hot to appreciate it. An announcement from the stage of raised greensward assured everybody that "God's good sunlight" was a splendid thing for them, and suggested that the use of umbrellas and sunshades was not to be recommended —if only because these might be painful to the backs of other people.[34]

Price-White's disappointed pastoral recalls some of the responses to the Coombe *As You Like It*, where the perfect pastoral evoked by the theatrical event was unobtainable due to disruptive meteorological circumstances beyond the theater-makers' control. He went on to commend the audience's ability to endure the heat, attributing their compliance to the "true British grit of the majority" who obeyed requests not to use sunshades despite discomfort (presumably some odd persons without British grit failed to comply).[35] Of those who did comply, he notes that "many contented themselves with covering their heads with four-knotted handkerchiefs" in communally spirited physical performances of weathering that managed not to hamper others' view of the stage, their comfort, or pleasure.[36]

The ambitious landscaping work undertaken at Regent's Park reveals that Reinhardt was not the only director with aspirations of an ideal theater in the open-air. In praise of the immense human exertion behind the lawned stage at Regent's Park, Sydney Carroll took a curtain call with his *Twelfth Night* cast and wished audiences to know "that every sod on this stage comes from

---

[31] Margaret Lane, "London's Roofless Theatre with Auditorium of Grass," *Daily Mail*, June 2, 1933, 7.
[32] Lane, "London's Roofless Theatre," 7.
[33] "Picture Gallery," *Daily Mail*, June 6, 1933.
[34] F.G. Prince-White, "Shakespeare Played in Radiant Open-Air Setting," *Daily Mail*, June 6, 1933, 7.
[35] Prince-White, "Shakespeare Played in Radiant Open-Air Setting," 7.
[36] Prince-White, 7.

Richmond"—ten miles away.[37] A note in the program for *Twelfth Night* also thanked the construction and haulage company Geo. E. Cloke Ltd. for supplying a granite rockery. Although the reception of the new theater at Regent's Park was on the whole in the tenor of those reviewers who posited "no naturally lovelier or more fitting setting,"[38] not everyone was initially impressed with the imported assemblage landscape. T., writing for the satirical magazine *Punch*, hoped that in the future "the rather unimaginative huddle of laurel and privet so dear to English park-gardeners" might be replaced with something "more imaginative and formalized."[39] For T., the production was most impressive where human interventions were greatest in the park, commenting that "It was a little curious and significant that the scene took on beauty from the moment when the electricians set to work upon it, so superior is art to park nature!"[40]

The weather changed. *As You Like* It, the second production at the Open Air Theatre, was "rehearsed during thunderstorms."[41] Reinhardt would have been aware of this inclement weather when he visited the theater for *As You Like It* during his stay in England, as the unsettled conditions affected his Oxford *Dream* too. It was with the cumulative experience of his trip to England, then, that he made his remarks about audiences as stoic weatherers, enthusiastic for Shakespeare in the open-air.

Similar observations of tenacious audience behavior continued to be borne out for the remainder of a largely warm and dry 1933. *As You Like It* was followed by the *Dream* as changes in the weather worried theatergoers at Regent's Park from one moment to the next, from within the context of a mostly dry summer. Theilade, now famous from her fairy dancing in Florence and Oxford, delighted London audiences at Regent's Park, where she performed "with the effortlessness of light [...] beautifully in key with the other-wordly atmosphere."[42] With manly patronizing, *Punch*'s Eric Keown pitied the fragile dancers' bodies in the wet theater, defenseless against the cold:

---

[37] David Conville, *The Park: The Story of the Open Air Theatre, Regent's Park* (London: Oberon Books, 2007), 18. Born in Melbourne, Australia, Sydney Carroll was the theater "impresario" behind Regent's Park Open Air Theater, with Robert Atkins. Their *Twelfth Night* in "black and white" transferred from the West End to a makeshift theater in Regent's Park in 1932, which led them to open the theater proper there in 1933. Carroll was not an "auteur" figure like Reinhardt, in the sense that while he directed a number of plays, he was largely a theater producer and manager, with a background in acting and theater journalism.
[38] F. Bonavia, "The Open-Air Theatre," *Daily Telegraph*. June 6, 1933, 6.
[39] T. "At the Play," *Punch Historical Archive*, June 14, 1933, 666.
[40] T. "At the Play," 666.
[41] M. Willson Disher, "Open-Air Play Success," *Daily Mail*, June 30, 1933, 13.
[42] W. A. Darlington, "A Memorable Production," *Daily Telegraph*, July 6, 1933, 8.

Despite a savage drop in temperature, which corresponded oddly with *Titania's* penetrating analysis of a similar climate and which made us chiefly sorry for the sparsely-clad little fairies at the bottom of the garden, one felt that any weather was worth braving to see this play so profitably removed from the artificialities of the conventional indoor setting.[43]

A wet production of *The Tempest* ended the 1933 season. J.E. Sewell of *The Daily Telegraph* thought it unfortunately apt that "the weather gods, after smiling so blandly" for the summer, might now "scowl" upon the final production.[44] "The desolate, dripping rows of deck-chairs ranged before the beautifully prepared stage yesterday afternoon were a melancholy sight,"[45] Sewell wrote, also commenting that "for some of the scenes at least, the sibilant instance of the rain outside was a very natural accompaniment."[46] His observation of partial complementarity between weather, performance, and fiction serves as a reminder of the different temporalities of theatrical time and that of the immediately experienced world, whatever the possible collisions. Collisions of the French "temp" as "time" and "temp" as "weather"—to draw on Michel Serres's now-prolific observation—can only ever be fleeting, even in an accommodating open-air theater dramaturgy like Shakespeare's.[47]

At the end of a hot summer, E. V. Knox for *Punch* was thrilled by the rain and the adventure of escaping to the undercover area, explaining that "this was the first time I had trodden on wet sward [an expanse of grass] for a month or seen real wet stuff, falling from the sky."[48] So rehearsed were theatergoers in performing weathering at open-air Shakespeares and such was the excitement caused by the rain after successive hot days that Knox later dramatized audience behavior in a sketch based on *The Tempest,* transmuting weathering as social performance into a new imaginary theatrical performance, adapting the stormy shipwreck in Shakespeare's play:

> "The Tempest" (REGENT'S PARK)
> *Scene 1. — A Park in London. A tempestuous noise of rain is heard. Enter* MYSELF *and a* Boatswain.
>   *Myself*: Boatswain!
>   *Boatswain*: Here, Master. What cheer?

---

[43] Eric Keown, "At the Play," *Punch*, July 12, 1933, 51.
[44] J. E. Sewell, "'The Tempest' in Regent's Park," *Daily Telegraph*, September 13, 1933, 8.
[45] Sewell, "'The Tempest' in Regent's Park," 8.
[46] Sewell, 8.
[47] Michel Serres, *The Natural Contract*, trans. E. MacArthur and W. Paulson (Michigan: University of Michigan Press, 1995), 27.
[48] E.V. Knox, "At the Play," *Punch*, September 20, 1933, 320.

Myself: Good. Speak to the audience. Fall to it yarely, or we run ourselves against the tent-pole. Bestir! Bestir!

Enter—Members of the audience.

Boatswain: Hey, my hearts! Cheerly, cheerly, my hearts. Yare! Yare! Mind the water running off the roof. Let me give you a carriage-rug, master, to put over your knees. Wait for the producers whistle. Blow your nose softly lest you disturb the players!

Miss MARGARETA SCOTT *speaking rapidly* (OFF) *to* Mr. JOHN DRINKWATER.

> If by your arts, my dearest father
> you have
> Put the wild waters in this roar, allay them.[49]

Knox's "prologue" turns the production of *The Tempest* into a metatheatrical story-within-a-story, where Shakespeare's text becomes a plot inside the story of theatergoers' performances of weathering.

Over a quarter of a million visitors weathered Shakespeare at the Open Air Theatre in Regent's Park that same summer. Several thousand people saw Reinhardt's *Dream* in Oxford in 1933. Weathering as an audience performance was routinely expressed in writing responding to the staged Shakespeares, documenting a repertoire of physical and discursive social performance practices that uniquely praised nationally given capacities to smile politely and make the most of the event, whatever the weather.

Do Your Worst: London, 1934

The respective successes of the 1933 open-air Shakespeares in Oxford and at Regent's Park appear to have bolstered their directors' self-assurance, for the following year the theatrical landscaping was even more confident and ambitious than before. In May 1934, Carroll reopened Regent's Park with the announcement that the theater had been "reconstructed and vastly improved, entirely re-turfed, the rake on both auditorium and stages […] increased," making it "possible for all to sit with the greatest ease and comfort and see the play without any neck craning or disturbance from heads or hats."[50] Everything was bigger at the Open Air Theatre in 1934. The width of the stage was increased to eighty feet. The

---

[49] E. V. Knox, "At the Play," *Punch*, September 20, 1933, 320. Mr John Drinkwater played Prospero and Miss Margareta Scott played Miranda.

[50] Sydney Carroll, "Regent's Park Open Air Theatre Season Programme Note," (1934), n.p.

auditorium's capacity was increased to 3,000 seats. The reserve undercover stage area was enlarged. Bishop catalogued this expansion for *The Daily Telegraph* readers, itemizing the nonhuman materials utilized for the enhancements to the theater: "Ten thousand yards of earth have been deposited, and there is now a beautiful turfed slope to the stage, which ensures a perfect view from all the 3,000 seats."[51] Upgraded electrical rigging for the outdoor theater "entailed installing 50 miles of wiring, all of which had to be buried, 49 arc lamps of 1000 watts each, and 50 intercommunicating telephones between the various light stands."[52] Carroll's admission of his inability to control the weather—"While we cannot of course guarantee that we shall be favored with the same marvelous weather as we had last year, but the portents are sufficiently encouraging to make us anticipate quite a reasonable spell of summer weather"[53]—is revealed as false modesty when viewed in light of the scale of the theater's environmental undertakings. Daring and risk increased exponentially along with hubris in the summer of 1934. The gulf between extravagant materials—those on show and those buried beneath the earth—and perceived environmental risk was vast.

The film star Madeleine Carroll launched the summer season at Regent's Park from the stage, having recently returned to London from California. When Ben Greet, emerging from semi-retirement to play Master of the Greensward, introduced her as having just visited the "most beautiful country in the world," she countered that "England was the most beautiful country," and looking around at the stage and amongst the audience, claimed the pleasure of opening "the world's most beautiful and delightful open-air theatre."[54] The weather held fine for the summer of 1934. Despite *Punch* reassuring audiences that "a propitiatory offering is made to Jupiter Pluvius in the form of emergency tents for wet weather,"[55] Bishop noted that these were hardly needed: in fact, "during the whole season the [indoor] enclosure has had to be used on only fifteen occasions."[56] The lawn was maintained green and tidy, such a triumph of cultured nature that the *Daily Telegraph* made a joke of it: "The greensward over which Sir Philip [Ben Greet] presides is rapidly becoming a misnomer. The stage now resembles the Trent Bridge wicket on the last day of the test."[57] Accordingly, *Punch* found Regent's Park to be "too kind and sylvan a setting for the Forest of Arden; it is

[51] George Bishop, "London's Open-Air Theatre Stage Re-Levelled and Re-Lighted," *Daily Telegraph*, May 2, 1934, 8.
[52] "The Open Air Theatre," *Daily Telegraph*, June 7, 1934, 17.
[53] Carroll, Program Note, n.p.
[54] "Open-air Shakespeare," *Aberdeen Press and Journal*, May 22, 1934, 6.
[55] *Punch Historical Archive*, June 6, 1934, 638.
[56] George W. Bishop, "The Open Air Theatre," *Daily Telegraph*, September 17, 1934, 8.
[57] "Master of the Greensward," *Daily Telegraph*, June 14, 1934, 19.

Figure 2.3 "During the Interval. Spectators Examine the Pitch." Photograph courtesy of *Punch*.

a rich garden no one would want to leave."[58] George Warrington, writing for *Country Life*, recalled that "At the beginning of last season Mr. Carroll said to the elements: —'I am going to have an Open Air Theatre and you can do your worst.' Whereupon the elements, respecting a man who stood up to them, promptly did their best and have gone on doing it this season also."[59] Warrington's weather rewarded the eccentric pluck of an Englishman with conviction.

Bringing Hollywood Back to Nature: California, 1934

Whilst backstage workers watered and rolled the lawn at Regent's Park, Sibley convinced Reinhardt to bring his *Dream* to California where it would play at the Hollywood Bowl, the San Francisco Opera House, and the Faculty Glade and Greek Theatre at the University of California, Berkeley, as part of what was to have become an inaugural Californian Shakespeare Festival. Amongst her Californian contacts, Sibley championed Reinhardt's attempts to create "the most beautiful open-air theatre" on a scale far surpassing Regent's Park's. As Carroll extolled the virtues of English nature from the Regent's Park stage, Sibley busily promoted Reinhardt's "most lavish"[60] *Dream* to be performed in "a setting

---

[58] "As You Like It," *Punch*, June 6, 1934, 638.
[59] George Warrington, "At the Theatre: Open Air Fancies," *Country Life*, June 30, 1934, 75.
[60] "Lavish 'Dream' Fantasy on at Bowl Tomorrow," *Los Angeles Times*, September 16, 1934, 10.

as appropriate as Nature and man could find"[61] and on a "Scale of grandeur that has never been rivalled."[62] Sibley applauded the American state's plentiful natural resources, including "abundant fruit growing on every side, oil spurting to the skies, the gold in our hills,"[63] as the ideal conditions for Shakespeare in the open air, in speeches anticipating the festival.

Far surpassing the impressive Regent's Park upgrades, reviews of Reinhardt's *Dream* at the Hollywood Bowl marveled at its scale. As at Regent's Park, the dimensions of the improvements were itinerized in responses to the production. The stage area of the Hollywood Bowl was increased to a size of "136 feet in length and 122 feet wide," upon which were placed "805 square yards of natural sod."[64] "Extending from the rear of the stage to a slope of the Hollywood Hills [was] seen a suspension bridge 250 feet in length and sixty-five feet above the ground at its greatest height, masked in shrubs."[65] Four thousand lighting arcs illuminated the vast landscape. The cast featured nearly four hundred people, including torch-bearers and dancers. Nearly twenty thousand people were in the audience to see the first performance, with some reportedly "climbing into the hills when they could not find regular standing room."[66] More multitudinous still, "Dotting the hillsides" were "myriad fireflies made possible by the installation of 30,000 electric lights."[67] Mortal *luciola* forgotten, electricity now dependably powered nature. Although the existing energy supply was insufficient to cater for the production's voracious appetite, a "special transformer" was acquired to "carry the 'extra load'" at the Hollywood Bowl.[68] The whole endeavor was deemed miraculous and Reinhardt was the miracle-maker.

Most decadent of all, perhaps, was that "Masking the stage at its sides and rear [were] seen seventy huge live oak trees uprooted at Calabasas," an area north of Hollywood.[69] These trees (over thirty tons apiece) were hauled twenty miles to the Bowl and transplanted there to complete the stage landscape. The *Los Angeles Times* featured a photograph of diminutive workers transporting one such gargantuan oak to the theater.[70] Just as Reinhardt's Boboli garden fireflies never made it from

---

[61] "Opening Performance of 'A Midsummer Night's Dream' Reveals Possibilities for Hollywood Bowl," *Los Angeles Times*, September 18, 1934, 25.
[62] *Wilmington Daily Press Journal*, September 1, 1934, 3.
[63] Catharine Sibley, "Nationwide Broadcast of the Reinhardt California Festival," October 9, 1934.
[64] "Lavish 'Dream' Fantasy on at Bowl Tomorrow," *Los Angeles Times*, September 16, 1934, 10.
[65] "Lavish 'Dream' Fantasy on at Bowl Tomorrow," 10.
[66] Catharine Sibley, "Nationwide Broadcasts of the Reinhardt California Festival," October 3, 1934, 3.
[67] "Lavish 'Dream' Fantasy on at Bowl Tomorrow," 10.
[68] "Lavish 'Dream' Fantasy on at Bowl Tomorrow," 10.
[69] "Lavish 'Dream' Fantasy on at Bowl Tomorrow," 10.
[70] "For Max Reinhardt Festival," *Wilmington Daily Press Journal*, September 8, 1934, 5.

Florence to Oxford, the transplanted Californian oaks were disposable. They were destroyed as soon as the seven performances ended.[71] Reassurances were given to audiences about where the human-made shell for the concert stage would be stored safely while Reinhardt's *Dream* was taking place at the theater, but nowhere is there mention of what happened to the trees, or to what became of their stumps in Calabasas.[72] Having lost so many ancient oaks to the film industry in the early twentieth century, Calabasas now has a protection order on its trees.[73]

Reinhardt's *Dream* reached peak excess in Hollywood. One man appeared to have the vision to master nature, aesthetically and imaginatively—with the help of Shakespeare (and Mendelssohn's music)—and to command extensive teams of laborers to realize the logistics of his miraculous vision. Consonant with Theilade's prior reception for dancing in the *Dream*, she was described as "the little Danish dancer, who whirls like a bit of thistledown as the first fairy."[74] So far were early notions of environmentalism, let alone a changing climate, from consciousness, around Reinhardt's *Dream* at the Hollywood Bowl, that Titania's tirade on the "seasons altering" was cut.[75] Instead of taking audiences through flooded fields, famine, and illness caused by extreme weather, she spoke to Oberon:

> These are the forgeries of jealousy:
> And never, since the middle summer's spring,
> Met we on hill, in dale, forest, or mead,
> By paved fountain or by rushy brook,
> Or in the beached margin of the sea,
> To dance our ringlets to the whistling wind,
> But with thy brawls thou hast disturbed our sport.
> (*A Midsummer Night's Dream* 2.1.81–7)

Oberon responded with "Do you amend it then, it lies in you" (2.1.118) missing out the thirty lines that have been pored over by ecocritics as Shakespeare's imaginative response to the Little Ice Age.[76] Some more of Titania's speech must

---

[71] Five performances were planned at the Hollywood Bowl but two additional performances extended the run.
[72] "Reinhardt Plans Great Change in Amphitheater," *Los Angeles Times*, August 20, 1934, 12.
[73] William Randolph Hearst, once fiancé to Chapter One's Eleanor Calhoun, made a fortune from trading in oak trees. The devastating forest fires of 2018 also reached Calabasas.
[74] "Rehearsals with Reinhardt Remind of Four-Ring Circus: There's Nothing Director Cannot Do, from Teaching Dances to Out-roaring a Lion," *Los Angeles Times*, September 9, 1934, 5.
[75] Promptbook marked by Catherine E. Sibley for Max Reinhardt's 1934 California tour. Prompt M.N.D. 23. The Folger Shakespeare Library.
[76] For ecocritical analysis of "the seasons alter," see Chiari, *Shakespeare's Representation of Weather, Climate and Environment*, 40–6.

have been heard at Regent's Park for *Punch*'s Eric Keown to note that her lines jarred with the freezing-looking fairies. But, that the seasons could alter—let alone that humans were implicated in that alteration—was so far from knowledge in California in 1934 that the lines were simply removed: a neat pencil line runs through the prompt copy of the text.

Reinhardt's *Dream* in Hollywood resolutely deployed a nature/culture distinction in an absolute triumph of culture: the double "pomp" Shakespeare's Theseus anticipates (*Dream* 1.1.15 and 19). Like Theseus, Reinhardt's work implicitly endorses the mastery of nonhuman nature (and women, although it would be grossly unfair to compare Reinhardt's dealings with Sibley and Theilade to Theseus's violent treatment of Hippolyta). Arthur Miller of the *Los Angeles Times* argued that "Reinhardt takes his audience into the very heart of nature by banishing every vestige of the stage and letting us see instead the swelling earth growing and its grass and trees."[77] More than the tearful audiences at Coombe, who were imagined weeping in response to nature in harmony with the pastoral vision of Arden, Miller surmised that "Shakespeare himself, confined by the limited theatre of his time, would weep tears of joy could he see his most charming play as Reinhardt presents it."[78] He concluded: "Through supreme art and vast imagination Reinhardt has brought the Bowl back to nature."[79]

After the *Dream* at the Hollywood Bowl, Reinhardt's production was performed indoors at the San Fransisco Memorial Opera House, where the indoor/outdoor binary was obliterated from the inside: Reinhardt had giant trees placed inside the theater. At the University of California, Berkeley—in a return to the promenade staging first trekked by audiences in Salzburg—the audience followed the actors from the Faculty Grove, where the woodland story was performed, to the nearby Hearst Greek Theatre for the play's palace scenes. The demand his production put on resources continued to intensify in the making of the film of the *Dream*. Technicians who worked on the film recalled—in awed, celebratory mode—that to light the forest set, "enough electricity was used to illuminate a city of 10,000 persons."[80] Although they had "sixty-five truckloads of natural trees and shrubbery" to decorate the film set's fairy world, the forest remained stubbornly difficult to illuminate because, they explained: "Artificial trees are easy to light, but natural leaves sop up radiation

---

[77] Arthur Miller, "'Dream' to Be Even Finer," *Los Angeles Times*, September 22, 1934, 3. This Arthur Miller is not to my knowledge the playwright of the same name, who would have been nineteen at this time and studying in Michigan.
[78] Miller, "'Dream' to Be Even Finer," 3.
[79] Miller, 3.
[80] D.W.C., "The Solid Fabric of A Midsummer Night's Dream," *New York Times*, October 20, 1934, X4.

like a sponge does water."⁸¹ Even with access to the most extravagant resources 1930s California could offer and without a germ of environmentalist awareness in feeling-distance, enough light could not be produced to penetrate the foliage of the real trees to Reinhardt's satisfaction. Living leaves were ultimately sprayed with aluminum paint to let in the light.

The open-air Shakespeares across this chapter demonstrate growing attempts to engage audiences beyond the elite aristocracy for whom The Pastoral Players' work was made. Across all of the productions and locations, many reviewers highly commend the fact that thousands of schoolchildren accessed Shakespeare through the performances.⁸² Ironically, Warner Brothers wanted to move away from the "shirt-sleeve" class of shooting-range films for which it was known. Their backing of Reinhardt's *Dream* as a film was an attempt to find favor with higher-class audiences.⁸³

Conclusion

Eleanor Calhoun and Lady Archibald Campbell argued that Shakespeare's nature and genius were quintessentially English at Coombe in 1884. So Felix Felton perceived Reinhardt's *Dream* with the Oxford University Dramatic Society in 1933, remembering Reinhardt's fulfilled ambition "to produce a play by Shakespeare in Shakespeare's own countryside."⁸⁴ The contrasting climates and material environmental circumstances of Salzburg, Florence, and California, pivoting around Reinhardt's English *Dream*, help to locate what is specific about the cultural construction of an English performance of weathering Shakespeare in the open-air. The likelihood is that Reinhardt was not thinking in terms of an English environment or ecology at all before he arrived in Oxford in June 1933. Leah Broad refers to Reinhardt's *Dream* in Oxford as a "bold statement of intent" responding to the rise of fascism and his own need to flee Austria and Germany.⁸⁵ But in light of Reinhardt's Florence production for Mussolini

---

⁸¹ D.W.C., "The Solid Fabric," X4.
⁸² "The change in the weather did not affect the enjoyment of an audience that included over 1,500 school children at the Open Air Theatre in Regent's Park yesterday afternoon," (*Daily Telegraph*, June 20, 1934, 8). "Over 200,000 people have visited the Open Air Theatre this summer, including 25,000 to 30,000 school children from various parts of the South of England" (*Daily Telegraph*, September 17, 1934, 8).
⁸³ D.W.C., "The Solid Fabric," X4.
⁸⁴ Felix Felton, "Max Reinhardt in England," *Theatre Research* (1958): 140.
⁸⁵ Leah Broad, "A Midsummer Night's Dream," BBC Arts, August 3, 2017. https://www.bbc.co.uk/programmes/p05bc49k.

and its subsequent westward travel, the Oxford production of the *Dream* feels as much a convenient offer and afterthought by a man making the best of escalating turmoil on the European continent as an intentional declaration of defiance. Indeed, *The Guardian* mused that Reinhardt's agreement to direct for the Oxford University Dramatic Society demonstrated England's first case of "profit[ing] from the bigotry of Hitlerite Germany," obliquely inferring that Oxford might not have been the director's first choice of location under different geopolitical circumstances.[86] Newspapers throughout 1933 and 1934 speculated about what Reinhardt would direct next, when, and where, including confident pronouncements from Reinhardt himself of future performances that never came to pass. Clues pertaining to both the geopolitical circumstances that set Reinhardt on the move and the grabby nature of theater-making and the resources it requires at short notice are present all along. Why, for instance, didn't Reinhardt simply attempt to enlist English glow-worms—the native *lampyris noctiluca* might have been successful—rather than shipping them from Italy? After all, there are glow-worms in *Hamlet, Pericles, Venus and Adonis, The Merry Wives of Windsor,* and *A Midsummer Night's Dream* and, unlike the rhododendrons brought to Coombe, it is likely that Shakespeare did encounter glow-worms in England. Although these insects are under threat now, they would still have been plentiful in the English countryside at the time of Reinhardt's production in 1933. The answer might be both as simple and as complex as the historical and political circumstances that underwrite Reinhardt's aesthetic choices and their environmental repercussions, as well as the scurry of hungry, I-want-it-get-it-for-me-quick nature of theater-making that discards stuff as easily as it desires it. That he did not pursue the possibility of utilizing English glow-worms for the *Dream* in Oxford, which we know, suggests that the aesthetic effects the fireflies produced for the Florence *Dream* may have simply inspired Reinhardt's attempt to ship some on a whim. And, then in England, he also accumulated ideas for materials before moving on to California. Like the performing fireflies apparently inspired by Florence's climate and habitat, the giant trees for the Hollywood Bowl production appear inspired, if not by the trees flanking the steps in the Boboli Gardens, then certainly by the trees that were so admired in Oxford. More than a metaphor for human relations with nonhuman life and matter, Reinhardt's production left material imprints on the earth in the impression of soil exposed under sod stripped for stages, tree stumps, and miles of buried electric cables. The appearance of control was illusory. The process of

---

[86] "Summer Term at Oxford," *Manchester Guardian,* May 1, 1933, 6.

theater-making is a hustle. As Reinhardt requested oak trees for California, his castle Leopoldskrone was bombed in Austria, damaging its heavy oak doors.[87] His *Dream* in the open-air begins to feel like the proverbial long-necked swan, duck legs paddling frantic beneath the shiny veneer of spectacle. Reinhardt's *Dream* is an attempt to escape the circumstances of war while it undertakes a misguided attack on nonhuman nature; even as it imagines itself glorifying nature through artifice.

The assurance with which landscapes were sculpted for performance grew exponentially between 1933 and 1934, continuing to resemble the spectacular theater of the nineteenth-century, but created by natural objects as much as scene painting or stage machinery. Natural resources were physically manipulated, altered, transformed, or decimated to satisfy the aesthetic vision of creatives with access to sufficient financial resources and workers. Trees were uprooted, hauled miles away and transplanted, tons of soil were shifted, and grass turf was extracted and moved elsewhere. Audiences were impressed by the efforts (what the laborers undertaking the physical work of moving the trees might have thought of the digging and transplanting we can only imagine). Second, size mattered in reception: the size of the cast, orchestra, corps de ballet, the size of the stage, the size of the audience, the quantity of lighting fixtures, the length of the wires, the wattage of the bulbs, the capacity of the generator. The degree and confidence with which material objects and nonhuman nature were manipulated attest to fantasies of control and mastery over nature, the superiority of art over nature, to perceptions of abundance and subsequent exploitation, where lavishness and excess were advantages, and where waste and decimated landscapes were inconsequential. Spectacle impressed those who encountered the performances, with many arguing that art outdid nature by improving the already-there.

In the contemporary context of anthropogenic climate change, Reinhardt's work is interesting because he appeared to think that he was working with nature to prove himself against the Nazis when really he was destroying it. What was happening at Regent's Park was motivated by similar but different impulses—an extension of imperialist fantasies of control over nature, gesturing toward military practices. Across the range of productions by Reinhardt and at Regent's Park, in England, and beyond England, journalists praise the exhibition of sheer size, scale, lavish, and energy-intensive visual spectacle. As Lucian Boia points out—in the quotation I included in the introduction—this

---

[87] "Nazi Bomb at Max Reinhardt," *Daily Telegraph*, June 7, 1934, 15.

imagined but false split between "social and moral causes" *and* "environment" as determining endures at the heart of many of our environmental problems today. It was always yes, social and moral causes, yes *and* weather.

Some of the accounts of these performances refer specifically to "English" climates—"wayward English climate,"[88] and others to climates that are "British"[89] but the effect is the same linking of particular audiences to a history that conjoins national characteristics with the weather, reinforced by social and staged performances of weathering. Unmatched resilience by temperate people born into temperate weather was, by the 1930s, one of the "stories that England [was still] telling itself about itself."[90] Weather was deployed to reinforce perceptions of national identity, environmental mastery, and military control—as seen in the uses to which Lord Dunboyne was put at Regent's Park. Future chapters will show how this sense of a community of performers and spectators united against the weather later acquires references to a "Blitz" or "Dunkirk" spirit after the Second World War. In their own time, these open-air productions were received as evidencing Man's unique ability to sculpt and control nonhuman nature by deploying lavish material resources in spectacular displays of mastery: antidotes to economic depression and the rise of fascism. Moreover, the accounts of weathering as performance that survive the performances disclose attempts to know and mitigate weather to come, despite exhibiting still anxious preoccupations with what might be coming from the skies.

While Sibley continued to write about Reinhardt's genius for the rest of her working life—his *Dream* having made a lifelong impression on this audience member—she was still chasing funds owed to her years after the production ended. Far from fragile, Theilade lived and danced to 102. The dying lights of the Italian fireflies quietly attest to the variegated stakes of it all.

---

[88] T. "At the Play," *Punch*, June 14, 1933, 666.
[89] F. G. Prince-White, "Shakespeare Played in Radiant Open-Air Setting," *Daily Mail*, June 6, 1933, 7.
[90] Simon Featherstone, *Englishness: Twentieth-Century Popular Culture and the Forming of English Identity* (Edinburgh: Edinburgh University Press, 2009), 5.

Part Two

3

Shakespeare-Inspired Nature-Theaters: Minack and the Willow Globe

This chapter looks at performances of weathering amongst audiences in today's "street theatre of daily coping" at two theaters built for Shakespeare from nature.[1] One is carved into sea-cliffs, the other growing in the earth. The first is a world-famous tourist attraction, the second much smaller in scale. Notwithstanding their respective historical, geographical, contextual, and operational particularities, I would like to start by acknowledging some of what Minack on the coast of Cornwall and the Willow Globe in Llanwrythwl, mid-Wales share, before considering their local differences. At heart, these are both purpose-built outdoor theaters originally intended for mostly non-professional performance. They are located in remote, rural areas with distinctive climates, landscapes, flora, fauna, and theater audiences. Both are inspired by Shakespeare's works and designed to home his plays. Both nature/theater projects are geographically distant from the mainstream theater in London and major regional theater scenes, but, complicating this remoteness, their Shakespeare inspiration might be said to chafe with some of the experimental and political theater produced in Cornwall and Wales in the twenty-first century. The fraught postcolonial histories and celticity of their landscapes are often but not always at odds with the Englishness of the encounter with Shakespeare in the open-air. Moreover, conflicting senses of Cornishness, Welshness, and Englishness jostle for position in the context of globalization.[2]

Typically, audiences at both of these theaters remain seated for a performance's duration, watching on-stage activity that emulates a "traditional" indoor theater

---

[1] Richard Mabey, *Turned Out Nice Again: On Living with the Weather* (London: Profile Books, 2013), 90.
[2] For Shakespeare's references to Cornwall, see Alan M. Kent, *The Theatre of Cornwall: Space, Place, Performance* (Bristol: Redcliffe Westcliffe Books, 2010) and "Art Thou of Cornish Crew?": Shakespeare, *Henry V* and Cornish Identity. *Cornish Studies*, 4 (1996), 7–25. For Welsh Shakespeare, see Willy Maley and Philip Schwyzer, *Shakespeare and Wales: From the Marches to the Assembly* (Farnham and Burlington: Ashgate, 2010).

experience. From their respective stages in 2014, actors in *The Tempest* at Minack and *The Merry Wives of Windsor* at the Willow Globe made only superficial gestural references to the places in which they performed and the Shakespearean texts were occasionally trimmed but largely unaltered. *The Tempest* at Minack and *Merry Wives* at the Willow Globe were not examples of site-specific theater that "privileges place," as in Fiona Wilkie's definition of site-specificity.[3] Nor did they accord with Mike Pearson and Michael Shanks's proposition for site-specific works that "are inseparable from their sites, the only contexts in which they are intelligible."[4] As unaltered iterations of a pre-existing classical text, these productions would have been intelligible at sites other than those in which they were performed. I contextualize first Minack and then the Willow Globe, referring to embodied and imagined responses to the theaters, finding that weathering Shakespeare at Minack and the Willow Globe was performed alongside theatrical events grounded in material landscapes. Following the landscape geographer John Wylie's proposition that *"practices* of landscaping"—by which he means "practices, habits, actions and events, ongoing processes of relating and un-relating that come before any separation of 'nature' and 'culture'"—"are in actuality the cause and origin of our ideas of what is 'nature' and what is 'culture,'"[5] this chapter's ethnography suggests that weathering as performance is a practice of landscaping that continues the nostalgic work of the pastoral in ways that can be both ecopolitically "regressive" and "progressive." To illustrate this point at each theater, I incorporate a section of responses to a particular Shakespearean scene in each play that has its dramatic setting in an outdoor space: first, *The Tempest*'s opening storm at sea and, second, *The Merry Wives of Windsor*'s duping of Falstaff in Windsor Forest. My story is told, as much as possible, with the words of people who were circulating at the theaters in the summer of 2014.

Minack: A Beautiful and Demanding Landscape

David Abram theorizes depth in landscape, venturing that "Depth is not a determinate relation between inert objects arrayed within a static space, but a dynamic tension between bodies, between beings that beckon and repulse one another across

---

[3] Fiona Wilkie, "The Production of 'Site': Site-Specific Theatre," in *A Concise Companion to Contemporary British and Irish Drama*, eds. Nadine Holdsworth and Mary Luckhurst (Oxford: Blackwell, 2008), 89.
[4] Mike Pearson and Michael Shanks, *Theatre/Archaeology* (London: Routledge, 2001), 23.
[5] John Wylie, *Landscape* (London and New York: Routledge, 2007), 11.

Figure 3.1 The Minack Theatre. Photograph courtesy of the Minack Theatre Archive.

an expanse that can never be precisely mapped."[6] He is trying to get away from landscapes as theatrical backdrops and seeking to grasp the ecophenomenological *in*ness of being-in-landscape, how it shifts with the body of the (sometimes human, sometimes nonhuman) perceiver. This kind of depth induces queasiness at Minack, cut into the cliffs where the vast Atlantic meets the Cornish coast. On a clear day, Minack's expansive horizons stretch uncontained, obscured at other times by mist, fog, and rain, altering what is perceptible from the auditorium and what it feels like to be there. Seagulls make luminous white flecks where sunlight meets the clouds. Cormorants skim stretches of sea, before diving down into impossibly turquoise water. Below, above, at eye level, moving of their own accord and moving with the dizzied eye of the perceiver, birds fly, float, disappear, and re-emerge from the waves that batter the theater's edges. As evening unfolds, boats and beaches fade to shadows, outlines, then memories. Occasional wings blink at the furthest reaches of electric stage lighting. In darkness, the sea makes itself known to audiences in the sounds of waves meeting rock and the taste of salty spray.

---

[6] David Abram, *Becoming Animal: An Earthly Cosmology* (New York: Vintage Books, 2010), 98–9.

Since Rowena Cade located an amateur production of *The Tempest* on the sea cliffs at Porthcurno, Cornwall, in 1932, there have been ten full productions of Shakespeare's island play at what later became a hazardous and captivating coastal theater.[7] While John Gillies argues, "There is little sense of realistic landscape in *The Tempest*, and that landscape varies according to the mind that perceives it," the "real" Atlantic Ocean and its relationship with the unmapped sea of Shakespeare's play have always been inseparable from the cultural imaginary upon which Minack trades.[8] "Such stuff as dreams are made on" (*The Tempest* 4.1.156–7) is the subheading for Minack's souvenir DVD and, although Downing Cless points out that Shakespeare probably never encountered a real, living dolphin, Minack audiences do, regularly, spot dolphins (and other marine life), as they look out to sea. Sea-life and sea-liveliness as well as Shakespeare draw audiences to this theater.[9]

Nowadays, Minack opens from May to September, hosting musicals, operas, and contemporary plays, as well as Shakespeares. Audiences tend to comprise committed "Friends" of the theater, Cornish residents, school groups, and huge numbers of tourists—who reprise the pastoral performances of Chapters 1 and 2 by visiting Minack as part of rejuvenating holidays. Theater manager Phil Jackson estimates that the tourist/local split between audiences during the busiest months is about 70/30, while this can be closer to 50/50 on the fringes of the season, when locals, many of whom work in tourism, are freer to attend. Minack's extended auditorium accommodates in excess of 700 people, with modest ticket prices dividing first-come-first-served seating between lower and vertiginous upper terraces. Some queue for hours to get the best view, although it is not uncommon for people in the upper terraces to leave at the interval, when they get too cold, or to catch the last bus back to Penzance. Day-visitors can attend the visitor center, subtropical gardens, café, and gift-shop that keep the unsubsidized Minack Charitable Trust financially independent.

Michael Dobson (2011) and Alan Kent (2010) make separate critiques of Minack in terms of Shakespeare and Britain, resonating with the weather-histories circulating in Chapters 1 and 2. Separately, Dobson and Kent see Minack performing a cultural imperialist function, although Dobson's context

---

[7] The productions of *The Tempest* at Minack include: 1932, local players; 1952, Bedford School Dramatic Society, 1963, City Literary Institute Shakespeare Players; 1976, West Cornwall Arts Centre; 1982, Woodlands Theatre Company; 1992, Drama Workshop of Waltham Forest; 2002, Derby Shakespeare Theatre Company; 2007, Winchester College Players; 2014, Moving Stories; 2020, The Hertfordshire Players.

[8] John Gillies, *Shakespeare and the Geography of Difference* (Cambridge and New York: Cambridge University Press, 1994), 112.

[9] Downing Cless, *Ecology and Environment in European Drama* (New York: Routledge, 2010), 95.

is amateur Shakespeare and Kent's is Cornishness. Dobson argues, "Minack labels the whole of the British mainland as Shakespeare's, in a posture at once of beckoning lighthouse and of defensive sentinel."[10] Kent is troubled by Minack for two reasons: one is the predominance of "imported" canonical English plays at the Cornish theater and the other is the "cultural imperialist difficulty" of a theater created by a "middle-class Englishwoman" significantly altering the Cornish landscape prior to laws protecting the heritage coastline.[11] Kent is right that Minack's mythologized founder Rowena Cade could not construct such a theater in the more regulated twenty-first century, although globalization means that popular American musicals—cultural imports of another kind—have often outweighed Shakespeare and English canonical texts in recent decades. But while Dobson and Kent make important points, *The Tempest* at Minack suggested that weathering Shakespeare complicates the relationship between theater, sea, and landscape (even when Moving Stories' production paid little heed to the historical trajectory of Shakespeare's most postcolonially adapted play).

Waiting for a performance at Minack, I spoke to John, who described feeling as though he had left England as he descended into the theater and gazed out to sea (which, of course, some Cornish people might argue, he had)[12]:

> I think one of the things that strikes you is you wouldn't think it was England. It seems to be full of subtropical plants. The sun is shining. The beach is sandy. The sea is a pale warm-looking blue. As I say it doesn't feel like England at all. That's nothing against England. But it's very different to most of England so the feel of the place is ... it's quite different to England and that's very attractive.

Most of the audience members to whom I spoke agreed that Minack was "beautiful," "stunning," "unique," "wonderful," or "breath-taking." Beautiful was demanding, though. The theater might have looked beautiful, but it felt like hard work. The lived experience of Minack was physical in a manner to which theatergoers were often unaccustomed. Indeed, Minack has a lower threshold of disability than most theaters because the lived practices it requires of its audiences are more demanding on a body. Responses given to performances at Minack alluded to a landscape composed of "vivid entities not entirely reducible to the contexts in which (human) subjects set them, never

---

[10] Michael Dobson, *Shakespeare and Amateur Performance* (Cambridge and New York: Cambridge University Press, 2011), 189.
[11] Alan M. Kent, *The Theatre of Cornwall: Space, Place, Performance* (Bristol: Redcliffe Westcliffe Books, 2010), 635.
[12] Audience members, who participated anonymously in this research, have been given alternate first names to give proportionate weight to their views amid the authority of named practitioners and scholars.

entirely exhausted by their semiotics," to borrow from Jane Bennett again.[13] They attended to the actual "materials" of the theater, for which Tim Ingold argues—stone (granite and concrete-as-faux-granite) and sea at Minack—and more "abstract" cultural materialities, although I try to let both speak through their conversations.[14]

Being in landscape, Tim Cresswell ventures, turns landscape into place.[15] For place-phenomenologist Edward Casey, "knowledge of place begins with the bodily experience of being-in-place."[16] The bodily experience of being in a landscape, Christopher Tilley—another place philosopher—argues, "acts as ground for all thought and social interaction."[17] Many theatergoers were unused to the exertion of ascending steep, uneven steps in dark evening air and were breathless as they arrived back in the car-park after a performance. Jennie laughed as she paused, part way up from her seat at the bottom of the auditorium, "It's hard work! Well, I'm 70, so the steps were very hard." Ben and Mary also described their encounter with the theater in terms of a challenge for the body, "You need to work up to it. You need to get in training, I think. [*laughter*]/Cushions and cups of tea!" Any grievances about the physical experience of attending a performance at Minack quickly transitioned into aesthetic appreciations of the landscape, usually returning to utterances of "beauty." Kellie explained, "It's tiring on the way out but it's exciting views and when the weather's great like it is today it really makes it something else." David continued, "Inevitably the seats are hard so that's a bit of an endurance test but, having said that on one side, you couldn't ask for a better experience." And Ben panted, "It was lovely having the background ... backdrop behind ... I'm out of breath ... that's part of the experience." Giles connected the physical experience of weathering the theater to an aesthetic appreciation of performance in the landscape when he said:

> You need some stamina—getting up from below [*laughter*]. And you need to be prepared, you know, in terms of how comfortable you feel and refreshments. The winds and the elements, which are always important, particularly, are of significance when you see a performance of something in the background during a significant soliloquy, you know.

---

[13] Jane Bennett, *Vibrant Matter: A Political Ecology of Things* (Durham and London: Duke University Press, 2010), 5.

[14] Tim Ingold, *Being Alive: Essays on Movement, Knowledge and Description* (Oxon and New York: Routledge, 2011), 32 (original emphasis), argues that materialist thinking has "hindered" the "proper understanding" of materials.

[15] Tim Cresswell, *Place: A Short Introduction* (Oxford: Blackwell, 2004), 10.

[16] Edward Casey, *Getting Back into Place*, 2nd ed. (Bloomington and Indianapolis: Indiana University Press, 2009), 46.

[17] Christopher Tilley, *Interpreting Landscapes: Geologies, Topographies, Identities* (Walnut Creek, California: Left Coast Press, 2010), 26.

While some people were aware that Minack had been originally created for Shakespeare, only a few were visiting specifically for his plays. Vague allusions to a "Shakespearean" performance space were commonplace. Steve and Patsy, who were waiting for the performance to begin, conversed:

> Steve: It's just like a Shakespearean theater, really but cut out of the rocks.
> Patsy: Yes, the arches, I guess, give it like a … like almost a Roman appeal.
> Steve: It's just totally unique, as Patsy said. We have never seen anything like it before and we've been to Shakespeare's theater in London and this is just totally different.

Enthusiasm for weathering Shakespeare at Minack was relative to enthusiasm for the theater, its architecture and location. In diminishing importance, theatergoers indicated that they were drawn by the unique situation of the Cornish theater, the timing of their holidays, the weather on a given day, Shakespeare generally, and, lastly, the particular play being performed. Typifying this sequence, Laura commented on what drew her there: "Well, obviously the setting. The setting and the play. We like Shakespeare. We're not good with Shakespeare but we enjoy watching. Especially on a day like today."

Stone and Sea: *The Tempest* at Minack, 2014

The theater phenomenologist Bert States draws on Victor Shklovsky to ponder what makes "stone *stony*?"[18] Tim Ingold answers that stoniness "*emerges through the stone's involvement in its total surroundings—including you, the observer—and from the manifold ways in which it is engaged in the currents of the lifeworld.*"[19] Many audience members at Moving Stories' *The Tempest* in July 2014 had some prior knowledge that Minack was originally constructed for a production of this particular play. Danielle was excited because, "Oh, I mean I absolutely wanted to come to Minack and when I saw *The Tempest* was on, which it proved to be … absolutely made it. This theater is absolutely made for this play." Nicolette also felt that the thematic resonances between the play and the theater were important, saying, "Well, *The Tempest* lends itself very much to performance here. I believe it was the very first play that was performed here. It relates very well." Deirdre and Gerry made connections between the landscape and the play, verbalizing the materiality of the stone and sea with reference to *The Tempest* at Minack:

---

[18] Bert O. States, *Great Reckonings in Little Rooms: On the Phenomenology of Theater* (London and California: University of California Press, 1981), 21 (original emphasis).
[19] Ingold, *Being Alive*, 32 (original emphasis).

Deirdre: I thought it was excellent. Apparently it was the first play that was put on here and I felt it ... yeah ... it was ... You've got all the rocky shore and the waves and ... Yes, it was perfect for me.

Gerry: I think in terms of location ... This is the perfect location for *The Tempest*. I don't think there can be many better locations than this one.

For Dan Brayton, Shakespeare's ocean is "real and imagined, pre-existing and constructed, natural and anthropogenic."[20] Amongst audiences at *The Tempest* at Minack these natureculture overlaps infused all attempts to disentangle the layers of representation in discussions around the performance. Shakespeare's play famously opens with "A tempestuous noise of thunder and lightning heard" (*The Tempest* 1.1), in a storm conjured by Prospero that Brayton argues represents "a European fantasy of mastery over nature."[21] Gwilym Jones argues that the play's opening storm scene—scripted for an indoor space—is accurately represented and "deliberately written to draw attention away from the aesthetic framework of the play."[22] Early modern audiences, Jones observes, would have first encountered the opening storm as "real," as Shakespeare wrote it, before learning of Prospero's magic: the tempest is only revealed to be supernatural by Miranda's entrance into it (and, indeed, as Jones points out, while the audience's first encounter with the storm "renders" it naturalistic, it is also retrospectively exposed as "metatheatre," along with the masque Prospero orchestrates).[23] Moving Stories' production of *The Tempest* for Minack, directed by Emma Gersch, opened with Ariel (Alex Rand), standing on a concrete-passing-for-granite platform and facing the sea with arms outstretched, and disclosed the supernatural source and metatheatrical framing of the storm from the outset. Nevertheless, for a moment the sight of Rand's back and black hair whipped upward by the wind seemed impressively at home in the landscape, ready to command the elements at Prospero's bidding and seeming to lend credence to Prospero's magic as "real." The audience looked down as Rand as Ariel reached out to sea, gesturing toward the ocean beyond the auditorium. For a moment, Shakespeare's airy spirit, the audience, and the place where the land meets the water were swept by the same winds in a convergence of actual and fictitious weather temporalities.

Peter described his response to anticipating the theatrical storm with reference to the solid and liquid composition of the Minack landscape:

---

[20] Dan Brayton, *Shakespeare's Ocean: An Ecocritical Exploration* (Charlottesville: University of Virginia Press, 2012), 178.
[21] Brayton, *Shakespeare's Ocean*, 186.
[22] Jones, *Shakespeare's Storms*, 149.
[23] Jones, *Shakespeare's Storms*, 136 and 143.

The start of the whole thing where you are getting into it … being brought into a frame of mind that the storm is raging. There's going to be this massive shipwreck that's coming and you're looking down, you're seeing the rocks, you're seeing the waves. I think that's what struck me.

Olivia explained, "I think in the first act when the storm was … when Prospero conjured up the storm, the tempest … And I think in terms of location here and the tempest being conjured up, that was perfect interaction between text and location." Sabina was captivated by the opening scene for similar reasons. She said, "At the beginning where there was the tempest it was great because there was the waves on the rocks and it felt like really, really good with the play."

Any fantasy of theatrical mastery or supernatural magic was short-lived and the moment *before* the theatrical storm was the most suspenseful for audiences. Despite knowing that a real tempest occurring as Ariel performed the storm "to point" (*The Tempest* 1.2.195) was impossible—given the vast bright horizon and the weather forecast—for a tiny moment, it looked like his actions might actually have transformative power. Rand swung his arms powerfully as Ariel. No storm materialized. With each successive gesture, the nature of theatrical representation at Minack became more apparent. On the stage, Shakespeare's Boatswain roared at the ship's crew, "A plague upon this howling. They are louder than the weather or our office" (*The Tempest* 1.1.35–6). Actors staggered about, simulating the accurately rendered rough seas Jones identifies in the text, at once conceding the limits of theater in the landscape—by behaving as though Ariel's powers had reached them when it was clear that they hadn't—and inviting the audience to join them in the fiction. The storm that did ensue was composed of actors' voices, pre-recorded thunder, and crashing waves played over Minack's water- and wind-proofed sound amplification system. A slightly choppy sea breaking on the rocks behind the stage highlighted the distance between theater and reality and the edges of human imagination in a material landscape. Gulls screeched in the air and recorded gulls screeched over the airwaves. Light breezes puffed along to recorded gales and actors yelled Shakespeare's lines at one another, out to sea, and into the audience, creating a polyvocal soundscape that acknowledged the environment prior to, in concert with, and beyond the shipwreck.

Some theatergoers commented on the production's efforts to incorporate the landscape into the performance by way of Ariel's physical gestures. Brian noted the conjuring of the storm and felt that this was effective, "Because they definitely … they didn't ignore the fact that they were outside and looking onto the ocean. Ariel cast his magic out onto the ocean and they would look out onto the ocean and yeah

… It was very linked in that way." Rosie also felt that Moving Stories utilized the space in a way that enhanced the opening storm, saying, "This play is out of the ordinary. I think, the language and nature … It's quite good how they used the space for making the storm at the beginning, how they integrated it with the place." Complementarity, occasioned by moments when Shakespeare's text felt suitable in the landscape, temporarily allowed the play to feel at home within a larger assemblage of lively matter, but audiences seemed capable of noticing the nonhuman environment's capacity to act beyond the representational work to which the theater put it.

The "friction" between what was "*of* the place" and what was "brought to the place"—as Mike Pearson and Michael Shanks articulate the effects of site-specific performance—was furthered by the aural simulation of the imaginary storm, the aesthetic effectiveness of which divided theatergoers.[24] Some heard the recorded sound effects as integrated with the sounds of the Atlantic—both the live sea sounds and indexing possible sounds that same sea might make in different weather conditions—delighting in the overt theatricality of mimicking nature with technology. Ana felt that "because you could listen to the sound effects and probably some of them were coming from the sea but it really did add to the atmosphere." Kathy and Arun also commented on the experience of hearing the recorded effects with the real sea:

> Kathy: We didn't know if the sound effects were sound effects or if they were the sea. I was completely into it.
> Arun: Well the sky suddenly darkened towards the end and they started playing thunder across the thing and I wasn't sure if it was thunder out on the bay or on the sound system. It was so integrated … It was beautifully …
> Kathy: It enhanced it all. It brought it all in together.

But for Harry, the recordings were superfluous given the presence of the sea below the auditorium:

> Well anything done here is rather special because of the environment but I didn't really think it contributed to the play. The play was almost separate from the environment. They were even playing sounds of the sea, which was unnecessary. The relationship should have been really strong because it's to do with being on an island and you feel, sitting here, that you could easily be on an island but … no. I didn't think it kind of gave out to the surroundings.

Harry was discomfited by the disjuncture between the production and the environment, but his unease was still secondary to the pleasures of the practices of landscaping he undertook at Minack. As Jane Bennett proposes, "to acknowledge

---

[24] Pearson and Shanks, *Theatre/Archaeology,* 111 (original emphasis).

nonhuman materialities as participants in a political ecology is not to claim that everything is always a participant, or that all participants are alike" and *The Tempest* as a Shakespearean text in performance was one participant with shifting influence in relation to the living, material environment and the efforts of audiences weathering the play.[25] There was no wholesale appropriation of the environment into the theatrical illusion and subject/object distinctions were harder to identify than an "assemblage" that comprised granite, concrete, sea, gulls, sound-system, Shakespeare, grass, weather, actors, and audience members, amongst whom affective agency was received as distributed in a way that did not privilege human activity.

Theatergoers ascribed the various theatrical and extra-theatrical sounds differentiated importance but noted them all. Complementarity between the play's thematic content and the material environment recurred throughout the many conversations I had, the real sea temporarily allowing *The Tempest*'s imagery to seem at home in its presence. Simply, it was good to see a play about the sea at the sea. Owen went as far as to consider the loneliness of island life, describing the relationship between the play and the landscape as, "Very closely linked. Especially because it's this play. It's very helpful to literally have it on a seaside island. It helped relate that isolation that they must have felt … seeing that there is nothing in front of us apart from the barren seascape." Lucy acknowledged the contradiction of the "natural" feel of the "unnatural" theater:

> Well with *The Tempest* in particular, obviously it's set on an island. It kind of does give you that feeling. It's just not a standard theater background basically. It is kind of a natural setting. I know it's all artificially built but it does feel like a natural setting where you're sat.

There was a sense that the landscape enhanced the reception of the spoken words, bringing the material presence of stone and sea into focus through the lens of the play. Ian reflected on what he felt was gained by being at the sea for the play, saying, "The themes that Shakespeare brings … most of them are natural as well in the kind of metaphors with the sea and nature versus nurture, which is a good place to have that idea." Deirdre and Gerry also mused on the experience of the language in the landscape:

> Deirdre: For me I find the words, Shakespeare's words are wonderful.
> Gerry: I'm just thinking for the right words, never mind Shakespeare's words! But the language … I really enjoyed listening to the language of Shakespeare. So much of the vocabulary is related to ocean and tempest and storm and that's what's so special about it.

---

[25] Bennett, *Vibrant Matter*, 108.

Shakespeare's terraqueous text was encountered as having a relationship with Minack and its seascape, independent of the actors' staging, suggesting that audience members drew their own connections between text and space, without the performers doing much more than the play in the place. The sea enhanced the play's elemental imagery, which never subsumed local specificity into Shakespeare's sea.

Prospero's tempest appeared all the more improbable when performed so close to the sea. As the opening scene progressed, the diminishing promise of a Shakespeare/ocean collaboration drew attention to the sea's independence and the place's independence prior to human intervention. It also acted as a reminder of human bodily vulnerability in the face of real storms. Whether or how Moving Stories' production of Shakespeare's island play aspired to incorporate the sea into the production at Minack, and whether or how it was received and imagined as doing so, the sea at Minack was received as in excess of Shakespeare, "never entirely exhausted by its semiotics," to return to Bennett, refusing to privilege human theatrical performance and shaping social performances of weathering.[26] The Atlantic provided an attractive accompaniment but it also generated its own affects, only momentarily absorbing the performance. *The Tempest*'s "obsession [...] not with getting back to nature, but with controlling it," as Jones identifies it in its early modern context, is mined theatrically and ultimately undermined in the theater that has literally excavated a landscape out of love for the play.

Whichever way you look at it, there is hubris or humility in performance at Minack. Hubris to think that performance can bring the sea, the weather, and the Shakespeare together, and humility in learning that such a coincidence is more easily imagined than the sea is harnessed in the service of theatrical performance. Staging *The Tempest* at the edges of the Atlantic temporarily appropriated the vertiginous edges of Cornwall as Prospero's island, inscribing Shakespeare's narrative onto the landscape—a landscape historically appropriated for Shakespearean pursuits, etched with memories of this island play—and, anthropocentrically, seeking to put the sea to work in the service of the play. The result could be seen as naturalizing a claim for all of Cornwall as Shakespeare's—echoing Dobson's and Kent's concerns about Minack as a culturally imperialist outpost. But there also seemed to be something in excess of Shakespeare that had to do with the coming into consciousness of an ecological encounter with the materiality of landscape as place in its own right

---

[26] Bennett, *Vibrant Matter*, 5.

in conversation with culture. It was less that the ecology of Minack colluded with Shakespeare to bolster an English imperialism, and more that the clarity of the landscape as material, prior to, during, and beyond the production meant that Shakespeare's invasive stamp on Minack was fairly faint. To attend *The Tempest* at Minack was also to attend to the materiality of the theater, as well as to one's own embodied maneuverings in weathering the space. Theatergoers liked the moments when the performance was sympathetic to nature and when nature appeared sympathetic to performance. And they liked being at the performances even when they were not captivated by the performances themselves. No one expected Shakespeare to outperform nature.

The creative efforts of Moving Stories therefore facilitated a pastoral escape for audiences at Minack, using *The Tempest* to encourage audiences into recognizing what is solid and liquid in stories and performances. Henri Lefebvre, the philosopher of space, skeptically contends that "the tourist, the passive spectator, can grasp but a pale shadow" of a (socially produced) space, in comparison with those who come to know them through the repetition of work.[27] For Lefebvre, tourism is a *"consumption of space"*—a fair portrayal of transient audiences—but he also concedes the transformative potential of such consumed tourist spaces. Lefebvre hypothesizes that in spaces "set aside for leisure, the body regains a certain right to use," and he allows that even if such spaces "have the middle classes as their only foundation, their only vehicle, and that these middle classes offer models of consumption to the so-called lower classes, in this case such mimesis may, under the pressure of the contradiction in question, be an effective stimulus."[28] Not all tourist spaces can be said to have the middle classes as their foundation anymore—if they ever did (although theaters arguably do)—and the class-based hierarchical model of influence with which Lefebvre thinks is surely outdated, but it seems to suffice not to diminish the ecological possibilities of the tourist experience of Minack. Later chapters attend to what the ecopolitical potential of such an "effective stimulus" might be (although Lefebvre does not!) but if the pastoral is a "British critical dead end," to be bypassed with "anti" or "post" pastorals, then it is instructive that even a Marxist like Lefebvre finds something useful in escape.[29]

---

[27] Henri Lefebvre, *The Production of Space*, trans. Donald Nicholson-Smith (Oxford: Blackwell, 1991), 137.
[28] Lefebvre, *The Production of Space*, 353–4.
[29] Terry Gifford, "Pastoral, Anti-Pastoral, and Post-Pastoral," in *The Cambridge Companion to Literature and the Environment*, ed. Louise Westling (Cambridge: Cambridge University Press, 2014), 26.

I leave Cornwall now, travel up through England, cross the Severn Valley Bridge, and drive into Wales and the Brecon Beacon mountains in search of another theater built from nature for Shakespeare.

The Willow Globe: A Midgey and Magical Enclosure

Actors Sue Best and Philip Bowen formed their theater company Shakespeare Link in 1992, gaining charitable status in 1994 for broad social objectives linked to Shakespeare and education. In 2006, they planted a living willow theater modelled on the reconstructed Shakespeare's Globe in London on their working, organic farm, Penlanole. Surrounded and sheltered by the Wye and Elan Valleys, the Willow Globe, Glôb Byw (meaning living Globe), fuses the idea of found space with a constructed theater. Local landscaper and actor Ben Aires recalled the original marking out of the plans on the ground, speaking of a relationship between people and the green plot chosen for the theater before the willow rods were planted:

> I think Penlanole is officially translated as meaning something like "the head of the bright place." We think people have been settled here for a really long time. The willow theater itself—right from the moment it was marked out on the ground—had children playing in it. Way before it actually was completed as a circle or anything, it was attracting people to it.

As David Abram reminds us, though, "culture can impose its patterns only within the constraints set by the biosphere itself" and lime had to be added to the soil to assist the willow in its initial growth.[30]

The Willow Globe is composed of inner and outer circles woven in deciduous willow arches, forming a twenty-sided geometric structure. There are two entrances at the back of the auditorium, two either side of a tiring house and a balcony, also planted in living willow. Around the thrust stage, staggered wooden benches seat up to 150 people. The gentle movement of the willow rods makes a softer frame than the wooden O of Shakespeare's Globe or the camouflage walls of Regent's Park's Open Air Theater in London. Rising beyond the tops of the willow, trees stretch to the sky from the fields beyond. The Willow Globe is literally alive. The theater grows fourteen feet a year and takes two people three weeks to prune every March. Birdsong fills the theater, loudest at dawn and dusk, and the insistent whisper of wind in the willows continues through

---

[30] Abram, *Becoming Animal*, 127.

the night, as do bleating sheep and occasional vehicles on the A470.[31] Swallows and blackbirds fly through the boughs, midges hover in still weather, and people do Shakespeare in the summer, all sharing the same living habitat. Blackfly have been occasional, unwelcome squatters.

In the foyer space between the square willow walls and the theater itself, a meadow is planted with wildflowers that would have grown during "Shakespeare's Day."[32] A grazing field doubles as a car-park (the Willow Globe is a smaller operation than Minack, open only on performance days) and stables provide indoor performance space, a library, wardrobe, box office, and a licensed bar. When I attended *All's Well That Ends Well* in May 2013, the theater's arches were semi-translucent and sunlight flashed through the moving leaves, with thousands of light shafts streaming from the circumference to dapple the interior. I returned on a wet weekend in May 2014 for *The Merry Wives of Windsor* and

Figure 3.2 The Willow Globe, May 2014. Photograph courtesy of Mark Nesbitt.

---

[31] I can attest to this noise throughout the night, having camped on the farm.
[32] Ursula Bowen, "The Shakespeare Meadow," Unpublished: 2012: 1–2, a retired lecturer in Environmental Biology, had suggested a wildflower meadow to complement the theater and encourage biodiversity. The remit for the Willow Globe's "organic tribute to the bard!" was extended from flowers named in Shakespeare's plays to "native wildflowers which would have been growing in Elizabethan hay meadows" to accommodate volunteers' enthusiasm for the project. Bowen passed away in 2015 and the garden has been dedicated to her memory.

again in a warmer June that year, when the arches were more densely filled, separating the inside of the outdoor theater from the farm outside.

Radnorshire is the least densely populated county in England and Wales and Shakespeare Link and the Willow Globe provide a gathering place for a diverse rural community with common interests in Shakespeare, theater, and nature.[33] As well as an annual Shakespeare performed by the resident Willow Globe Company, the theater acts as a receiving house for touring performances. Theater Company The Factory and director Tim Carroll, with whom Best and Bowen have a long-established relationship, visit often. In 2013, a group of LAMDA graduates camped on-site for a week and created a production of *The Taming of the Shrew* for the theater. Although Best grew up in Wales, she and Bowen have largely English theater backgrounds. Both toured with Michael Bogdanov's English Shakespeare Company before settling in Penlanole. As a result, many of the sounds of Shakespeare at the Willow Globe are in Received Pronunciation, with occasional Welsh accents audible. At first glance, the criticisms that Kent levelled at Minack might appear transferrable to the Willow Globe with respect to Welshness, as another nature-theater built for Shakespeare in a postcolonial part of Britain. But the activities at the Willow Globe are more outward looking than easy accusations of cultural imperialism might imply. Theater-makers and theatergoers contextualized the ways they spoke about Shakespeare and performance there with an "ecocosmopolitan" sense of itself as a place on a "planet."[34] The theater's green ethos looks to the future as much as it draws on the past: an interest in Shakespeare's environments is complemented by wider environmental interests—from the environment future generations will inhabit and back to the environments referenced within Shakespeare's plays. Outside the stables, a noticeboard outlines the theater's green energy objectives and modestly suggests that the Willow Globe is "probably the first static theater facility in the UK powered by a stand-alone energy system": the theater is powered by on-site solar panels and a wind turbine. Best and Bowen program an eclectic range of performances and workshops at the theater, many of which directly address ecological concerns: alongside *Merry Wives* and other Shakespeares, for example, the 2014 season included a reworking of José Antonio Jauregui and Eduardo

---

[33] The population density of Brecon and Radnorshire in 2010 was approximately twenty-three persons per square kilometer, according to the 2011 Census, making it the least densely populated constituency in England and Wales. Office for National Statistics (National Park, Parliamentary Constituency and Ward Population Estimates, Mid-2010), 2011. http://www.ons.gov.uk/ons/dcp171778_239440.pdf

[34] Ursula K. Heise, *Sense of Place and Sense of Planet: The Environmental Imagination of the Global* (Oxford and New York: Oxford University Press, 2008), 205.

Jauregui's *Humans on Trial: An Ecological Fable* (performed by local young people) and a series of creative-writing workshops linked to seasonal agricultural cycles. Furthering this sense of planetary responsibility, Shakespeare Link and the Willow Globe are contributing an ecodramaturgical *Cymbeline* to Randall Martin's global "*Cymbeline* in the Anthropocene" project in 2020/2021 (analysis of which does not fit within the purview of this book, but which reinforces the theater community's aspiration to "eco-cosmopolitanism").[35] Best and Bowen are committed to pursuing Shakespeare Link's socially engaged educational charitable objectives. Bowen explained, "What I really want to do with Shakespeare Link is help people understand they do not necessarily need to go to those big theaters all the time to enjoy the plays—the plays are for all of us."[36]

While the distinction between people who worked on the land and those who visited the landscape was fairly clear at Minack, labor and leisure were more closely integrated at the Willow Globe. This is not to suggest that there is an entirely consistent "insider" community at the Willow Globe, but that a greater proportion of the people attending the theater here is also involved with other aspects of the theater's work, with fewer tourists. As at Minack, audience members performed a haptic experience of weathering the Willow Globe in embodied and discursive responses to Shakespeare. Whereas Minack's proximity to the sea means that it is relatively safe from midges, insect attack was a greater cause of concern at the Willow Globe. Ursula and Peggy discussed their preparations for weathering the performance: "We've got a winter coat on and something to put on your knees and something to sit on. A cushion. / And something to protect you from the midges, which can be very nasty. Last time I came I got thoroughly bitten. All in my hair for days afterwards. Avoiding that this time." Paul mentioned the midges too, saying, "I can't remember how many performances we've come to … We've suffered the midges, we've suffered the cold, we've been distracted by the birds flying over but it's always been worthwhile and a great experience." Aires, who prunes the willow in the springtime, brought the memory of the task with him to a summertime performance. Recollecting his task, he shared, "It's evil. Evil in the biting wind and the snow and stuff and you're going up there on these really big ladders and you have to full reach as well." As at Minack, the embodied encounter with the Willow Globe invariably affected responses to seeing Shakespeare performed within the theater. If quaint Shakespeare was anticipated, the lived experience of the theater left audiences bitten and bruised.

---

[35] Heise, *Sense of Place and Sense of Planet*, 205; https://www.cymbeline-anthropocene.com/
[36] Philip Bowen, Interview with the author. Penlanole, May 25, 2013.

Seasonal changes at the Willow Globe were considered aesthetically as well as physically in terms of the theater's growth. Naomi, who had visited the theater earlier in the year, observed, "When I saw the space it was pretty bare so now it's much greener, which is great. It's filled out. So of course the space is carefully woven and as it fills out in the summer it becomes even better and better." Nathan, who regularly performs with Shakespeare Link, also spoke about how seasonal changes affected the way sound reverberated against the willow in the theater:

> It's different in this theater, especially when it's like this—it's not fully grown. So there's a lot of gaps and you can kind of feel your voice disappearing through the walls so it's quite hard to balance being loud enough for everyone to hear. When it's fully grown in a couple of months it will be almost completely opaque and then it will hold it in. Apart from the bit above you so then you feel like you're more in some sort of bowl or maybe at the bottom of a green well almost.

Fairies of the Willow Tree: *The Merry Wives of Windsor*, 2014

Owing to Best's and Bowen's lifelong interests and expertise in Shakespeare and the ways in which Shakespeare is inscribed onto many parts of the farm at Penlanole, audiences at the Willow Globe referenced Shakespeare much more than they did at Minack. Responses to the final scenes of *The Merry Wives of Windsor* in May and June 2014 echoed those moments of complementarity between performance content and setting identified at *The Tempest* at Minack, arising from a perceived thematic suitability rather than as a result of a sought-after ecodramaturgical relationship between the play in performance and the living theater. No less vehement about the unique qualities of the outdoor theater space than Minack audiences, audiences at the Willow Globe tended to describe the space in more personal terms. Where Minack felt vast and awesome, the Willow Globe felt intimate, contained by porous willow walls. For Richard, being at *Merry Wives* evoked memories of childhood hideaways created in nature.

> It reminded me a bit like a den or something that I would have as a kid. And as kids we would go out into the fields or the nearby woods or whatever and make a little den, a little kind of shelter or what-not. I think because there was a lot of shade in it and because it was quite tall and kind of sheltered a little bit. But I mean, saying that, there was no roof on it, obviously. It felt like a little kind of hideaway but at the same time it felt like a kind of an outdoor patio or somebody's back garden.

The final scene of *Merry Wives* sees Falstaff, dressed as a stag, waiting for a midnight encounter with Mistresses Page and Ford. His designated meeting spot is Herne's Oak in Windsor Forest, a tree that has its inspiration in what is now understood to be a made-up myth, invented by Shakespeare, about the ghost of Herne the Hunter.[37] At the oak tree, local children disguised as "urchins, oafs and fairies" (*The Merry Wives of Windsor* 4.4.48), led by Mistress Quickly as their queen and Pistol as a hobgoblin humiliate Falstaff in an act of good natured community-orchestrated revenge. The Willow Globe's production featured local children of varying ages, wearing masks and raggedy green, white, and silver robes. Led by Mistress Quickly and circling Falstaff, they sang together "pinch him and burn him and turn him about, / Till candles and starlight and moonshine be out" (*Merry Wives* 5.5.101). As with *The Tempest*'s storm scenes at Minack, many theatergoers at *Merry Wives* commented on the Herne's Oak scene at the Willow Globe, noticing complementarity between the play's fictional locale and the theater's living willow walls. Sitting in the theater after the performance, for example, Winnie reflected:

> You know, it's *The Merry Wives of Windsor*. It's fairly light but there's also, you know, lots of sort of deep meanings there if you chose to search them out. Particularly perhaps the last scene with all the fairy sprites and the woodland creatures and you're in the middle of a woodland setting in the middle of the countryside and there are lots of references to the countryside in the play.

Randall Martin's ecocritical reading of *Merry Wives* argues for the significance of naming an ancient oak as "Herne's" and the conservationist impulse to establish a folk myth for the tree in the context of widespread early modern deforestation.[38] This Willow Globe production bore no visible traces of enacting knowledge of early modern deforestation, but Martin's argument nevertheless resonated through the contemporary performance in the way that audience members drew parallels between the significance of Herne's Oak as a "magical" tree and the significance they attributed to the willow. As Herne's Oak is important for Windsor inhabitants in *Merry Wives,* so the Willow Globe was important for theatergoers, who played with personifying the theater in support of Bowen and Best's environmentalist ethos. Where, as Vin Nardizzi proposes, early modern theaters were literally shaped by a (real and perceived) scarcity of wood and timber at that time, the Willow Globe is a created as a contemporary space where audiences can bring their (real and perceived) anthropocene anxieties

---

[37] Randall Martin, *Shakespeare & Ecology* (Oxford: Oxford University Press, 2015), 51.
[38] Martin, *Shakespeare & Ecology*, 51–3.

about the scarcity of natural resources and can envision a less resource-intensive flourishing of culture in its living architecture.[39] I am not proposing anachronistic continuities between the wooden and willow Os here, only seeking to note an environmental resonance in the timbre(er) of theater histories.

Where Minack's expansive landscape was often described as "breath-taking" at *The Tempest,* alluding to expansive, awesome sublime landscape, the Willow Globe was more often discussed in terms of "magic" and intimacy. Simon, for instance, said of the theater, "It's got a kind of magic to it" and Jennifer described the space as, "Really magical. It's sort of another world. It's really special." Like Shklovsky's "stony" stones, the willow's "willowyness" inflected responses to the performance.[40] Megan pointed to the willow's contribution to making "magic" when she reflected:

> Well I think it's quite a magical space because of the willow. The Willow Globe. It is quite unique. I've only ever seen it in, you know, planned gardens really, but to have it as a theater setting is really quite, quite special, I think. It adds to the atmosphere and makes it something a bit more—I don't know—more grassroots.

She elaborated, "Well, I think being in the open air adds a dimension to it. It kind of, I don't know what the word is really, it kind of makes it more earthy and mysterious. Because you're sort of in the elements." Jane also reflected on a thematic complementarity between the Windsor Forest scene and the Willow Globe in terms of magic, saying, "It's a very natural environment. It's very beautiful, very simple, very magical. So the last scene with the deer and the fairies, you know, we know what it was all about. It adds to the atmosphere." So many casual allusions to "magic" at the Willow Globe come perilously close to being warily written-off as Philip Auslander's critique of "traditional, unreflective assumptions that fail to get much further in their attempts to explicate the value of 'liveness' than invoking clichés and mystifications like the 'magic of live theatre.'"[41] But, as Robert Watson argues in his historicist ecocritical analysis of *A Midsummer Night's Dream,* "In biology as in so many areas of early modern science, 'magic' is the place-holder for phenomena with pending explanations,"[42] and, thinking through the pretend "magic" used to torment Falstaff in *Merry*

---

[39] Vin Nardizzi, *Wooden Os: Shakespeare's Theatres and England's Trees* (Toronto, Buffalo, London: University of Toronto Press, 2013), 16.
[40] States, *Great Reckonings in Little Rooms,* 21 (original emphasis).
[41] Philip Auslander, *Liveness: Performance in a Mediatized Culture* (London: Routledge, 1999), 2.
[42] Robert N. Watson, "The Ecology of Self in *A Midsummer Night's Dream,*" in *Ecocritical Shakespeare,* eds. Lynne Bruckner and Dan Brayton (Farnham and Burlington: Ashgate, 2011), 36.

Wives in light of Jane Bennett's argument for lively and animate matter, it is possible to propose "magic" at the Willow Globe standing in for the "earthy, not quite human capaciousness" of the willow, a living material that exceeded its semiotics.[43] This magic appeared to derive in part from a sense of the willow's life apart from the architectural task to which people had put it and from an awareness of lively nonhuman materiality as vital to this experience of *Merry Wives*. Experiences deemed "magical" were given specificity by the phony folk myth of Herne the Hunter in the play and supported by the physical presence of local children dressed as fairies.

Richard commented that the willow took on some of the magical properties of Herne's Oak, or that Herne's Oak took on some of the magical properties of the Willow Globe. He referred to music, costume, and particularized the children at Herne's Oak as "fairies of the willow tree," before reaching for an ancient nature-based religious aspect to the play in the theater. I share Richard's thoughts at length because his search for words illuminates an encounter with the living theater in conversation with the play in performance:

> I felt towards the end when they had the big Falstaff ending, you know, with all the kids dressed up … What were they dressed up as? Fairies. They kind of … with the whole kind of willow and kind of outdoor effect … it kind of added a bit more to it. Do you know what I mean? I mean it all kind of works in with the nature of it. I mean there were … I don't know … they were fairies of the willow tree. I don't know, you know, it all seemed very natural and kind of … I suppose it's … I was going to say it's a bit like pagan kinds of things, a bit like … pagan. And a bit more connection with their surroundings and things, you know, especially as you have Falstaff as the deer and the stag, you know. And you had all the kids out and all the masks and everything and the music worked really well too because they started playing some very eerie music and different sounds.

In addition to magic, gently anthropomorphized ways of speaking about the Willow Globe went further than acknowledging the willow as animate and imbued it with human characteristics, extending Martin's argument for the conservationist potential of naming a tree to create a local legend around it. Individuals at *Merry Wives* often suggested a collective sense of investment in the care and growth (literal and metaphorical) of the physical theater. Some of the language used to describe the theater was evocative of words that might describe a child's growing up. Dot shared, "And I've been coming here for years because I used to do the costumes. So I've seen it from the willow being that high

---

[43] Bennett, *Vibrant Matter*, 3 and 5.

[*gestures towards the ground*] to what it is today," while Trevor and Mel, who were visiting from London, remarked, "I used to live here when it was first planted. / So we've seen it grow up." Lizzie and Alice also felt pride about the duration of their relationship with the Willow Globe, saying, "We've seen it develop over the years and grow and grow—physically as well as in reputation—and it's just so idyllic up here that you could be absolutely anywhere in the world but we've got it on our doorstep. How fantastic is that?" Characterized as a child, the Willow Globe was also personalized with a playful character by Ben:

> It is itself a really magical looking structure, as I'm sure you've noticed —especially this time of year when it's been cut back and it's looking all sinewy. It kind of looks like something out of a Terry Pratchett book. You can almost expect that overnight it might wander off somewhere else and come back again. So there's all of that before you even start thinking of the drama.

Nardizzi argues that in encountering woodland scenes amid the wooden pillars and structures of early modern theater spaces, historical audiences were encouraged "to see one thing (a post) and another thing (a tree) simultaneously" as actors "revivif[ied]" the wood, "suggesting that in these moments there is no distinction between 'nature' (living wood) and 'culture' (lumbered wood)."[44] In a further pleasing resonance between early modern and modern Globes, Shakespeare's textual references to woods and trees when performed at the Willow Globe do not "revivify" dead wood so much as bring the "life" of the living willow into focus through the play. Thomas Symes, who directed *Merry Wives*, described the theater as cheeky:

> It's like a cheeky space, I think. So you can do kind of cheeky stuff with it, which is really nice. And I think it wants to be playful … And because the willow is a tree and it kind of falls and rustles and there's just something about it which is very … It's not stuffy and it's not conventional. It just feels quite childish and playful as a space.

In his work on the cultural function of literary pastorals in 1971, Peter Marinelli argues that the innocent figure of the child replaces the shepherd, explaining that whereas "the shepherd needed an external world of lovely fresh nature in which to appear; residing only in time, the child can survive as an emblem of innocence without it." Rhetorically, he wonders what will follow, taking over from what he calls the "child-cult" of the pastoral.[45] Marinelli might find these figures of pastoral conflated in the comments at the Willow Globe where the living theater

---

[44] Nardizzi, *Wooden Os*, 21.
[45] Peter Marinelli, *Pastoral* (London: Methuen, 1971), 81.

takes on the figure of the child. Responses that imbued the theater with human characteristics might be carefully considered alongside Jane Bennett's provocation that we "cultivate a bit of anthropomorphism—the idea that human agency has some echoes in nonhuman nature—to counter the narcissism of humans in charge of the world."[46] She elaborates that "an anthropomorphic element in perception can uncover a whole world of resonances and resemblances—sounds and sights that echo and bounce far more than would be possible were the universe to have a hierarchical structure."[47] Anthropomorphizing the Willow Globe was not a violent, appropriative way of humanizing nonhuman nature but instead suggested audience members scrabbling for a language to articulate the significance of the living theater within human frames of reference. Humans may have planted the Willow Globe, culture may have imposed itself upon the physical space—before the land was used for a theater it was a farm, and before that it was something else—but nature was acknowledged as continuing to act of its own accord, contributing to how audience members heard the fairies singing to Falstaff at Herne's Oak. Where the production of *Merry Wives* at the Willow Globe did not seek to enact an ecocritical reading of the play, weathering Shakespeare in the theater stimulated responses to the place that were at once connected to and in excess of the performance.

In addition to claiming that Shakespeare's nature was suitable in this contemporary nature because of the correspondences between willow and magic in the contemporary moment and Herne's Oak and magic in the past, there were also many who extended this sense of complementarity between the content of Shakespeare's play and the configuration of the Shakespearean playing space. Charlie felt that early modern theater practices supported outdoor performances today. He described Shakespeare's work as, "Earthy. A lot of it. Not all of it, but a lot of it is earthy. It just lends itself ... I mean if you look at the Globe that was an open top. This is based on the Globe. So that was the same sort of outdoors almost, wasn't it?" When Barbara described the Willow Globe as "so cleverly thought out ... the use of the willow to make the shape" her companion, Emily, followed by emphasizing the space's Shakespearian credentials, "And the fact that it is actually a fifth of the size of Shakespeare's Globe theater in London ... of the original theater in London. It's done to scale. It's not just put up in any old way. It's deliberately a fifth of the size." They went on, noting the same distinction that was made at Minack between an "unnatural" theater with a "natural" feel: "I

---

[46] Bennett, *Vibrant Matter*, xvi.
[47] Bennett, *Vibrant Matter*, 99.

think there is the timelessness of it as well. You know, there is the sense that this isn't a building that was built in 1950 or something. This is ... of course it's made, but you could have had the same thing in Shakespeare's time." Shakespeare is, of course, unlikely to have either experienced or imagined a living willow theater, although Christopher Tilley argues tentatively that sounds, smells, sights, light, and darkness do in a "limited sense [provide] a direct bodily connection with the past" and we do know that Shakespeare experienced willow, imagining a "willow cabin" at Olivia's gate in *Twelfth Night* (1.5.238), if this matters.[48] What might matter more was that Shakespeare performed at the living Willow Globe facilitated continuity between then and now where now was nice because it was like then and if then was like this we'd like some more of that now please.

Collectively, audience remarks associating the present experience of the Willow Globe with an "authentic" or "original" Shakespeare might well be considered within frameworks of nostalgia, what Susan Bennett refers to as a drawing on "the past as a figure for the desires of the present."[49] For Bennett, "Shakespeare performs the role which links the psychic experience of nostalgia to the possibility of reviving an authentic, naturally better, and material past."[50] As far as Shakespeare and a pastoral nostalgia are concerned, particularly in a British context, the tendency is toward regression; the absent past of Shakespeare's day is hazy, rosy, selective, and in danger of veering toward nationalism. Without losing sight of the risks of nostalgia, though, I would like to suggest a further progressive context for nostalgia among Willow Globe audiences that, in light of the environmental crises outlined at the start of this chapter, incorporates not just a gazing back to an imagined Elizabethan golden age but also what Kate Soper calls a "provocatively contradictory avant-garde nostalgia."[51] Soper offers avant-garde nostalgia in light of "the Romantic reflection on vanished or vanishing times and spaces,"[52] rejecting romanticized calls for a "return to nature" but contending that "aspects of [Romanticism] could be harnessed to the development of a new politics of consumption organized around more sensually rewarding and ecologically progressive conceptions of pleasure and fulfilment."[53] Heeding Raymond Williams's warning against outright

---

[48] Tilley, *Interpreting Landscapes*, 30.
[49] Susan Bennett, *Performing Nostalgia: Shifting Shakespeare and the Contemporary Past* (New York: Routledge, 1996), 3.
[50] Bennett, *Performing Nostalgia*, 7.
[51] Kate Soper, "Passing Glories and Romantic Retrievals: Avant-garde Nostalgia and Hedonist Renewal," in *Ecocritical Theory: New European Approaches*, eds. Kate Rigby and Axel Goodbody (Charlottesville and London: University of Virginia Press, 2011), 23.
[52] Soper, "Passing Glories and Romantic Retrievals," 23.
[53] Soper, 17.

condemnations of nostalgia, Soper warns of the dangers of the "simple-backward look" *and* the "simple progressive thrust."[54] An avant-garde nostalgia, she posits, might contribute in our present ecologically threatened moment "by reflecting on past experience in ways that highlight what is pre-empted by contemporary forms of consumption, and thereby stimulate desire for a future that will be at once less environmentally destructive and more sensually gratifying."[55] The thrust of her argument is that longing for a more pleasurable, sustainable past (even an imagined past) might prompt desire for a more pleasurable and sustainable future. While the pleasures of which Willow Globe audience members spoke were often yoked to a perceived connectedness to Shakespeare's day—nostalgically approximating the current conditions of performance with perceptions of past performances—this longing was located within a wider theme that encompassed pleasure arising from "nature" more broadly.

Selwyn and Georgia conversed about the present nature and the nature of Shakespeare's day. Selwyn began, "It feels realistic like it might have been in Shakespeare's day" and Georgia went on to talk about the birdsong that was audible as she was speaking, elaborating on pleasure derived from this perceived getting "closer" to Shakespeare in nature: "And it's lovely. You can hear the swallows and the birdsong. The swallows are usually diving around amongst the willow." Paul drew more specific parallels between the wildlife of "Shakespeare's day" and the once-endangered red kites that fly across the circumference of the Willow Globe. He said:

> I think it's an extraordinary experience in which the living world shares in. We've got the kites, which were still present in London and were flying over the theater in London when Shakespeare wrote the plays and here we are again seeing them in mid-Wales so that's a lovely context.

Shakespeare's references to kites were well-known by Willow Globe audiences; Goneril is a "detested kite!" (*King Lear* 1.4.224), a "hell-kite" takes Macduff's family (*Macbeth* 4.3.218), and Autolycus warns, "when the kite builds, look to lesser linen" (*The Winter's Tale* 4.3.23); a reminder that this now-protected bird of prey was, in Shakespeare's day, considered a scavenging pest that might steal your underwear as it was hanging out to dry.[56] Kites were persecuted to near-extinction under the sixteenth-century vermin acts and their reintroduction

---

[54] Soper, 24.
[55] Soper, 24.
[56] Kerridge, "An Ecocritic's Macbeth," 193–210, discusses the natural history of red kites, their past as pests and their present as restored wildlife in a reading of *Macbeth*, hoping for an ecocritically inflected production of the play.

to Wales's Elan Valley is one of Britain's conservation success stories. David Attenborough's introduction to the otherwise admonitory 2013 State of Nature report begins with the "good news" that "red kites and sea eagles soar where they have been absent for centuries."[57] As Paul responded to the kites at the Willow Globe, he did so within the context of having to weather the theater as well as his perceptions of the original performance conditions of the plays. There was delight in the continuity of nature so nearly lost that was part of the pleasure he derived from the performance. Jane also responded to the kites and to birdsong:

> For me I think, I imagine Shakespeare must have performed outside a lot when the natural world was much more around you. So to me, this takes the environment back to how it would have been when Shakespeare performed. Like birdsong. Birdsong around the Globe in London now is virtually nil. I mean here with the kites. Shakespeare mentions kites in his words and I think wow to me it is the setting brings it more into how Shakespeare would relate to it.

Together, these not-uninformed perceptions of Shakespeare's (more biodiverse) natural world and the pleasure they derived from the present performance at the Willow Globe suggested both loss and desire. To return to Soper, they were "reflecting on past experience in ways that highlight what is pre-empted by contemporary forms of consumption" and, in the process, enjoying a pleasurable present.[58] Responses to Shakespeare at the Willow Globe therefore simultaneously supported the assertion that Shakespeare conspires with a conservative nostalgia to revive "an authentic, naturally better, and material past"[59] *and* an avant-garde nostalgia that might "stimulate desire for a future that will be at once less environmentally destructive and more sensually gratifying."[60] Nostalgia meandered between ahistorical longings for a blurry but better Shakespeare's environment and desire for a more pleasurable and environmentally engaged present.

Conclusion

This chapter has argued for the affective potential of two nature-theater architectures, whose designs instigate performances of weathering that inflect how audiences encounter Shakespeare's plays within them. Performances of

---

[57] David Attenborough, "Foreword," State of Nature Report (2013), 8 https://www.rspb.org.uk/Images/stateofnature_tcm9-345839.pdf.
[58] Soper, "Passing Glories and Romantic Retrievals," 24.
[59] Bennett, *Performing Nostalgia*, 7.
[60] Soper, "Passing Glories and Romantic Retrievals," 24.

weathering undertaken by audiences at Minack and the Willow Globe were patchily continuous with their cultural antecedents at the Pastoral Players' *As You Like It* in 1884 and 1885 and Max Reinhardt's *Dream* and at Regent's Park in the 1930s, albeit here within the context of vastly different knowledge pertaining to the environment. For many theatergoers, performing weathering at Minack and the Willow Globe brought ecology into the light through the frame of the plays, which partially and temporarily succeeded in being at home in the theaters. In both theaters, audiences were capable of imaginatively encountering the fiction whilst remaining attentive to life and matter that pre-exist and survive the architecture. Rather than this life and matter simply bolstering an ideologically English Shakespeare, it undid some of the perceived mastery of human creativity and intervention. Theatergoers often perceived relations between the play, theater, and environment without collapsing one into the other. In concert with Shakespeare, however, the theaters assisted with encouraging this awareness of ecological interdependence and distributed rather than hierarchical agency. Human theater-makers and actors created imaginative spaces as the pretext for audiences attending the theaters, and an appreciation of that human effort is palpable amongst audience responses to weathering Shakespeare there. These are bright places bursting with work and environmental potential run by passionate people who care about the possibilities for theater and performance in their communities, with an intuitive, working regard for the weather.

The pastoral nevertheless persists at Minack and the Willow Globe. At Minack, tourists and locals reaffirm awe in the presence of the expansive landscape. Minack offers a dramatic escape "experience," but the escape necessitates a bodily awakening to the practices of landscaping, whether the weathering is pleasurable or not. Even if visitors grasp only a "pale shadow"[61] of Minack, many return to the theater after years and replay vivid memories of the shadow. The lived experience of the actual pasture (on a farm with sheep) at the Willow Globe facilitates a more intimate relationship with nonhuman nature. If Minack evokes a nostalgia that circuits back to the iconography of its founder Rowena Cade sitting in an upturned wheelbarrow and Shakespeare's *The Tempest* by the sea, underscoring the sublime experience of the landscape, then pastoral nostalgia at the Willow Globe evinces a more clearly articulated avant-garde ambition, where hope for the future permeates care for the past. I am inclined to agree with Todd Borlik, who points out that the "yearning for a life in harmony with nature which finds expressions in the pastoral, may have

---

[61] Lefebvre, *The Production of Space*, 353–4.

political and psychological motivations, but this does not prevent the mode from voicing a real empathetic engagement with the biophysical world."[62] Audience responses to weathering Shakespeare at Minack and the Willow Globe point to the contradictory affects that performance in the open air can bring about, fluctuating between environmentally appropriative, exploitative, and conservative, and self-consciously generative of ecological relations, alert, attentive to and affected by the weather.

If the present-day environmental potential of Shakespeare's play in performance is limited to what is in the play, however, then those texts that offer thematic convergences with the sea or the willow at Minack and the Willow Globe remain limited to a narrow range within the Shakespearean canon. Perhaps, with knowledge of how these plays work in the theaters, we could also conceive of works written specially for them, works that do not so much "privilege place,"[63] but works that would be "intelligible only at these sites"[64] and still produce affects in the gaps between a "conflicting/indifferent/and reciprocal"[65] relationship between action and space. The next chapter looks at three productions designed to "collaborate" with non-theater spaces outdoors in ways that are more than referential, noting some of the differences in performances of weathering that they instigate from their audiences.

---

[62] Todd Borlik, *Ecocriticism and Early Modern English Literature: Green Pastures* (New York and London: Routledge, 2011), 209.
[63] Wilkie, "The Production of 'Site,'" 89.
[64] Pearson and Shanks, *Theatre/Archaeology*, 23.
[65] Bernard Tschumi in Mike Pearson, *Site-Specific Performance* (Basingstoke and New York: Palgrave, 2010), 38.

4

Wandering in Woods: The Natural Place for the Play

HELENA: My brother made me go and see a production of it, one of those god-awful outdoor things where you have to follow the actors around some park. It was a freezing night and I had no jacket. Shakespeare was a filthy bugger anyway. All that talk about getting the love juice in your eye. I could hardly keep a straight face.[1]

Shakespeare has been out walking since Max Reinhardt's production of *A Midsummer Night's Dream* at Salzburg in 1932, long enough to be a joke in David Leddy's *Susurrus* (2009), a site-based audio performance referencing the *Dream* and created for Edinburgh's Botanic Gardens in Scotland. Leaving the theater architectures of Minack and the Willow Globe, this chapter focuses on performances in outdoor spaces that were neither designed nor designated for theater and where practitioners stated an intent to "collaborate with space" formally, by taking their audiences on walks around parks. These are spaces Dan Kulmala classifies as "urban pastoral: a civic green world of social distinction like an old city park that belongs (or belonged) to an upper middle class or elite neighbourhood."[2] The productions at which I look are Sprite Productions' *A Midsummer Night's Dream* (2014, directed by Charlotte Bennett), Taking Flight Theatre Company's *As You Like It* (2014, directed by Elise Davison), and Teatro Vivo's *After the Tempest* (2013, directed by Sophie Austin). Each of these works set out to establish a "reciprocal" relationship between action and space, the theater companies interchangeably naming their work "promenade," "site-specific," and "immersive" to reflect this intention. While these were still not "ecodramaturgical" works in their aspirations, as before, weathering Shakespeare demanded an active physical engagement with the imaginative work of

---

[1] David Leddy, *Susurrus* (Glasgow: Fire Exit Ltd., 2009), 39.
[2] Dan Kulmala, "'Is All Our Company Here?': Shakespeare Festivals as Fields of Cultural Production," *English Language and Literature Studies* 5, no. 1 (2015): 4.

theatrical representation from audiences, who followed the actors from scene to scene. Somewhat counterintuitively, the more performances were thought of as "collaborating with space," the more the effect appeared to be a greater sense of audience engagement with the stories of the plays.[3] I found theatergoers invested in what Gay McAuley refers to as Shakespeare's "onstage fictional places,"[4] raising questions about who a nature/performance "collaboration" serves and what it achieves environmentally. In the following accounts, I walk on often-beaten tracks, wander from the path, trace others' desire-lines, and find occasional bits of wildness in cultured parks.

Sara Maitland restores an emphasis on *where* fairy stories are set in *Gossip from the Forest* (2012), reclaiming the "real" forests in which the stories unfold from psychoanalytic readings that ask them to stand for some kind of subconscious narrative of the mind.[5] Maitland argues instead for the geographical site-specificity of northern European fairy tales of the Teutonic tradition as they evolved in British contexts. She seeks "to match up what is in the forests with fairy stories, see how the themes of the fairy stories grow out of the reality of the forest, and the other way around too—show how people see the forests in a particular way because of the fairy stories."[6] Preceding Maitland's inquiry by several years, Salman Rushdie's introduction to Angela Carter's magic realist fairy tales in *Burning Your Boats* (1995) draws attention to Carter's distinction between the damp, homey English "wood" of Shakespeare's *Dream* and the terrifying "forests" of Northern European fairy tales.[7] If, then, as Catherine Belsey advances, the persistence of Shakespeare's perceived timelessness (despite so many arguments to the contrary) derives from the oral tradition of fairy tales he reworks in many of the plays—so that the amended plots and characters are always vaguely familiar—it comes as little surprise that taking audiences for walks under trees to encounter these plays today imaginatively locates Shakespeare in the woods of English fairy tales.[8] This chapter extends Maitland's endeavor to weathering Shakespeare at open-air performances that take their audiences for walks in the woods. Roger Deakin's popular nonfiction *Wildwood: A Journey through Trees* (2007) ventures that the transformative settings of Shakespeare's

---

[3] Pearson, *Site-Specific Performance*, 38.
[4] Gay McAuley, *Space in Performance: Meaning Making in the Theatre* (Ann Arbor, Michigan: University of Michigan Press, 1999), 30.
[5] Sara Maitland, *Gossip from the Forest: The Tangled Roots of Our Forests and Fairy Tales* (London: Granta, 2012), 7.
[6] Maitland, *Gossip from the Forest*, 20.
[7] Salman Rushdie, "Introduction," in Angela Carter, *Burning Your Boats: Collected Short Stories* (London: Vintage Books, 1996), xiii.
[8] Catherine Belsey, *Why Shakespeare?* (Basingstoke and New York: Palgrave, 2007), 11–20.

Arden and Athens are both examples of the "English wood," where people go "to grow, learn and change."⁹ While the *Dream* and *As You Like It* share the pastoral retreat to "woods outside Athens" and the "Forest of Arden" respectively, Teatro Vivo's adaptation of *The Tempest* also brought its audiences under trees in parks to signify the play's island location. In response to all three productions, audience members suggested that a few trees stood in for generic fairy tale forests: given geographical specificity as English woods by Shakespeare. As I will elaborate, the ambulatory nature of the staging employed by the theater companies elicited a substitution of one tree for a forest and one forest for a Shakespearean wood, which drew audiences deeper into a form of theatrical "ecomimesis,"¹⁰ losing the park trees by recasting them as Shakespeare's, only to rediscover them in their own right through the fairy tale environment.

This chapter's ethnography therefore gently touches conversations about realism in scholarship on ecotheater and literary ecocriticism. Obviously, early modern plays with elements of magic—the *Dream*'s fairies, *The Tempest*'s Prospero, and even some of the events of *As You Like It*'s Arden—performed in cultured parks in the twenty-first century, are far from "realistic" in the sense of actually representing events that might happen (or might have happened) in such a location, but audiences nevertheless alluded to theater encounters that "felt real." Their performances of weathering, undertaken as journeys through the parks, raise questions about the triangulated relationship between the ecopolitics of theatrical representation in contemporary mobile open-air Shakespeares, the nineteenth-century humanist tradition of theatrical realism (and naturalism as an associated philosophical approach to theatrical representation at this time), and enchanting experiences on curated patches of forest floor.

More Believable in a Way: *A Midsummer Night's Dream*, 2014

Sprite Productions' tenth anniversary performances of *A Midsummer Night's Dream* in July 2014 at Ripley Castle, North Yorkshire, began in the castle's Edwardian walled garden. Vivaldi's *Four Seasons* reverberated across a plush lawn where audiences picnicked in the sunshine, held between clematis-clad

---

⁹ Roger Deakin, *Wildwood: A Journey through Trees* (London and New York: Penguin, 2007), x.
¹⁰ Timothy Morton, *Ecology without Nature: Rethinking Environmental Aesthetics* (Cambridge, MA: Harvard University Press, 2007), 8.

walls and herbaceous borders. After the *Dream*'s expository court scenes, audience members gathered their picnic chairs and followed Shakespeare's mechanicals through a greenhouse filled with cacti and exotic ferns—a threshold between the cultured garden and the grounds beyond—into the castle's ornamental woodland. Shakespeare's lovers kept to the marked footpaths but the fairies drew them deeper in, deviating from official routes and leading to damp and mossy clearings. In pursuit, chair-carrying, twig-trampling audiences navigated branches and exposed roots, while fairies beat drums to usher us from one place to the next. Substantial gatherings of up to 150 people were encouraged to "pack in tight like penguins" before scenes commenced when theatergoers were settled.[11] Titania's bower nestled in a giant yew. The lovers quarrelled under an ancient oak. One audience member ostentatiously hung his coat on a branch, only to put it on again shortly afterwards: it was cold in the shade. Others peered through foliage, flicking leaves to amend the frame through which they saw the scenes.

Maitland is struck by the simultaneity of "the nineteenth century Romantic aesthetic in gardening, which led to the development of ornamental forests and woods" in both Britain and Germany—respective homes of the damp wood and terrifying forest—and "the re-emergence of fairy stories" following the publication of the Grimm brothers' collection in 1812.[12] She argues that the ornamental woods and fairy tales arose from "the same cultural movement and influenced each other profoundly."[13] At Ripley, audiences walked past specimen trees marked by small plaques near to the ground—*Wellingtonia, Sequoiadendron giganteum, Planted 1860s, with seeds from Canada*—keeping up with Shakespeare's fairies. Repeatedly, theatergoers talked about how "real," "vivid," "believable," and "natural" these woodland scenes felt. Charlotte spoke to me after the performance, saying, "Well, I mean, much of the play is set in a wood so to perform in a wood you can't get much better than that. Even though it's drama, you can't get more real than that." Despite the proviso—"even though it's drama"—she and her partner William expanded upon their delight in seeing fairies where they might be if fairies existed:

> Charlotte: The fairy queen when she was in the woods and the lovers were playing in front of her and she was asleep.

---

[11] I attended Sprite's *Dream* the same weekend that Le Grand Depart for the Tour De France passed through Ripley. Huge crowds lining the streets for the cycling event were another reminder of the relative popularity of open-air Shakespeares.

[12] Maitland, *Gossip from the Forest*, 279.

[13] Maitland, 279.

> William: When they were lost in the woods as well. That was excellent.
> Charlotte: Because they were! They weren't on a stage—they were lost in the woods! And the fairies were in the woods.

Carmel echoed Charlotte and William's conditional enthusiasm for how "real" the woodland scenes felt when she said, "I thought that it was a really vivid way that a fairy queen would have a bed in a wood." James explained that the trees made the play "more believable in a way because the surroundings are a natural theater and especially this one because they're in the wood. It really lends itself, I thought." For James, the woodland environment lent credence to the unlikely, carefully qualified with "in a way." Alex also felt that the woodland scenes were "natural," although she continued to imagine the wood as a theatrical setting, remarking, "I thought the kind of trees and the kind of set scenes were great. Well, you could do it on a stage but it's contrived on a stage. Here it is natural. It's there, isn't it?" Thomas stated that the ornamental English wood was the "natural" place for Shakespeare's *Dream*:

> I think the environment was terrific. The forest, the bowers, the trees, the artificial lights on it as the evening went on. The fairy lights, I thought, looked very well and really brought up the environment and the twisted trees and gnarled knots of the trees were, yeah, that was very effective. So if the actors or the lovers were in the forest having a quarrel and you had fairies, they were where you would expect to find them. It was actually the naturalness of that. They used the setting well and I didn't feel there was an artifice.

Thomas's words alluded to the materiality of the forest— "gnarled knots" and "twisted trees"—although the promenade staging appeared to subsume these material things into the fiction, encouraging them to stand in for Shakespeare's things in an anachronistic fairy-tale experience. Alex and Joey referred to the *Dream* as an "organic" experience in the woods:

> Alex: I liked when they were in the trees with Titania and then with her, the child, the fairies, I like that.
> Joey: That was a really appropriate scene, you're right. And the building of the scene too seemed very natural. It seemed like it was not just a set but also part of the grounds.
> Alex: It was organic.
> Joey: It was organic.

The natural place for the play was not any kind of Elizabethan stage, it seemed, but woods where the events of the play—human and fairy—might have unfolded in Victorian costume, if they had unfolded in Victorian costume:

notwithstanding differences between real woods near Athens, the Athenian (English) woods of Shakespeare's early modern imagination, and the imported eighteenth-century woods—planted with seeds of imperial conquest around pre-existing one-thousand-year-old oaks—on the grounds of a fourteenth-century castle at a time when the re-emergence of fairy tales in popular consciousness influenced ornamental landscaping. Sprite supplanted Ripley's "real" woods with Shakespeare's Athenian woods, and the woods of early modern drama with a transhistorical fairy tale locale.

The reported experience of the play therefore touches traditions of theatrical and literary realism—conceived as "a broad spectrum of representational strategies intended to produce an effect of verisimilitude on stage and page."[14] In calling for an "eco-theater," Una Chaudhuri draws on Raymond Williams's 1980 essay on "Social Environment and Theatrical Environment: The Case of English Naturalism" to note that the "ideological discourse" of theatrical realism in the nineteenth century "thrust the nonhuman world into the shadows."[15] These anthropocentric shadows are compounded by Elin Diamond's feminist critique of realism, which argues that "Because it naturalizes the relation between character and actor, setting and world, realism operates in concert with ideology,"[16] reinforcing the status quo and limiting scope for rupture or dissidence. Relatedly, since literary ecocriticism's "early devotion to realism,"[17] critics have shied away from earnest attempts to depict nature, often in nonfiction writing, founded on assumptions that to describe the world accurately in prose was to encourage care or even politicization in the reader. Of course, Sprite's staging of the *Dream* looked very different to the kinds of realist stages that replicate moments in the world in order to reveal social relations and their structuring politics. Audience members nevertheless repeated the terms "real" and "natural" often in response to the performance in the woods at Ripley. When people suggested that the play "felt real" under the trees, they appeared to mean that if the fictitious events represented *could* happen (or could have happened) anywhere, they might as well have happened in these woods—not that they

---

[14] Roberta Barker, Kim Solga, and Cary Mazer, "'Tis Pity She's a Realist: A Conversational Case Study in Realism and Early Modern Theater Today," *Shakespeare Bulletin* 31, no. 4 (2013): 573.

[15] Una Chaudhuri, "'There Must Be a Lot of Fish in That Lake': Toward an Ecological Theater," *Theater* 25, no.1 (1994), 23–31, 24; Raymond Williams, "Social Environment and Theatrical Environment: The Case of English Naturalism," in *Culture and Materialism* (London and New York: Verso, 1980).

[16] Elin Diamond, *Unmaking Mimesis: Essays on Feminism and Theater* (London and New York: Routledge, 1997), 4.

[17] Dana Philips, "Review Article *Ecology without Nature*," *The Oxford Literary Review* 32, no. 1 (2010), 152, points out his and Greg Garrard's early skepticism of ecocritical realism in Dana Philips, *The Truth of Ecology* (Oxford: Oxford University Press, 2003) and Greg Garrard, *Ecocriticism* (London and New York: Routledge, 2004).

had been duped into thinking these events were actually happening now. Dan Rebellato's argument for "Theatrical representation as metaphorical" is perhaps more apt an observation for noting that rather than holding illusory "*mistaken beliefs*" about what they saw, audience members were capable of knowing that "two objects are quite separate, but [... thinking] of one in terms of the other."[18] Nobody believed that they were literally transported to Shakespeare's "woods outside Athens" for the duration of the play, but audience members accepted the invitation to think about one set of trees in terms of a wood (and the wood of this metaphorical substitution was not an Athenian wood or a Northern European forest, but the environment for an English fairy tale). Opting in to metaphorical theatrical representation, audience members simultaneously suggested a writing-over of nature, space, and time. While much of what they had to say concerned the place of performance, these responses focussed primarily on the fictitious woods. Although the play brought the world out of the shadows (or brought people into the shadows to see the world), as Diamond suggests, responses to the production elided any history of the castle's grounds—official or otherwise—and reimagined Shakespeare as a universal fairy story.

Out walking alone, David Abram worries that "although our bodies are in the forest, our verbal thoughts are commonly elsewhere."[19] He admonishes himself with Henry David Thoreau's self-censure, "What business have I in the woods if I am thinking of something out of the woods?"[20] In response to the *Dream* in the woods, we might wonder, "What business have I under this tree if I am thinking of some make-believe enchanted woods?" Sprite brought its audiences into the woods, using the space as a container for the work and writing over Ripley's stories with Shakespeare's. By accepting one nature as a metaphor for another, audience members demonstrated the kind of ecomimetic aestheticizing that Morton argues is the outcome of every attempt to faithfully represent nature.[21] But the idea of the fairy tale through which they saw the trees as woods also enabled them to see the trees in the woods. If, following Maitland's logic, the woods of fairy tales have always been real woods—and not a stand-in for human subconscious (just as Vin Nardizzi argues that Shakespeare's wood-words reference the materials used to build the playhouses)—then the trees persist in the production's attempts to integrate what was already "at site" with what was

---

[18] Dan Rebellato, "When We Talk of Horses: Or, What Do We See When We See a Play?" *Performance Research* 14, no. 1 (2009): 24–5 (original emphasis).
[19] David Abram, *Becoming Animal: An Earthly Cosmology* (New York: Vintage Books, 2010), 191.
[20] Abram, *Becoming Animal*, 192.
[21] Morton, *Ecology without Nature*, 31.

"brought to site" in ways that acknowledged the lively and affective capacities of the woods themselves.²² Klara transitioned from thinking about the material props that were used by the actors back to a reflection that human life in the woods was not prior to the life of the trees: "And the attention to detail. It was almost like a festival-like feeling with streamers coming from the trees and there was a little Christmas tree as well. And a rocking horse. Just lots of little details. It looked like the forest was really alive. Which of course it is." Lina noted dust moving in the wind in the wood, visible in occasional sunbeams descending through the canopy: "The trees were all around. And the fact that they were all around. It [the production] was not quite interactive, but the elements were interactive with us. I mean, you could see the dust flying in the rays of light coming down." Irrespective of how the woods were framed as fairy tales or stripped of history, they were still encountered as living. Tim Ingold reminds us that "the creeping entanglements of life will always and inevitably triumph over our attempts to box them in" and these trees endured in their own arboreal materiality through the fairy forest.²³

Going further than asking a few trees to stand in for a forest, the following production undertook gentle and differentiated environmental work that encompassed both the representation of people and nonhuman nature as audiences weathered Shakespeare on a walk in the park, following the actors into the woods for *As You Like It*.

You're on the Journey That the Characters Are On: *As You Like It*, 2014

Taking Flight Theatre Company works with "groups of people who have traditionally been under-represented in theatre" (2014), creating inclusive performances that challenge perceptions of (dis)ability. The company's open-air production of *As You Like It* was performed in public parks in Wales and the South-West of England in 2014 and featured a multi-racial cast of differently abled actors. Live audio-description was available via radio-mic for visually impaired audience members and sign-language was incorporated into all aspects of the performance. The routes the production took through the parks were wheelchair accessible, but rather than accessibility impeding a depth of

---

[22] Mike Pearson and Michael Shanks, *Theatre/Archaeology* (London: Routledge, 2001), 211.
[23] Tim Ingold, *Being Alive: Essays on Movement, Knowledge and Description* (Oxon and New York: Routledge, 2011), 125.

engagement with the spaces, director Elise Davison sought to "encourage audiences to look in all the nooks and crannies," creating what felt like very mobile adventures.[24] Areas designated for performing scenes in the parks were signaled by bunting colored to match extravagantly textured costumes, designed by Becky Davies. Prior to the performance, a tactile exploration of the costumes and park paths was available for anyone with a visual impairment.

I joined audiences for *As You Like It* at three different venues: Cyfartha Castle in Merthyr Tydfil, Thompson's Park in Cardiff, and Blaise Castle and Dairy Estate in Bristol. Audiences for these performances varied between small groups of ten people, or thereabouts, up to nearly one hundred at some of the busier performances. At Cyfarthfa—a nineteenth-century castle on 150 acres of landscaped grounds attesting to past industrial prosperity—audiences gathered at a bandstand where deciduous trees blocked out traces of the town below. Taking Fight shared the hot summer space with an ice-cream van, picnickers, and a packed paddling pool. Once we left the bandstand in search of Arden, the castle was hidden from view. In daylight, the actors spoke directly to their audiences, acknowledging our presence and that of other park users, including—on one occasion—a silver Honda that had taken a wrong turn. The following week at Thompson's Park audiences assembled around a pond with a decorative fountain, whose statue by Welsh artist William Goscombe John has been stolen and replaced on multiple occasions. Thompson's Park's neat lawns, flower-beds, and playing fields were designed during the late eighteenth century. Today, the park is a short walk from Cardiff's buzzy Chapter Arts Centre in the residential area of Canton. Here, audiences traced Arden by following the park's paths too, pausing by wooden benches where a few trees came to stand in for the forest. Joggers, children playing ball games, and dogs and their walkers passed from time to time. Lastly, I visited Taking Flight's *As You Like It* on the grounds of the eighteenth-century Blaise Castle, where audiences waited in a grassy amphitheater for the performance to begin. Disgruntled explorers went on a map-less search for faraway pub toilets. As at Cyfarthfa Castle and Thompson's Park, Blaise Castle's sloping paths led to Arden. Stopping under a few trees signaled the forest.

This *As You Like It* commenced with an interactive fairground set-up where theatergoers had their fortunes told, competed in a duck race, fired balls at a coconut shy, and arm-wrestled *As You Like It*'s Charles the Wrestler. Local outreach groups performed a song that transitioned from the fair into the Shakespearean text. During

---

[24] K. Price, "Inclusive Theatre Company Taking Flight Launches Alfresco Shakespeare for Everyone," *Wales Online*, 2013. www.walesonline.co.uk/whats-on/theatre/taking-flight-launches-alfrescoshakespeare-3416944.

the play's opening court scenes, every time the word "Arden" was uttered aloud, musicians wearing antlered and rabbit-eared headdresses howled in anticipation, spooking Rosalind, Celia, and Touchstone, and visibly aligning the production with the tradition of enchanted forest Shakespeares (despite Arden's anthropomorphized critters not being "magical" in the same way as the *Dream*'s fairy-populated wood). Our feral guides led us through each imaginary Arden, signing and singing, and actors roamed in the nearby distance. Phoebe wandered looking for her flock, chased by Silvius. Orlando wrote poems and attached them to trees.

Michael Dobson speculates that "everywhere one looks under the surface of English outdoor Shakespeare one finds the desire to sit in an English field and say, 'This *is* Arden,'" alluding to the literary and performance history of an Arden that exemplifies nostalgic expressions of rural Englishness—those that can be traced back to The Pastoral Players at Coombe Woods in the 1880s.[25] Audiences at Taking Flight's *As You Like It* certainly indicated that standing under a tree in a park facilitated an imaginative response to Arden rather than uncovering the parks' Welsh histories. But Taking Flight's *As You Like It* also extended Arden beyond these historical limitations. To whom does Arden belong? What do its inhabitants look like? And, in a world with diminishing woodlands, what remains of Arden under a few trees? In this section, I move between responses given across all three parks, as what was environmentally unique about this work—arising from the company's formal approach to working in the weather combined with its mission of inclusivity—was identifiable amongst audiences at all of its venues.

Responses to Taking Flight's *As You Like It* initially shared much with those who responded to Sprite's *Dream*. At each park, a few trees stood in for larger woods, substituting the parks' "real" trees with Shakespeare's forest. Gwyn, for example, explained that the park surroundings complemented the play's content, "Well it's set, isn't it, in the forest, the Forest of Arden? So I just liked the use of the trees and the landscape around you. It just seemed to all fit together quite well." Tracy described delight at being in the park and alluded to a "real" Forest of Arden, also echoing some of the responses to Sprite's *Dream*:

> I suppose the idea of it being *As You Like It,* part of it is set in the Forest of Arden, which is very rural, and I suppose all the trees and the greenery helped me to imagine what the Forest of Arden might have been like and how the actors used the trees as well, you know, to stick love notes on, so, yeah, I feel like that added a lot to the story.

---

[25] Michael Dobson, *Shakespeare and Amateur Performance* (Cambridge and New York: Cambridge University Press, 2011), 188 (original emphasis).

Cheryl imagined the forest under a few trees, saying, "I mean, you really felt as though you were in the middle of a very good wood." Mark and Donna likewise felt that a small cluster of trees enabled them to imagine themselves in Arden:

> Mark: Like under the tree probably made you feel quite like you were in the middle of a forest. Yeah. Yeah.
> Donna: Particularly, the scenes here, when you first came into the forest, you do get that sense that you're in the forest.

Jess added that being under the trees was a pleasurable experience, given the day's warm weather: "Especially with this story … This story is set in the woods so that helps loads. That just makes it much nicer on a nice day. It's just much more pleasant than being anywhere else. Inside or anything."

As for audiences at Sprite's *Dream*, references to the nonhuman nature of the parks in which Taking Flight performed were abundant, tending not to excavate strata of social space but to paint a bright version of Shakespeare's pastoral over the surface. By encouraging audience members to see one or two trees for Arden, individual trees became metaphors for generic fairy tale woodlands inhabited by enchanted animals. The act of moving through the parks de-privileged place as it privileged the play. Cyfarthfa Castle, Thompson's Park, and Blaise Castle were always secondary to Arden. Lynn and Donna discussed trees and birds remaining distinct from but also imagined as complementary to *As You Like It*:

> Lynn: Also I think nature is a really strong theme within the play and they reflected that really nicely with the animal headdresses and animal noises and so that fit really well with the being outdoors and being in nature.
> Donna: There was times when the birds just worked with it as well—you know, the sound of the birds I enjoyed.
> Lynn: The parts when the shepherd in the fields was great and also the pinning of the pages to the trees, sort of … That was a nice match from paper to wood.

Holly recognized the artifice of the performance, but enjoyed the imaginative labor of asking the park to stand in for Shakespeare's forest:

> When there were moments up in the forest. The trees and walking up and down the mountains worked really well. Well they weren't mountains, the little hills of the park worked lovely when we were watching the scene. The shepherdess scenes worked lovely in this sort of environment.

Uniquely in response to Taking Flight's work, as a development of their comments about imagining a few park trees to be standing in for Arden, audience members frequently related that they felt "part of" the performance as a result of sharing the journey with the actors. Beth remarked, "The performance drew you in and took you on a journey around the park" and Jess interrupted her, thinking of the park's topography, saying, "So the fact that they were surrounded by trees and I liked all of the up and downs as well so the audience felt like they were on a journey with the actors or with their characters." Beth continued, suggesting that Taking Flight's formal attempts to collaborate with the park drew her further into the play, "It felt like you were engaged all of the time. You're sort of made to be involved in it. You're an active participant in it, which was a good thing. It made you follow the story more in that way." In a similar vein, Dale offered:

> There was a beautiful atmospheric echo that happened when the actors were really getting into it. The environment, the promenade of the environment, up and down the hills made it feel a lot more like you were traipsing through forests and made you feel much more involved in the show.

Sarah and Tim also enjoyed walking the same route as Shakespeare's characters, literally following in their footsteps:

> Sarah: I think the landscape helps. You know, as opposed to it being just a flat stage with a background. It's more interactive, you know, you feel like you're on the journey that the characters are on.
> Tim: Yeah. You feel part of it really.
> Sarah: I think just in general the setting with, you know, *As You Like It* takes part in a forest so having the trees and having the rolling hills it helps to put you in the right position and frame of mind to … to be not just a part of the show itself but to kind of relate it to the performance.

Since the publication of Jacques Rancière's *The Emancipated Spectator* (2009), the politics of what it means to "participate" in performance, what it means for an audience member to be "active" and what makes them "passive," who has power or agency, and what modes of interaction are affective, superior, or politically "emancipatory" have become well-trampled intellectual ground.[26] Michael Dobson finds promenade Shakespeares anything but liberating, arguing that "the exercise of attending a promenade Shakespeare today is characteristically not one of emancipation […] but one of subjection, made

---

[26] See, for example, Claire Bishop, *Artificial Hells: Participatory Arts and The Politics of Spectatorship* (London: Verso, 2012); Stephen Purcell, *Shakespeare and Audience in Practice* (Basingstoke and New York: Palgrave, 2013), 134; Gareth White, *Audience Participation in Theatre. Aesthetics of the Invitation* (Basingstoke and New York: Palgrave, 2013).

explicit by figures around the fringe of the play who serve as authoritarian mediators between the play's world and that of its helpless spectators."[27] Dobson claims that promenade Shakespeares simply replace restrictive theater seats with "a more elaborate and better-agreed set of restrictions."[28] While I don't disagree that restrictions are in place at this type of mobile performance, care is needed not to undermine audiences' abilities to describe the conditions of their participation for themselves, otherwise we run the risk of obstructing the agency that "emancipating" performance is anxious to promote: we want you to have agency (really, we do) but only when attending the theater that we think is good for you. It is not my intention to comment upon whether the audience was emancipated or not, but I would like to suggest that the unprompted choice to express their engagement as "participatory" at Taking Flight's *As You Like It* was environmentally significant. Participation did not appear to mean that audience members felt as though they were shaping the action of the play nor that they were interacting meaningfully with the fictitious characters, but seemed to have more to do with recognizing their physical and imaginative contribution as an audience to the theatrical event as a whole. Their performances of weathering were generously given, knowingly opting-in to being ushered around more than helpless or curmudgeonly aloof. The mobile staging, received as participatory, challenged its audiences to extend historically limiting conceptions of Arden.

Bree Hadley, writing on *Disability, Public Space and Spectatorship* (2013), ventures that "interventionist"[29] performance in public space can generate "a chance—not a certainty—that spectators will start to reflect, reconsider the scripts that underpin their social interactions."[30] While the text of Shakespeare's *As You Like It* is far from "interventionist" in the way that Hadley conceptualizes this kind of performance, there was sufficient evidence in audience responses to Taking Flight's production to suggest that the company's approach to staging facilitated an oblique intervention anyway. *As You Like It* intervened in the parks inasmuch as people who might not usually be thought of as able to use them in certain ways—as audience members or as Shakespearean actors—embarked on journeys

---

[27] Michael Dobson, "Moving the Audience: Shakespeare, the Mob, and the Promenade," *Shakespeare Bulletin* 23, no. 2 (2005): 19–28.
[28] Dobson, "Moving the Audience," 26.
[29] Bree Hadley, *Disability, Public Space Performance and Spectatorship: Unconscious Performers* (Basingstoke and New York: Palgrave Macmillan, 2013), 8–17.
[30] Hadley, *Disability, Public Space Performance and Spectatorship*, 15.

through the places, performing Arden as they went. Rosalind, for example, played by Alison Halstead, was half Orlando's height—meaningful casting for a play that describes Rosalind as "more than common tall" (*As You Like It* 1.3.112). Chain in hand, she walked to Orlando (Connor Allen) and without breaking eye contact with him, took hold of both his outstretched hands, climbed onto his upper legs one foot at a time, placed the chain around his neck and leaned back in a counterbalance; "Wear this for me—one out of suits with fortune, / That could give more but that her hand lacks means" (*As You Like It* 1.2.235–6). Charles the wrestler recovered from his defeat and played romantic music on the flute. Leaves rustled in sycamores sheltering the bandstand at Cyfarthfa Castle. Later in the play, Rosalind's "Do you not know I am a woman, when I think I must speak?" (3.2.242–3), often a cue for laughter, received no audible response from the audience members around me; the line that relies on stereotypes for its laugh became redundant in a production that otherwise challenged them.

Largely, no one amongst the audience members to whom I spoke referenced disability directly but used language that was imprecisely positive, tagged onto their discussions about trees and allusions to participation: implicitly reconsidering how the imaginary Arden was populated. Sara and Tim conversed:

> Sara: It's demanding on your back but it's worth it.
> Tim: Yeah, it's worth it and it helps that we're in a ground with, you know, varying abilities, disabilities, you know. […] So moving around is hard but it's good because it involves everyone. It's a little arduous getting up the hill but it's … it does involve everyone and I think that's definitely something to commend.

Holly offered, "I think it brings new people along. The children were enthusiastic. I mean it's opening up a new diversity. It's opening up to new ideas. It's fresh and it's out there," and Chantelle explained, "You really do feel that it's more open, more free and that no one is judging you." Taking Flight's production made a more inclusive version of the green world feel, if not real then at least possible under a few trees. Within the frame of a fairy tale, performances of weathering painted a repopulated Arden over the parks, catering for differentiated access needs in a world with fewer trees. This *As You Like It* didn't look back to something better but upward into trees and around at one another, finding more inclusive ways of living with less and celebrating what there is.

Also disrupting the performance history of the canon of open-air Shakespeares under trees, the final example in this chapter adapts its play, edging closer to ecodramaturgical intentions as audiences continue to perform their weathering out on a walk in the park.

Figure 4.1 Alison Halstead and Connor Allen in Taking Flight's *As You Like It*, 2014. Photograph courtesy of Jorge Lizalde Cano.

You Notice Things You Haven't Noticed Before: *After the Tempest*, 2013

Teatro Vivo is a theater company based in South East London, aiming to "turn everyday environments into magical worlds."³¹ *After The Tempest*, their ninety-minute adaptation of Shakespeare's *The Tempest* was created with support from the London Parks and Green Spaces Forum and toured to five different parks in July and August 2013.³² Aware of the inherent contradictions of trying to make

---

³¹ Teatro Vivo, "About Us," 2019 http://www.teatrovivo.co.uk/about-us/.
³² Adaptation is another contested term. I use it here in keeping with Daniel Fischlin and Mark Fortier's definition of a work "which, through verbal and theatrical devices, radically alter[s] the shape and significance of another work so as to invoke that work and yet be different from it," eds. Mark Fortier and Daniel Fischlin. *Adaptations of Shakespeare: A Critical Anthology of Plays from the Seventeenth Century to the Present* (London and New York: Routledge, 2000), 4.

site-specific performance for different parks, director Sophie Austin explained that she wanted "to create a play that would be one thing in one park and entirely another in another park."[33] Austin aspired to use the production to intervene in existing narratives of the parks, explaining:

> I think it's about doing something different with the park. Because a park is generally somewhere you go during the day to walk your dog or to stretch your legs or to run around you know but we're inviting you to come to the park after it's closed often and to be in the place when you shouldn't be.[34]

The premise for *After The Tempest* was that the island's spirits—left behind after Prospero and Miranda's departure—were re-enacting the events of Shakespeare's *The Tempest* on location to celebrate a year's independence from its former leader. Booking a ticket for Teatro Vivo's production prompted an email invite from Ariel to the island's "Independence Day" celebrations. The invite communicated light-hearted practical advice for weathering Shakespeare and advocated a responsible approach to being in the parks:

> This humble theatrical event will take you to the most far-flung and beautiful parts of our land, so please bring sensible footwear and be aware that some of the more junior spirits may find it amusing to burst rain clouds overhead from time to time, so umbrellas may be a wise precaution. Finally, as the Island slowly recovers from its fettered history, please respect our "leave no trace" policy, and take nothing but pictures, kill nothing but time, leave nothing but footprints and keep only memories.

Upon arrival, actors handed audience members either a feather or pinecone to wear, creating groups of "air" and "earth" spirits who—after the shipwreck—followed separate paths through the parks and encountered events in a different order, meeting together again for the final scenes. Ariel (Kas Darley), the island's new and tyrannical dictator, orchestrated the re-enactment as propaganda for the island's subjects while Caliban attempted to enlist the audience in a coup d'état. The re-enacted scenes the audience were to witness, Ariel solemnly informed us, would return to the very places on the island where they first occurred, ghosting the park spaces with fabricated historical waymarkers and—as with Sprite's and Taking Flight's work—writing over the parks with the story of the play. As the actors guided their earth or air spirits between the Shakespearean scenes—fairly faithful textual renditions—they improvised

---

[33] Sophie Austin, Interview with the author, October 9, 2014.
[34] Austin, Interview, October 9, 2014.

provocative conversations in everyday language, directly addressing audience members with questions about political leadership, land ownership, marriage, and nonhuman nature. Regardless of which trail a person followed, discontented whispers crossed paths, undercutting the official narrative of the anniversary celebration. Through the disgruntled murmurings, it became apparent that Caliban coveted a power-position rather than intending to supplant Ariel with an egalitarian socialist state as he had led the audience to believe. The improvised dialogue asked us as an audience to notice things we might not otherwise have seen in the parks, while simultaneously pre-empting, reflecting upon, and challenging Shakespeare's text, asking, "What would be better than this?" (in relation to claims on the island) and "What are we going to do about it?" (through attempts to start the revolution). As with responses to Taking Flight's mission of inclusivity, however, the thematic resonances between *After The Tempest* and questions of access and control appeared only cursorily in audience responses.

The first of two places I joined audiences for *After The Tempest* was Barking Park, South East London, which in 2013 had undergone an extensive regeneration project with assistance from the Heritage Lottery Fund. The second was Holland Park, West London, which in 2013 was hosting the In Transit Festival of which *After The Tempest* was part: "A festival of new work responding to and reflecting the unique environment and character of Kensington and Chelsea."[35] The respective boroughs of "Barking and Dagenham" and "Kensington and Chelsea" occupied opposite ends of the 2013 London Poverty Profile.[36] It would be easy to assume that at Barking—with some of the highest unemployment and long-term sick benefits rate in London—*After The Tempest* functioned as an improving force, whereas at Holland Park—renowned as an elite opera venue—Shakespeare simply affirmed the park's high cultural status, despite that fact that marked poverty and affluence coexist in both areas. The audience responses to *After The Tempest* unsettled these historically concerning uses of Shakespeare, responding to the company's attention to space, their adaptation of the text—reframing and constantly questioning Shakespeare's narrative—and from their direct challenges to the audience. At Barking Park, social media posts signaled that chalk paw-prints would point the way to a makeshift box-office outside the park's newly opened café (where I spotted children covering them up with leaves and rubbing them out). The pre-booked audience at Barking Park was small—sometimes comprising fewer than fifteen people—but

[35] "In Transit Festival Holland Park," 2013, http://www.rbkc.gov.uk/subsites/intransit.aspx.
[36] "London Poverty Profile," 2013, http://www.londonspovertyprofile.org.uk/press/lpp-2013-barking-press-release/.

further park users, including many children, stumbled across the performance and some stayed to watch to the end. The audience included locals, as well as people who had seen Teatro Vivo's work previously and had traveled to support the company. Tina regularly visited the park to feed the ducks with her grandchildren. She had come to *After The Tempest*, "Because it was outside and because it was in this particular park and because it's quite close to where I live and I just wouldn't miss it." Izzy, who had traveled to support a friend in the cast, had never been to the park in Barking and her preconceptions of the place were disrupted by the play. She commented:

> I think what I'm going to most remember to be honest is just that I've never been to this park before and I didn't know Barking had a park. I've been out of the tube station before but I haven't ventured out so I think just how surprisingly beautiful the park is because it hasn't got a good reputation as a place. So surprisingly beautiful.

In contrast with Barking's busy high street and market, the journey from Holland Park tube station to the park took the walker down wide tree-lined roads, past extensive white houses, driveways with expensive-looking cars, restaurants, and wine bars. Actors dressed as elemental spirits met audience members near the opera café and escorted us to a wooded area off the marked paths. Even from our "wild" clearing, it was still impossible not to hear the orchestra warming up for the rarely performed *I gioielli della Madonna* by Ermanno Wolf-Ferrari or not to note the contrast between the waterproof-clad audience members for *After The Tempest* and the smartly dressed operagoers. There were no chalk paw prints on the paths at Holland Park, and Jenny, who had struggled to find the meeting place, laughed as she anticipated the promenade aspect of the performance, "We've already got lost finding our way here so if we have to navigate, we're buggered!" Before venturing from the meeting place, Freya compared the setting at Holland Park to "a manicured Hampstead Heath. It's a cute little park." Laura added, "But bits of it we walked through are really manicured and regal and beautiful. It used to be a private estate so that ... It was a Jacobean estate, I think, and I feel like I still see remnants of that, which is interesting. Yeah. It's beautiful." A conversation with Harry and Lucy, who were familiar with Teatro Vivo's work, suggested that Holland Park was an unusual venue for the company.

> Lucy: I guess, like, yeah, it's a leafy park in upper class London. [*Laughter*] It's not the surroundings I'm used to. Coming down High St Kenn ... It's a whole different part of London to what I'm used to really.
> Harry: It's nice that I suppose somewhere like Holland Park ... I suppose you associate with, you know, quite upper class.

Lucy: Yeah. You can hear the opera.
Harry: Yeah. It's nice that they've obviously let Teatro Vivo do it in the space and it's, I suppose, a novel way of seeing Holland Park.

Their journey to Holland Park had prompted feelings of their being out of place, suggesting that Holland Park's management was generous to "allow" Teatro Vivo to perform there. Bella compounded this sense of Teatro Vivo's nonbelonging in Holland Park when she said, "It's a different kind of park as well … not where they normally do stuff because it's like, it's quite a swanky area. And normally they don't like swanky places." For these audience members, the adaptation of Shakespeare—an affirmer of middle-brow culture at Ripley Castle—became the transgressor when juxtaposed with Holland Park's opera.

Locals Carol and Dave, however, were drawn to *After The Tempest* precisely because of its taking place in their local Holland Park. They explained:

Dave: The location here in Holland Park is quite magical. Especially once the evening starts to set in. This is a wonderful park, actually a magical park in my opinion.
Carol: So … he thinks there are fairies in it!
Dave: That magic was brought more … It worked with the production.
Carol: I think they were very lucky to have Holland Park. It may not have worked so well in some other park. But Holland Park's ideal for this kind of activity.

The reiteration of allusions to "magic" recalled Robert Watson's early modern "placeholder for phenomena with pending explanation" and the liveliness of the Willow Globe: here at Holland Park, Shakespeare was a fairy tale in the forest (refrain: a few trees stood in for a wood).[37]

Attempting to integrate "magic" with the materiality of the park, Darley as Ariel brought audience members to a tree—a London Plane in Barking Park and a silver birch at Holland Park—touched the tree and looked up into its branches. She explained that bark from "this very tree" had been used to make the "magic" flutes she would now distribute to members of the audience so that we could play them together to encourage Ferdinand (Tom Ross Williams) and Miranda (Natasha Magigi)—who were asleep in a tree—to fall in love. Elliot responded to the materials found in the park creatively incorporated into the performance:

---

[37] Robert N. Watson, *Back to Nature: The Green and the Real in the Late Renaissance* (Philadelphia: University of Pennsylvania Press, 2006), 36.

Figure 4.2 Natasha Magigi and Tom Ross Williams as Mirando and Ferdinand in Teatro Vivo's *After The Tempest*, 2013. Photograph courtesy of Sophie Austin.

> I liked the sleeping thing on the tree. It's just quite a well set out park with having the different sections so you kind of feel like they could just be on an island in a way and they're coming out of nature really. And there's very limited props what they had. A lot of it was made from wood and sticks that they found here and it incorporated a lot of what was around.

Izzy also suggested that she noticed nature she might not otherwise have seen because of the journey through the park at Barking:

> I thought that was … it's really, really beautiful and it kind of feels like, I don't know, it's kind of like, like it's not as boring because there's a lot of things to capture your visual attention and there's a lot of distractions but it's nice, you notice things you haven't noticed before because you don't take the time to look at them. So just scenery wise—just trees and it's nice when there were some

squirrels involved, getting in on the action. There was a scene by the tree where Caliban was talking about "The isle is full of noises" (*The Tempest* 3.2.130) and at that point there was a squirrel running up and down the tree and it was that kind of things are always going on and wildlife is all around you.

There are no squirrels in *The Tempest*, but—as in Taking Flight's reworking of *As You Like It*—fairy tales make as good a home as London parks for fluffy rodents. It was possible to imagine them standing in for the squirrels Shakespeare didn't write in *After The Tempest* in the woods.

Further conversations revealed that Carol and Dave—whose playful exchange on fairies in Holland Park is quoted above—had a prior personal relationship with Holland Park. This arose during our discussion of the performance's final scene, which was presented in scrubland on the outskirts of the park that had to be accessed through a locked gate off the public paths, through trees, stumbling in the dusk (where a frog had earlier taken me by surprise as I sat down in the long grass).

> Carol: And we've seen it [*The Tempest*] in Regent's Park. But, it's more poignant for us because we used to know the people that lived in the house that was here.
> Evelyn: Oh wow. And it's no more a house?
> Dave: No more a house.
> Carol: And it was a head-gardener's house.
> Dave: You can feel it underneath our feet.
> Evelyn: So when did it come down—the house?
> Dave: It must be ten years ago.
> Carol: So the gardener doesn't live here anymore ... I mean doesn't live on site. I don't know why ... but we knew the people that lived here.
> Dave: And the mum is dead now isn't she?
> Carol: So when we came in here it felt really sort of poignant.
> Dave: So there was another layer there as well.

Carol and Dave's experience of the space was socially situated in their own memories of people, ghosts of dwellings, and prior uses of the land, as well as the immediate experience of the play in the weather.[38] Extending this conversation, they recalled a convergence of the elemental themes in Shakespeare's play, the park landscape, the weather, and the time of day:

---

[38] Austin explained that park management were initially unwilling for the untended space to be used for the performance and that she had had to press for permission to use it. She was not aware that once there had once been a house on the site.

Carol: In the woods when they were asleep under the trees, I thought that was really good.

Dave: Especially the last bit as well because the location here in Holland Park is quite magical. Especially once the evening starts to set in. I think the ending … Ariel's speech at the end is one of Shakespeare's best speeches and to have it in a setting like this with the sun going down … having gone down … and little stars have just come out and it's such an effective speech and, in this location, it's the best experience I've had of that particular speech ever.

"Ariel's speech," to which Dave referred, was Prospero's "Our revels now are ended …" (*The Tempest* 4.1.148), reassigned to Ariel at the climax of the reenactment and delivered from the long grass in the locked, wooded, and overgrown area of the park. Izzy, Carol, and Dave, and the trees, squirrels, stars, and words they remarked upon in response to Teatro Vivo's *After The Tempest* return us to the notion the enchanted wood where this chapter began.

Woods in the Trees

In the context of a climate-threatened world, the idea of enchantment has been employed ecopolitically—by some more convincingly than others. "Enchantment" sounds fluffy, sentimental, or spiritual, recalling the romantic, Disneyfied constructions of picturesque landscapes and anthropomorphized wildlife that are dangerous between humans and for nonhuman nature. James Gibson makes ambitious claims for reenchantment—the "re" indicating a return to a nature deemed lost—describing an experience that might bring about "*transcendence*, a sense of mystery and meaning, glimpses of a numinous world beyond our own."[39] What Gibson sees as a contemporary culture of reenchantment is neither nostalgia for a lost Eden "nor simply another outburst of romanticism," because, he argues, in light of our growing knowledge of anthropogenic climate change, "it is fueled by a new sense of urgency."[40] Gibson confidently pronounces reenchantment's ethical potential, positing that "spiritual connections made to animals and landscapes almost invariably lead—often intentionally, sometimes not—to a new relationship to nature in general."[41] Timothy Morton, however, memorably refutes reenchantment propositions such as Gibson's by first citing poet and nature writer John Daniel:

---

[39] James W. Gibson, *A Reenchanted World: The Quest for a New Kinship with Nature* (New York: Holt, 2009), 11 (original emphasis).
[40] Gibson, *A Reenchanted* World, 10.
[41] Gibson, 12.

> The sky is probably falling. Global warming is happening. But somehow it's not going to work to call people to arms about that and pretend to know what will work. This is why you shouldn't teach kids about the dire straits of the rain forest. You should take kids out to the stream out back and show them the water striders.[42]

Morton demolishes what he perceives to be a dangerous naivety on Daniel's part, countering that "To speak thus is to use the aesthetic as anesthetic."[43] As far as Morton is concerned, reenchantment—especially when imaginably derived from an in-situ experience of nature—is a form of denial, paralyzing the urgency to act.

But while evidenced links between enchantment and environmentally conscious behavior (let alone ecopolitics) are tenuous at best, Jane Bennett's argument for a secular form of enchantment in *The Enchantment of Modern Life* (2001) appears potentially suited to an analysis of the lived experience of the woods of across the range of outdoor Shakespeares studied. Unlike Gibson's, Bennett's is "not a tale of reenchantment but one that calls attention to the magical sites already there."[44] Bennett assigns herself the role of disenchantment's "trash collector" and assembles the discards of modernity's compelling disenchantment narratives to tell an "alter-tale" of enchantment, which, she proposes, has been simultaneously present all the while (like Jan Golinski's weather—modernity never controlled the weather and it wasn't entirely disenchanted either).[45] Enchantment, Bennett argues more persuasively than Gibson, reinforces attachment to the world: we care for the world because we first feel attached to it. To be enchanted, as Bennett puts forward, "is to be struck and shaken by the extraordinary that lives amid the familiar and the everyday."[46] Enchantment "requires active engagement with objects of sensuous experience; it is a state of interactive fascination, not fall-to-your knees awe."[47] Bennett argues—with caveats aplenty—that enchantment may be essential for generating ethically generous behavior in the longer term. A person returning to regular life after an enchanted experience might be more inclined to behave generously toward human and nonhuman others. She summarizes, "I pursue a life with moments of enchantment rather than an enchanted way of life."[48]

---

[42] John Daniel in Morton, *Ecology without Nature*, 12.
[43] Morton, *Ecology without Nature*, 12.
[44] Jane Bennett, *The Enchantment of Modern Life: Attachments, Crossings and Ethics* (New Jersey: Princeton University Press, 2001), 8.
[45] Bennett, *The Enchantment of Modern Life*, 8.
[46] Bennett, 4.
[47] Bennett, 5.
[48] Bennett, 10.

While there remains much about which to be wary, I also seek to collect the enchanted trash—to reuse Bennett's idea—in the audience responses, and to offer a parallel counter story. I agree with Bennett's assertion of "the effect—always indirect—that a cultural narrative has on the ethical sensibility of its bearers";[49] that to continuously rehearse stories of disenchantment inhibits imagining alternatives. This is not to succumb to a reductive optimism by enthusiastically overstating a case for hope but an attempt to tell a messier story about the ecologies of audiences performing weathering at open-air Shakespeares on a walk in the woods. At Sprite's *Dream*, weathering Shakespeare was an aesthetic act, enabling the play to feel real in the woods. Taking Flight's *As You Like It* weathering Shakespeare meant participating in an event that allowed a new version of Arden to feel real, as audiences imagined themselves "participating" in creating the woods; aware that all weathering is not undertaken with the same resources, but realizing that—with care—it is possible to accommodate differing needs. At Teatro Vivo's *After The Tempest*, weathering Shakespeare was a transgressive act. The events of the play felt "real" inasmuch as everything around the play framed them as metatheater (the actors were really themselves as their characters and the scenes from *The Tempest* were framed as a re-enactment). By and large, across all three performances, the effect of moving through the parks tended to be the fostering of greater engagement with the stories presented. In practitioners' attempts to "collaborate with space," the collaboration tended to privilege the play, working so that the play felt at home there. The parks were perceived as the natural places for the plays, oftentimes performing the function of spatial containers for Shakespeare's stories, serving the performances. While audience members spoke a lot about the places where the plays took place—as Mike Pearson's measure of site-specificity imagined audiences might[50]—they did so by suggesting that the places supported the plays rather than the other way round. While the performances brought attention to places, they tended to do so in the context of the plays, writing over the parks with fairy tale iterations of Shakespeare's stories. Edward Casey's observation that "I can know I am here without knowing where I am"[51] falls silently because no one is there to hear it.

Each of the productions, however, also seemed to elicit enchanted responses, by playing with the poet Jeremy Hooker's notion of "ditch vision," summarized

---

[49] Bennett, 12.
[50] Pearson, *Site-Specific Performance*, 194.
[51] Edward Casey, *Getting Back into Place*. 2nd ed. (Bloomington and Indianapolis: Indiana University Press, 2009), 54.

by Richard Kerridge as "the imaginative habit of playing with scale in order to discover wildness and infinity in small spaces; the genre of daydreaming that sees in an overgrown railway bank the principle and possibility of wildness."[52] They asked audiences to see in one tree a wood, to look into the cracks and to affirm Rebecca Solnit's provocation that the "surprises, liberations, and clarifications of travel can sometimes be garnered by going around the block as well as going around the world."[53] Audience responses raised troubling questions about what was *in* the bits of wildness, in the ditches that stood in for Shakespeare's woods. We ventured into the woods, sought out wildness, and peered into the cracks only to find our human image—standing in for early modern theater standing in for fairy tales—reflected right back at us. Vin Nardizzi argues that the wooden theaters of early modern England "invited spectators—many of whom would have encountered discourses of resource scarcity [...]—to behold a wood in the theatre."[54] In the woodlands of the twenty-first century, the scenic verisimilitude of the trees as both Shakespeare's trees and "real" trees tended toward a performed enactment of ecomimesis, where "real" nature was presented through a highly mediated form of culture, aestheticizing Nature and preserving distance from it. But as Sara Maitland points out, the woodland settings for fairy-tales are actually more placed than we have previously cared to think,[55] and a woodland retelling of Shakespeare—however problematic in terms of its incongruity with early modern theatrical practice or the erasure of local and cultural histories—might also offer a decent example of "woods performing woods," grasping for their ontological status as "trees" through the fairy-tale optic with which audiences encountered them. If fairy-tale settings have been real woods all along, then maybe these trees, enchanting transient Shakespearean audiences, were a little less victims of ecomimesis and always more themselves than theater.

---

[52] Richard Kerridge, "Green Pleasures," in *The Politics and Pleasures of Consuming Differently*, eds. Kate Soper, Martin Ryle, and Lyn Thomas (London: Palgrave, 2009), 133.
[53] Rebecca Solnit, *Wanderlust: A History of Walking* (London: Verso, 2001), 6.
[54] Nardizzi, *Wooden Os*, 20.
[55] Maitland, *Gossip from the Forest*, 7.

Part Three

5

Green Atmospheres: Nature Playing (Along, Sometimes)

Jade: When I look at the clouds sometimes I think there must be a God.
Alex: When we had the really, really, really torrential rainstorm in …
Jade: In Newby?
Alex: In Newby, yeah. I looked up and I went, "Do you see this oh God?" and straightaway it basically stopped. I thought, "Fuck, maybe God's real." I mean I don't believe in him and I went through this whole religious thing in like four seconds on stage it was really odd.
Simon: And I just thought thank fuck it's stopped raining.[1]

The third and final part of this book considers what, if any, ecopolitical potential resides in the performances of weathering generated by open-air Shakespeares, given that their persistence runs parallel to the accelerated accumulation of atmospheric carbon dioxide, catastrophic anthropogenic environmental damage, and climate change. That conversations amongst audiences and actors turned to wildlife, light, landscape, and weather at all performances, irrespective of different meteorological conditions, biodiversity, time of day, topography, the choice of play, the varied aesthetic qualities of a production, and, not least, the socio-cultural histories of the places of the performances, will likely be apparent by now. This chapter takes themes common across the contemporary productions discussed in Chapters 3 and 4, inflected by the environmental event histories discussed in Chapters 1 and 2, as its matter. Alongside Shakespeare, theatergoers frequently referenced the subjects of what Raymond Williams identifies as a "green language" in late eighteenth-century British nature poetry[2]—wildlife, light, landscape, and weather—in conversations about the atmospheres of the theatrical events. As Jeffrey Cohen's collection *Prismatic Ecology: Ecotheory Beyond Green* points out, "green" has become shorthand for

---

[1] Helen Lawson, *A Summer Hamlet* (2003). Documentary Produced by Dusthouse.
[2] Raymond Williams, *The Country and the City* (London: Vintage Books, 2016 [1973]), 193.

anything with an environmental bent, "as if the color were the only organic hue, a blazon for nature itself."[3] While weather as encountered in person might more precisely be thought of as translucent and invisible, audiences incorporated it—as Williams does—into a green language as they spoke about the performance atmospheres.

Proximity, of course, does not equate to an unmediated relationship. As with the Pastoral Players in 1884 and the energy-intensive spectacles of the 1930s, atmospheres at these contemporary productions were verbalized through hazy ideas of an historical Shakespeare, authentic, and original practices—revealing imagined memories of a teleological cultural mythology that begins in Elizabethan playhouses—and with reference to literary and cultural pastorals. I also notice people attuned to the meteorological aspect of atmosphere in response to Shakespearean theater performed in the weather.

Aleatory Anecdotes

Penelope Woods recounts an anecdote of a pigeon landing on stage at the reconstructed Shakespeare's Globe during Tim Carroll's production of *Macbeth*, just as the actor Jasper Britton spoke Macbeth's lines: "Life's but a walking shadow, / A poor player that struts and frets his hour upon the stage" (*Macbeth* 5.5.23–4). Britton waited for the pigeon to fly off before finishing, "and then is heard no more" (*Macbeth* 5.5.25).[4] Thinking about how an audience might watch Britton watching the pigeon, Woods cites Werner Meyer-Eppler's definition of "aleatory" to name a performance process where the "large-scale course is determined, the case of individual elements however being dependent on chance."[5] In agreement with Meyer-Eppler, Woods observes that the solid frame around the sky influences the reception of nonhuman nature within the theater's circumference:

> Unlike interruptions to a performance in stately-home gardens, or at Minack in Cornwall or the Regent's Park Outdoor Theatre in London, the enclosed and purpose-built space of the Globe frames and determines a potential and significant momentary role for these interruptions within the performance,

---

[3] Jeffrey Jerome Cohen, "Introduction: Ecology's Rainbow," *Prismatic Ecology: Ecotheory beyond Green* (Minneapolis and London: University of Minnesota Press, 2013).
[4] Penelope Woods, "Globe Audiences: Spectatorship and Reconstruction at Shakespeare's Globe" (PhD thesis, Queen Mary University of London, 2012), 252.
[5] Werner Meyer-Eppler in Woods, "Globe Audiences," 250.

whereas they are more likely to be experienced as incidental and circumstantial, and hence not "determined" and "determining," at other outdoor theatre events.[6]

Such an encircled structure as Shakespeare's Globe generates aleatory effects that differ from those that might occur in more exposed outdoor performance spaces. The framed sky of the Globe's wooden O assists in keeping Shakespeare and his play at the heart of the theatrical event, Woods argues, affording the actor the choice to incorporate the pigeon into the frame or not.[7] Without the Globe's architecture, the myth of Britton's peristeronic confrontation circulated as a kind of grail—deferred potential and possibility—at the performances I attended. The actor Nathan Goode captured some of this anticipation when he enthused:

> And you never know, one day you might just get that opportune noise ... just at the right moment ... you know, you might just get that crack of thunder as one of the witches stands up in *Macbeth*. You never know ... you just never know. It makes it much more exciting.[8]

A deluge came down just as Prospero conjured his tempest. Lear stumbled across the blasted heath during a rainstorm, which cleared up after the interval. Sunbeams broke through heavy cloud as Hermione descended her platform, warm. Puck skimmed the surface of the lake just as the only cloud in a starry sky drifted to reveal a crescent moon. A duck quacked along in iambic pentameter. Someone was always delighted that they had been there. Someone always remembered: anecdotes traded and trumped. These anecdotes tended to be mythologized memories of what did happen, however, or excitement about what might happen, rather than examples of what happened just now.

In organizing responses thematically according to the four subjects of Williams's green language, this chapter is interested in atmospheres that precede anecdotes and the translation of atmosphere into a remembered event. What is the experience of the "incidental and circumstantial" at open-air Shakespeares when nature only haphazardly interacts with the play? How are encounters between nonhuman nature and performance perceived in the moment of reception if not as "determining" effects? How do atmosphere and memory intersect in performances of weathering? And why might Shakespeare matter when we attend to anecdotal performances of remembered atmosphere

---

[6] Woods, "Globe Audiences," 251.
[7] Woods, 256.
[8] Nathan Goode, Interview with the author at The Willow Globe, Penlanole, May 25, 2012.

in thinking about anthropogenic climate change? Chasing the pigeon back out through the wooden O, the following sections track atmospheres through a green language that emanates from but is irreducible to wildlife, light, landscape, weather, and Shakespeare.

Green Atmospheres

Undertaking the fieldwork for this book, I encountered theatergoers speaking about atmosphere in a wide range of ways. Sometimes, people referred to atmosphere in terms of the experience of being outdoors: "Being outside always adds to the atmosphere, doesn't it?" or "It's just nice being outside. It gives it an atmosphere that you can't really get in a theater." Sometimes, they referred to the informality of the atmosphere: "I like to come when the weather is nice. I think it's just more casual, more informal. It's a lovely atmosphere." Sometimes, they referred to the sociability of being outdoors with others: "The atmosphere of not only the actors but also the audience was very good." Sometimes, they referred to a pastoral atmosphere as complementary to Shakespeare: "The atmosphere of the outdoor theatre lends itself very well to Shakespeare because of the … oh, because of the sort of bucolic themes he explores." Sometimes, they referred to theatrical aesthetics in terms of atmosphere: "There was a beautiful atmospheric echo that happened when the actors were really getting into it." Lastly, sometimes they praised the atmosphere without filtering it through any context at all: "It was the atmosphere. It was the atmosphere!" It is necessary to admit at this point that I—naively—began the fieldwork with a view to asking a question about "the atmosphere in the audience" and without a clear sense of the term myself. With few exceptions, though, theatergoers raised atmosphere *before* I managed to ask the question, infusing its affective dimension with a tacit acknowledgment of its meteorological composition.

Energized scholarly attention to atmosphere as an aesthetic concept coincides with a re-attending to the air surrounding the earth—at interdisciplinary intersections between anthropology, ecocriticism, ecology, phenomenology, performance studies, anthropology, philosophy, human geography, and the social sciences.[9] For Gernot Böhme, one of the instigators of interest in atmosphere in phenomenology since the 1990s, the "vague use of the expression atmosphere in aesthetic and political discourse derives from a use in everyday speech which

---

[9] The Staging Atmospheres—Theatre and the Atmospheric Turn conference, Queen Mary University, London, December 8, and December 9, 2017, https://ambiances.net/seminars/london-2017-staging-atmospheres.html, hosted by Martin Welton and Penelope Woods, brought together some of this work.

is in many respects much more exact."¹⁰ Böhme explains atmosphere as neither independent nor "free floating" but as "something that proceeds from and is created by things, persons or their constellations."¹¹ He expands:

> Atmospheres are neither something objective, that is, qualities possessed by things, and yet they are something thinglike, belonging to the thing in that things articulate their presence through qualities—conceived as ecstasies. Nor are atmospheres something subjective, for example, determinations of a psychic state. And yet they are subjectlike, belong to subjects in that they are sensed in bodily presence by human beings and this sensing is at the same time a bodily state of being of subjects in space.¹²

Irrespective of where they were, audience members spoke about the "things" of a green language—of wildlife, light, landscape, and weather—suggesting that atmosphere proceeded from and moved in-between these constellations of persons and things. "Perhaps," ventures the geographer Ben Anderson, "the use of atmosphere in everyday speech and aesthetic discourse provides the best approximation of the concept of affect."¹³ What Anderson terms "affective atmospheres" extends these audience responses, contingent upon their (culturally contingent) open-air contexts, illuminating some of the affects of weathering Shakespeare in our present ecological moment. While there are many different ways in which "affect" has been understood and deployed, the following definitions are apposite here in that they reference environment beyond the subject: we might note Derek McCormack's description of "heterogeneous matters of *the sensible world* we often try and capture through terms such as emotion, mood, and feeling […] circulating within but also moving beyond and around bodies";¹⁴ or Anderson and Paul Harrison's thinking of affect as "the aleatory dynamics of experience, the 'push' of life which interrupts, unsettles and haunts persons, *places* or things";¹⁵ or Sara Ahmed's feminist, antiracist attention to "the messiness of the experiential, the unfolding of bodies *into worlds* and the drama of contingency, how we are touched by *what we are near*."¹⁶

---

¹⁰ Gernot Böhme, "Atmosphere as the Fundamental Concept of a New Aesthetics," *Thesis Eleven* 36 (1993): 113–26, 113.
¹¹ Böhme, "Atmosphere as the Fundamental Concept of a New Aesthetics," 122.
¹² Böhme, 122.
¹³ Ben Anderson, "Affective atmospheres," *Emotion, Space and Society* 2, no. 2 (2009): 78.
¹⁴ Derek McCormack, *Refrains for Moving Bodies: Experience and Experiment in Affective Spaces* (Durham and London: Duke University Press, 2013), 3 (my emphasis).
¹⁵ Ben Anderson and Paul Harrison, *Taking-Place: Non-Representational Theories* (Farnham: Ashgate, 2010), 16 (my emphasis).
¹⁶ Sara Ahmed, "Happy Objects," in *The Affect Theory Reader*, eds. Melissa Gregg and Gregory. J. Seigworth (Durham and London: Duke University Press, 2010), 30 (my emphasis).

A green language responding to the open-air Shakespeare experience depicts an "affective atmosphere," circulating within and around places, bodies, and things, made with weather.

Anthropogenic atmospheric pollution has forced humans to remember that the "forgotten" air—to draw on David Abram's borrowing of Luce Irigray's lament for modernity's invisible and "most taken-for-granted of phenomena"—can no longer be taken for granted.[17] For Tim Ingold (who extends Böhme's work), an atmosphere is an "all-enveloping experience of sound, light and feeling," with the "forgotten" air at its fore.[18] In atmosphere, Ingold writes, a person is "immersed in the fluxes of the medium, the body is enlightened, ensounded and enraptured."[19] Visibility, audibility, and tangibility were interwoven in responses to open-air Shakespeares where atmospheres were sensed from within what Ingold calls the "fluxes" of the weather.[20]

If Ingold's atmosphere is principally weather and Böhme's is foremost aesthetic, Derek McCormack's summary definition of "elemental spacetimes that are simultaneously affective and meteorological, whose force and variation can be felt, sometimes only barely, in bodies of different kinds," balances aesthetic atmospheres as always already weather.[21] McCormack (who draws on Ingold) argues that connecting "the affective as a field of potentially sensed palpability with the meteorological as the variation in the gaseous medium in which much of life on Earth is immersed" happens through a process of "envelopment."[22]

In a literary ecocritical context, Timothy Chandler (who draws on Böhme) ventures that in light of anthropogenic climate change, "the relationship between atmosphere in the aesthetic sense and atmosphere in the planetary sense becomes ever more important."[23] Timothy Clark's provocation that the phenomenological experience of place presents one of the greatest challenges to anthropocene ecopolitics—because it bounds subjects somewhere without a sense of elsewhere—remains a problem, even where atmospheres are

---

[17] David Abram, *The Spell of the Sensuous* (New York: Vintage Books, 1996), 258.
[18] Tim Ingold *Being Alive: Essays on Movement, Knowledge and Description* (Oxon and New York: Routledge, 2011), 134.
[19] Ingold, *Being Alive*, 134.
[20] Ingold, 135.
[21] Derek McCormack, *Atmospheric Things: On the Allure of Elemental Envelopment.* (Durham and London: Duke University Press, 2018), 4.
[22] McCormack, *Atmospheric Things*, 6.
[23] Timothy Chandler, "Reading Atmospheres: The Ecocritical Potential of Gernot Böhme's Aesthetic Theory of Nature," *ISLE Interdisciplinary Studies in Literature and Environment* 18 (Summer 2011): 553–68, 566.

encountered meteorologically as well as aesthetically.²⁴ Atmospheres identified by audiences were felt to be "simultaneously affective and meteorological," as McCormack suggests, but perceptions of the weathery mass of air surrounding the earth remained largely within the edges of phenomenologically encountered performance events and their local conditions, as Clark fears. If Shakespeare's imaginative geographies encouraged audiences to think about atmospheres elsewhere, perception did not often extend to the "planetary" consciousness Chandler proposes. Nevertheless, Chandler's approach to climate change, which extends atmospheres (affectively and meteorologically construed) to planetary space is a useful call to ecopolitics. Echoing Lucian Boia's revision to David Hume's rejection of environmental determinism discussed in the introduction, weathering Shakespeare in this chapter yokes meteorological and affective atmospheres: once again, it is "yes, climate" *and* "yes, social and moral causes too."²⁵ What follows attends to atmosphere as audiences grasped for it in words.

Wildlife

Birds, basking sharks, cows, dolphins, horses, midges, moths, squirrels, and sheep—including wildlife and agricultural animals conceived of as *wild*life in relation to the plays—variously featured in audience conversations about performance atmospheres. Birdsong was audible in the background of many interview recordings conducted at dusk and is sadly lost in transcription. It chirps throughout the chapter. The particular birds present at performances varied from place to place—sparrows cheeped at Coombe, a nightingale sang at Regent's Park, seabirds screeched at Minack, blackbirds whistled at the Willow Globe, and ducks quacked on park ponds—although, on the whole, audience members tended to speak of "birdsong" generically. Jess, for instance, responded to *As You Like It* at Cyfarthfa Castle by saying, "There were times when the birds just worked with it as well—you know, the sound of the birds I enjoyed." Mark liked the blend of organic and manufactured extra-theatrical sounds at *All's Well That Ends Well* at the Willow Globe, commenting, "I actually enjoyed the ambient background sounds of the birds and there was a bit of traffic." Rachel mentioned birdsong and wind at *A Midsummer Night's Dream* at Ripley Castle, telling me, "The birds are singing and the wind is blowing and it's just a

---

²⁴ Timothy Clark, "Phenomenology," in *The Oxford Handbook of Ecocriticism*, ed. Greg Garrard (Oxford and New York: Oxford University Press, 2014), 284.
²⁵ Lucian Boia, *The Weather in the Imagination* (London: Reaktion Books, 2005), 54.

great atmosphere." And Simon, at the Willow Globe's *Merry Wives of Windsor*, also spoke of birdsong with the sound of the wind (editing insects from his ideal performance experience): "It's so friendly and it's so magical with all the birdsong. When you hear an evening performance here and you get the birdsong particularly and the rustle of the wind in the trees and the willow. We won't mention the midges." Both Rachel and Simon's references to birdsong implicitly acknowledged the medium through which it was transmitted, merging social, aesthetic, and airy atmospheres in the one outbreath.

Mostly, wildlife was not remembered with reference to a particular moment in a play—as Britton's pigeon was at *Macbeth*—but simply as an acknowledgment of the nonhuman companions who co-created performance atmospheres, where human audiences and actors were the most fleeting of inhabitants. When asked about his experience of *All's Well That Ends Well*, Matt responded, "I loved watching a kite fly over. And then seeing how many other people noticed. I don't think they did. It was quite spectacular." The sighting of the kite was impressive and personal for Matt, separate from the play but contributory to the atmosphere of the theatrical event. For Gwyn at Cyfarthfa Castle, birdsong was part of the atmosphere of *As You Like It* but not specifically connected to the play. She explained:

> Outdoors I think you've just got that extra dimension of, you know, the birds were singing in the background, which you wouldn't have got, like, if you were watching this in a theater. Which although at first can be a bit distracting but you do sort of tune it out but it's just there.

Gwyn's suggestion was that birdsong was something she tried to tune out in order to tune in to the performance. It was a distraction but it also co-created the atmosphere enveloping the play.

Colin Jerolmack—coincidentally writing on pigeons—proposes that encounters between people and wildlife are, like weather-talk, inherently social more than they are "tied to an innate desire to commune with nature."[26] Audience members Joe, Mike, and Conor discussed a flock of geese that had flown over the stage in "V" formation during *Antony and Cleopatra* at Minack, performing the social nature of their shared experience of wildlife:

> Mike: Your eye does get taken away by seabirds or whatever and then you look down and you realise you're here to look at that. [*looks down at the stage*]
> Joe: Yeah. We had a noisy flock of geese going over and it was like "Oh, watch the geese for twenty seconds!" And it's like, "Oh, we'll spend twenty seconds with the geese rather than what's going on."

[26] Colin Jerolmack, *The Global Pigeon* (Chicago and London: Chicago University Press, 2013), 17.

Conor: Actually I nearly missed them because of my own peaked cap. And then suddenly I looked up and I thought, "Oh!" [*laughter from all*]

Mike and Joe were distracted by the geese but appreciated the interruption before returning to the play. The geese took Conor by surprise. His hat nearly blocked them out, but in a blend of social and airy atmospheres, their presence in the sky became a talking point during the interval.

Kaz at *Romeo and Juliet* laughed as he recalled farm animal sounds emanating from a nearby field: "We had … oh … sheep. Baa! All the way through the performance. Loud as you can, like screaming." When bird or animal noises entered the playing space (or when birds and animals went about their everyday doings in spaces that humans happened to be used for Shakespeare) without the actors "incorporating" them into the action, these sounds were largely received as "circumstantial," as Woods suggests.[27] Anne, at *Romeo and Juliet*, mentioned birdsong and dusk in the same breath, saying, "It's nice because you've got the light and you've got the birds singing. You've got the birds and the surroundings of the garden make it as well, don't they?" Ingold, whose atmosphere is presented along with an objection to the idea of an independent "soundscape," asks, "Are we not bathed in the fluxes of light just as much as we are in those of sounds?"[28] Many references to wildlife overlapped with light and darkness, connecting what was visible with what was audible in the space.

Light

Scott Palmer, writing on the phenomenology of light in the theater, cites Bertolt Brecht's disdain for misguided attempts to enhance Shakespeare's poetry with elaborate electric lighting: "The Elizabethan wrote us verses / About a heath at evening / Which no electrician can match, nor even / The heath itself."[29] Epistemologically, of course poetry is diminished by attempts to actualize it. But audience responses to light and darkness at contemporary open-air Shakespeares challenge the implication that the natural light of the world outside somehow fails to live up to the way a poet like Shakespeare wrote about it, that Shakespeare always out-heaths the heath itself. If Shakespeare was upstaged by a striking sunset and the sunset was noticed and remarked upon, whether or not

---

[27] Woods, "Globe Audiences," 251.
[28] Ingold, *Being Alive*, 128.
[29] Bertolt Brecht in Scott Palmer, *Light* (Basingstoke and New York: Palgrave Macmillan, 2013), 133.

it complemented a moment in the play, what did this say about the relationship between Shakespeare and the natural light outdoors?

In 1887, Henrietta Labouchere's scenes from *A Midsummer Night's Dream* at the Pope's Villa in Twickenham were admired for the experience of the dark gardens afforded by late evening start time, in contrast with retrospective grievances about Pastoral Players' daylight matinees of *As You Like It* at Coombe Woods in 1884 (Chapter 1). The triumph of electricity was a talking point at the open-air Shakespeares at Regent's Park and Max Reinhardt's *Dream* in 1934 (Chapter 2). Today's evening performances continue to contrast with the daylight matinees of Shakespeare's Elizabethan theater. As Alan Dessen explains, early modern performances signaled time through props, costumes, and spoken references to light and darkness: "dialogue, torches, nightgowns, groping in the dark, and failures in seeing—presented in shared daylight—[established] the illusion of darkness for a viewer."[30] Neglecting the need for performances to begin when most people are actually free to attend the theater, the contradictions between desire for historical accuracy and nostalgia for picturesque atmospheres derived from nineteenth-century pastorals pervade contemporary experiences of light. For the most part, today's open-air Shakespeares neither take place in the daylight conditions of matinees nor utilize the gamut of lighting technologies available to indoor theaters. The natural light accompanying evening performances tends to pass from daylight through dusk into darkness, and this progression alters with the changing weather and across the summer months. With the exception of audiences at the Willow Globe, where early modern practices were pursued and shared lighting embraced, the theatergoers consulted as part of this research did not usually consider daylight to be beneficial. Matinee audiences repeatedly indicated that something was lacking. Sam, for example, felt that dusk would have better suited *Romeo and Juliet* than bright afternoon sunshine:

> And this was obviously in the middle of the day, but some plays ... if they're early evening ... they would be even better because quite a lot of the scenes were happening at night or early morning. So if you've got that light where it's not quite dark ... you know ... somehow it's more ... a bit ... it brings it ... it brings it to you a bit more, doesn't it? The atmosphere.

Adrian, at a matinee of *Antony and Cleopatra*, maintained that Shakespeare simply did not work in the daytime: it was too difficult to concentrate. He explained: "In the evening when it gets dark it works, but not in the afternoon.

---

[30] Alan C. Dessen, *Elizabethan Stage Conventions and Modern Interpreters* (Cambridge and New York: Cambridge University Press, 1984), 75.

I mean the environment takes over. The actors have a very difficult job." Anomalously, daylight was an important part of the atmosphere Mike sought. He offered, "I think to get the most out of being here, it's got to be a warm summer's evening. It wouldn't work in the dark because of the environment around you as well," articulating the environment in primarily visual terms, lost with the loss of light.

Uniquely, evening performances at Minack start at eight o'clock. Phil Jackson, one of the theater managers, explains the time as both an aesthetic preference and a socio-economic necessity (Minack is a considerable drive from its nearest working town and the late start allows locals to travel to the theater). More than practical considerations, he insists that darkness is crucial for creating the desired atmosphere:

> At eight o'clock you get more atmosphere. Lighting comes in. If you did it at seven-thirty in the summer, in the first half of the season you could forget theater lights. You wouldn't need them so you wouldn't get the atmosphere. So at eight o'clock ... the lights ... by the second half the lights are kicking in even early in the season and it creates the atmosphere that the Minack generates. We've thought about seven-thirty. It used to be eight-thirty years ago. We've brought it back to eight—I don't know how many years ago—twenty years ago now. But again that was for atmosphere.[31]

If it is an atmospheric experience of Shakespeare that Minack seeks to accommodate, the disappointment that Jennie felt at a matinee of *The Tempest* corroborated Jackson's argument:

> I thought it might be a bit better at night because if you're in a theater situation and it's dark, it's a bit like watching TV and, actually, you can be there more with it because here if you see a noise you look around or you see a boat, you're more here aren't you? And then you're aware, you're quite aware a lot of the time that you're just watching the play rather than getting completely into it.

Some awareness of the historical origins of daylight performance occasionally explained away disappointment at a perceived absence of atmosphere. Jack, at a matinee of *Romeo and Juliet*, explained, "I did think it was slightly hot out. But the Globe is an outdoor venue isn't it and that's a bit more enclosed than this and it was intended for the outdoor performance, wasn't it? Without lights and all things like that." It was initially unclear as to whether Jack was alluding to the reconstructed or the early modern Globe—although thoughts of the latter theater led him to think about the natural light for which the plays were intended.

---

[31] Phil Jackson, Interview with the author. Minack, Cornwall. September 13, 2013.

Jack reconciled himself to watching the play in hot daylight by rationalizing that these were the conditions under which Shakespeare's own performances would have taken place. Quasi-historical authenticity partially compensated for dissatisfaction with the bright afternoon.

Martin, in early evening light, felt that the time of day facilitated a "democratic" relationship between actors and audience—"particularly in this first half because the lights haven't come on yet, the lighting's equal. We're all illuminated the same, so, in a certain way, there's a sort of equality to us and the performers," appearing to inherit the myth of a socially egalitarian early modern theater experience, accommodating all strata of people under the same sky. He also inferred that the shared experience of the play in the first half changed into something personal as the audience was gradually overtaken by darkness. On this darkening transition, Hattie said, "I like it also when it starts to get dark and it becomes more, sort of, atmospheric somehow." Phoebe, her friend, expanded that her focus narrowed as the light faded:

> As the sun goes down … the focus changes. Because of the way it's set with all the different entrances, you … I don't know … it's quite big, but because of the lights and it getting darker … I don't know … and by the end it's just the two of them in the middle on the stage and that's all you can really see. And the focus shifts.

Frances's remarks upheld Phoebe's thoughts, "And everyone is engrossed in it as well. Everyone is … it's got their imagination and everything I think. Especially now it's dark." The onset of darkness gradually privileged the play as audiences were separated from the performers by what Palmer calls "a fourth wall" of stage lighting.[32] In the shift toward isolation amid a crowd, this increasingly solitary experience echoed Gaston Bachelard's description of the poet Rainer Maria Rilke, out walking with friends and suddenly seeing a light flickering in a far-off hermit's hut. Despite being in the company of others, Rilke feels suddenly alone. For Bachelard, the "solitude symbolized by a single light moves the poet's heart in so personal a way that it isolates him from his companions."[33] Bachelard wonders, "When we are lost in darkness and see a distant glimmer of light, who does not dream of a thatched cottage or, to go more deeply still into legend, of a hermit's hut?"[34] Collective experiences of darkness obviously differ fundamentally from the isolation Bachelard describes, given that the lit performance space presents activity and not the quiet isolation of a solitary dweller. But, with the only light on

---

[32] Palmer, *Light*, 13.
[33] Gaston Bachelard, *The Poetics of Space*, ed. J. R. Stilgoe (Boston, Massachusetts: Beacon Press, 1994), 31.
[34] Bachelard, *The Poetics of Space*, 31.

the dreamlike space of the play, audience members appeared to feel disconnected from one another. The world of the play became a lighted bubble into which they peered, more like to gazing into the glass of a snow-globe than sharing space in a Globe like Shakespeare's. Kim summarized, "I was totally absorbed in it. More and more as it got darker actually." This darkness prompts a return to the idea of a fairy tale within the oral tradition discussed in Chapter 4—to the idea of a story told around the light of a fire after a day's work, the light far off in the woods—an atmospheric experience formed in history and culture as well as air and weather. As Sara Maitland reminds us, "many fairy stories begin with the protagonists spending a night up a tree in a forest and seeing from that height a 'small light' far off through the woods which they then follow to find their adventure and destiny."[35] Ingold proposes that "light is fundamentally an experience of being *in* the world that is ontologically prior to the sight of things" and provokes that although "we do not see light, we do see *in* light."[36] Light and darkness were part of the atmospheres of which audience members spoke: looking into light, they saw light from darkness.

If an open-air Shakespeare ends in darkness, does the practice come full circle only to replicate the darkened auditorium that decades of progressive site-specific practitioners have worked so hard to eradicate?[37] Although the latter part of an evening performance tends to be privileged by artificial lighting, night, Maurice Merleau-Ponty suggests, differs from artificially created darkness. Night, like atmosphere, "is not an object in front of me; rather, it envelops me, it penetrates me through all of my senses, it suffocates my memories, and it all but effaces my personal identity."[38] The audiences, gradually invisible to the actors, were aware of dropping temperatures, identities all but effaced. Sitting on damp ground in the night, breathing unfamiliar air was a physically different experience to occupying a seat in a darkened indoor theater. Audiences retained the sensory experience of being enveloped in an affective *and* meteorological atmosphere. "Groundweather"—Astrida Neimanis and Rachel Loewen Walker's word for how the ground remembers the day[39]—recalled warmth from beneath an audience seated on grass in the night. Audiences desired atmospheric rather than historical

---

[35] Sara Maitland, *Gossip from the Forest: The Tangled Roots of Our Forests and Fairy Tales* (London: Granta Publications, 2012), 123.
[36] Ingold, *Being Alive*, 96 (original emphasis).
[37] Mike Pearson, *Site-Specific Performance* (Basingstoke and New York: Palgrave, 2010), 16–17, proposes a list of "provisional distinctions" between auditorium and site-specific performance.
[38] Maurice Merleau-Ponty, *Phenomenology of Perception*, trans. D. A. Landes (London: Routledge, 2012), 296.
[39] Astrida Neimanis and Rachel Loewen Walker, "Weathering and the Thick Time of Transcorporeality," *Hypatia* 29, no. 3 (2014): 573.

experiences of light, but history and language infiltrated meteorology. If a sunset was sometimes more spectacular than the play, if the stars shone for Romeo to defy, or if he confronted them in broad daylight, the real heath usually out-heathed the discursive one. Alighting on the heath, I look next to landscape as another aspect of Williams's green language present in audience conversations.

Landscape

Una Chaudhuri argues that "the 'nature' that is landscape's subject is never free of cultural coding" and, across the audience responses to all of the open-air Shakespeares I attended, landscape was culturally coded as theater.[40] Whatever the place of performance, theatergoers repeatedly drew on the language of *scenery* and *backdrops*, suggesting that the landscape, perceived as framing the performance space, was considered a resource in the service of Shakespeare.[41] Baz Kershaw develops Jean Baudrillard's work on spectacle to suggest that "zoos and theatres […] rely on a crucial separation between observed and observer, they conjure up an act of 'looking-on' which tends to turn 'nature'—plant, animal, human—into spectacle and then, too often, commodity."[42] The scenery of which people spoke was commodified through this process of looking, coded first as landscape in a green language, then as theatrical scenery. Naomi described one performance as "mutually enjoyable, so it was a celebration of the play and the surrounding scenery." Nora referred to scenery too. What might she remember about the event? "Obviously the scenery. Obviously, you don't need, like, a setting. They're using the space … nature." Lisa likened her view from a picnic rug to tiered seating in an indoor theater: "I think we've got a particularly good seat because we've got the view over there of the hills." Philippa also spoke about the landscape as though it were theater: "I guess that's the beauty of not having too much set. If you … because you're not going to get any much better setting if you have a beautiful big lake or a stately home or a nice … you know, the views today are amazing."

Alex explained that the landscape and performance of *A Midsummer Night's Dream* were reciprocally enhancing, layering culture onto already cultured castle gardens:

---

[40] Elinor Fuchs and Una Chaudhuri, eds., *Land/Scape/Theater* (Ann Arbor: University of Michigan Press, 2002), 12.
[41] Una Chaudhuri, *Staging Place: The Geography of Modern Drama* (Ann Arbor: University of Michigan Press, 1995), 25.
[42] Baz Kershaw, *Theatre Ecology* (Cambridge and New York: Cambridge University Press, 2007), 303.

The setting enhances it, I'd say because it's already a beautiful setting and the performance makes it even more beautiful, especially with the use of space, you know. The first time I ever visited this space was for one of Sprite's performances and, you know, it's just a perfect way to showcase the park, the setting. It makes the exploration of the space more, more intimate and more cultural, you know and really adds to it, I think.

Liam chipped in: "It shows that it's more than a set of gardens, that you can actually make something live in that natural space," his language implying that landscapes are inert prior to human intervention.

Chaudhuri is wary too of the "persistent" idea that landscape offers "peaceful repose and even enhanced health,"[43] despite long-standing challenges to these assumptions, including those by Williams in *The Country and the City* (1973). Significant dangers have always lurked in Western conceptions of picturesque rural landscapes, inherited from eighteenth- and nineteenth-century landscape painting: the isolated egoistical position of the viewer outside of the picture; the concealment of labor (who is reposed?), the obfuscation of violence and exclusion (whose health is improved at whose cost?); the "deeply conservative" uses to which the pastoral has been put[44]; and the flattening out of life and biodiversity to satisfy the compulsion to tidy and trim. David Abram grieves, "Even if we venture beyond the walls of our office or metropolis, we often find ourselves merely staring at the scenery."[45] Amongst audiences, it was certainly possible to read evidence of landscapes appropriated as theatrical backdrops, consumed by sleepy, staring subjects who understood neither where they were nor how they were implicated in these places.

Aiden, however, in the audience for *Antony and Cleopatra* at Minack, voiced the complexity of talking about open-air performance, caught in overlapping metaphors.

> I was on occasions distracted by the scenery ... scenery as in surroundings rather than scenery within the play. I mean it's very difficult when you come here. You don't just sit there and look at the play. I mean it's a 360-degree panoramic experience so you've got the play and the surroundings.

Aiden identified a lack of adequate language to differentiate between fictional locales in the plays and the landscape as a way of encountering the performance location. He usefully distinguished between landscape as the built and/or imagined scenery complementing the drama (the real landscape perceived

---

[43] Fuchs and Chaudhuri, *Land/Scape/Theater*, 14–16.
[44] John Lucas, *England and Englishness* (London: Hogarth Press, 1990), 118.
[45] David Abram, *Becoming Animal: An Earthly Cosmology* (New York: Vintage Books, 2010), 92.

through the lens of the play) and the landscape surrounding the place of performance (thought of as independent to the performance), although both ways of thinking reflect anthropocentric readings of aestheticized landscapes.

Sometimes people commented more specifically on "scenery as in the play" as complementary to the Shakespearean content, recalling Minack and the Willow Globe, where the sea and willow were seen as making good homes for *The Tempest* and *The Merry Wives of Windsor* respectively, and the woodland productions of *As You Like It*, *A Midsummer Night's Dream*, and *After The Tempest*. None of the contemporary productions I attended utilized much-built stage scenery—in the way that Max Reinhardt's *Dream* deployed transplanted trees, for comparison—and, consequently, very few audience members remarked on constructed scenery. But while audience members described the scenery as a "backdrop" to the contrived human drama taking place, the lived experiences of atmospheric landscapes generated further contradictions. The scenery of which they spoke was usually perceived as in excess of the human performances in it. Stacy, for instance, reflected on scenery in atmospheric terms, saying, "The change of scenery with the different scenes was really exciting actually and it kind of added a new atmosphere to things." The landscape was exciting and atmospheric, despite Stacy's coding it as scenery. Similarly, for Maria at Minack, the sea formed a "generalized" nature backdrop into which she projected her feelings.[46]

> It's just amazing, I mean, being outside and the backdrop of the sea as well. It's just a wonderful concept really that the lady [Rowena Cade] had. That you could have outside theater with just this backdrop, you know. It's just that the sea is a calming influence anyway, I think. But, you know, and it is … it's just amazing isn't it?

In all of these instances, landscape framed performance, becoming scenery. Scenery was perceived as a resource but also as affective in its own right: atmosphere exceeded performances spatially and sensorially, enveloped by the duration of the play and theatrical event. Audiences could not just stare at the scenery because they had to weather the plays.

Weather

Throughout this book, I have been arguing that theatergoers and actors perform weathering as a heightened social, physical, and discursive practice in response to Shakespeare's plays in the open-air. If modernity forgot the weather (or if the

---

[46] Williams, *The Country and the City*, 193.

weather gave modernity the slip, as I discussed with reference to Jan Golinski's work on Enlightenment weather in the Introduction), atmospheres at open-air Shakespeares were never not meteorological. Regardless of the conditions, theatergoers invariably referred to their experiences, as Michael Dobson quips, "Complete with the weather."[47] In-situ, audience members spoke about the weather at the time of the interview: "It's actually one of the warmer nights I've ever been here. So I'm actually not freezing cold, which is really nice," and "I think everybody's a little bit cold and so if you look around one or two people are sort of hiding under blankets and everything." They reflected on how the weather made them feel during performances: "It is pretty chilly in the woods. It was nice to be out here and to get a little bit of warmth before we finish." And they spoke about weather as memories of previous outdoor performances: "It's the first time I've watched open-air theater and it hasn't rained. That's good. I've always tried in the past and it's always been cold and wet and miserable but today it's been lovely," or "I mean both times we've been here, the weather has been good. I don't know what it would be if it had been sighing down with rain." They spoke about the weather as affecting the mood of the actors and audience:

> Alex: But the sun peeking out allows, I think, the players in the play-within-the-play maybe were more playful. I don't know. I imagine ...
> Joey: It's like a big bonus.
> Alex: Yes.
> Joey: You know, and everyone gets excited about the weather and, you know, when it peeks out at that moment everyone rejoices and the performance is enhanced that way.

Comments like "It's a bit chilly. But there's really good views" or "It's cold and it's windy but it's breathtakingly beautiful. It's like nothing I've ever seen before" segued from the physical to the aesthetic experience of being a spectator in weather. More linked to the performances, "I thought the rain might be distracting but it wasn't. I think it did start to shape my imagination" and "For me it was when Mark Antony came in and he was wet and his hair was wet so you knew he was coming off a battle from the sea. For me that's when it kind of all came together" were direct references to weather influencing the reception of a play.

Amongst the audiences observed and individuals interviewed, a mixture of sensible and disproportionate preparations was occasioned by the desire to experience a Shakespeare play in the open-air. Waterproof clothing, flasks of tea,

---

[47] Michael Dobson, *Shakespeare and Amateur Performance* (Cambridge: Cambridge University Press, 2011), 196.

sunscreen, mosquito spray, hayfever tablets, down-filled jackets, camping chairs and deckchairs, bin bags, hats, scarves, rugs and blankets, and hot water bottles were used as material props to help protect the body from weather, pollen, insect-attack, and general discomfort. Discourses around alternative wet-weather venues, no-refund, and show-abandonment policies potentially compounded what Simon Estok terms ecophobia, "an irrational fear or groundless hatred of the natural world."[48] But would sunstroke acquired "naturally" during a heatwave have perpetuated any less ecophobia than "unnatural" cover-ups? Or were pragmatic responses superseded by the conscious choice to venture outdoors to watch a play—a synthetic activity anyway—opening space for a more complex affective ecopolitics? While it would be reductive to suggest that gradations of wet, cold, or windy conditions correlated with gradations of ecophobia, the human-animal world pitted itself against nature, setting up a kind of resistance to the weather in the hope that the play would be well-served.

Audience members frequently used violent, warlike, and nationalist language to describe the relationship between Shakespeare and the weather. Phrases such as "battling the elements" and "fighting the wind" were commonplace. I heard "the weather is our enemy" and "the British weather is merciless" often. Less often, but occasionally present at wet performances were allusions to "Dunkirk" or "Blitz spirit," and "British stoicism" in conversations about seeing the performance through to the end, whatever the weather. As Chapters 1 and 2 found, and as Stephen Purcell cautions, "Shakespeare as a source of national pride, is often in danger of becoming a symbol of nationalism."[49] The residual references to British resistance and fortitude during the Second World War demonstrated an extension of the growing nationalism in attitudes toward the weather at Regent's Park in 1933 and 1934, leading up to the war. Shakespeare, as the raison d'être for these contemporary open-air theater events, can compound ecophobia with the weather alongside the kinds of Britishness that veer toward a "creatively produced and staged" nationalism—to draw on Jen Harvie's formulation of nation-making as performative.[50] Timothy Morton aspires to "an ecological language opposed to the phantasmagorical positivities of nation-speak" and, certainly, the green language of theater audiences did not approach a language such as Morton envisages, where it retained patchy nationalism performed with the weather.[51]

---

[48] Simon Estok, *Ecocriticism and Shakespeare: Reading Ecophobia* (New York: Palgrave, 2011) 4.
[49] Stephen Purcell, "A Shared Experience: Shakespeare and Popular Theatre," *Performance Research* 10, no. 3 (2005): 74–84, 83.
[50] Jen Harvie, *Staging the UK* (Manchester: Manchester University Press, 2005), 2.
[51] Timothy Morton, *Ecology without Nature: Rethinking Environmental Aesthetics* (Cambridge, MA: Harvard University Press, 2007), 102.

One of the byproducts of an ecophobic language, where present, was that it promoted a supportive relationship between audience and actors. Anthropologists Sarah Strauss and Ben Orlove find that the "physical experience of the weather provides a common focal point in many societies, through both commiseration and celebration."[52] Requests that individuals refrain from using umbrellas to avoid blocking others' views of the stage were met with smiles. Introductions like "if it rains … you will get wet" generated laughter, establishing camaraderie. The audience would endure what the actors would endure and vice versa. The theater director Ralph Alan Cohen observes one such supportive audience-actor relationship in evidence at Shakespeare's Globe, noting that "when the rain falls on the standees, they respond with laughter and with an increased determination to enjoy the show, a determination that communicates itself to the actors, who raise their games in appreciation."[53] Audiences were resolved at the wet performances I observed, vehemently enthusiastic about the actors' perseverance, which generated a perceived bond between them. Reciprocally, the actors tended to praise the audiences for their endurance—speeding up their delivery of the text to relieve soaked spectators and vigorously applauding the audience from the stage.

At an especially soggy *The Taming of the Shrew* at Minack, I huddled with a group of friends under a door frame, looking out at the stage area. Tara mused, "In a way it almost makes you feel more connected especially as you're going through it as they're going through it." Eileen also empathized with the actors, saying, "I really felt for them in the wet. Their costumes were sopping but they kept going with so much energy!" Chris reflected, "You could tell that they were working really hard and it almost made the story more alive and urgent." Rain undermined mimesis, highlighting the artificiality of the performance practice and drawing attention to the labor of acting, as audience members empathized with actors as people rather than with their fictitious characters. Because the metaphorical battle between audience and weather was one where the human participants were ultimately powerless, the embodied experience of weather might more optimistically be regarded as reinforcing a sense of human powerlessness against the weather. This does not dilute the culturally conservative aspects of weathering as performance at open-air Shakespeares, but it muddies them a bit. Perceived threats from the weather made atmospheric experiences all the more knowably fragile, all the more ephemeral. The best of Shakespeare bellowed at the sky can't change the weather.

---

[52] Sarah Strauss and Ben Orlove, eds., *Weather, Climate, Culture* (Oxford and New York: Berg, 2003), 3.
[53] Ralph Alan Cohen, "Directing at the Globe and the Blackfriars: Six Big Rules for Contemporary Directors," in *Shakespeare's Globe: A Theatrical Experiment*, eds. Christie Carson and Farah Karim-Cooper (Cambridge, Delhi and New York: Cambridge University Press, 2008), 211–25, 223.

Green Pleasures

As I meander through references to weather, wildlife, light, landscape, and Shakespeare, uttered in a demotic green language, the impossibility of separating out stimuli for analysis is apparent. Weather and landscape were often contained in the same exhalation that surrounded the pigeon. Noelle offered, "And being in the natural environment as well is part of it I think. You know because things happen, like, you know, the wind blows or the sun comes out or a helicopter goes over and the actors respond to that which was really good." Naomi linked some of the language in *All's Well That Ends Well* to animal sounds and changing light, evoking atmosphere.

> When they talked about skies and heaven, I looked upwards and thought it was very evocative. That related the sounds to the surroundings and the sounds of lambs bleating in the background ... That was very atmospheric too and as the play was going on, the sun was going down and casting light on the stage.

The atmosphere Naomi described was ambiguous but not free-floating, emanating from persons—whose performance of Shakespeare's play was integral—skies, sounds, and surroundings: attributable to all. Joe, at *Antony and Cleopatra,* spoke of atmospherics without privileging any one stimulus:

> I think you've got to ... you've got to pay a lot of attention to what's going on down on the stage because wherever you're sitting you might miss a little bit of the action depending on the angle of where you're sitting. And, yeah, the sound sometimes with the wind and everything ... the sound ... the sound can be a little bit impaired. So you've got to be paying attention to that. And there's all the stuff going on around which is really interesting. You've got ... you know ... sort of, boats going by. You've got things happening. I sometimes watch the tide coming in and out over there. During half of a show you can see how much the tide's come in and out. So it's kind of like you've got everything going on around you with the show going on as well. So you've got to be really active in your attention if you want to pay attention to all of those things. I mean maybe I should be just concentrating on the show. But I think there's other things that I'm interested in in the environment that I want to see as well while I'm here.

Joe seemed interactively attuned to a polyvocal environment. He expressed a desire to take in the multiple stimuli in an atmosphere where all inhabitants had something to say, including what he could see, hear, and feel. The world apart from the play communicated in material languages that did not originate with the performance, but that were coproduced with it and experienced as atmosphere.

Richard tried to verbalize the atmosphere at *The Merry Wives of Windsor*, speaking to me about light, wind, and wildlife with particular reference to a moment during the play:

> I think when the two wives got together for the first time and they were kind of thinking about what they were going to do to Falstaff, there was a ... I think it was either a dimming of the sunlight—the light went dim—and it was kind of like almost something's going on here, it's a bit darker now, I don't know, or there was some kind of change, like a bit of a breeze or something like that, you know, and I thought that was interesting. There was a little bird, or it was either a blackbird—it was some kind of blackbird anyway and it would fly in this kind of specific path every now and again. Did you see it? It would just shoot across and that was just like a little added extra, do you know what I mean? At one point where there was a ... I think it was a kestrel that was flying high. Did you see that?

Richard brought together seeing, hearing, and feeling, conflating the event's ecology and aesthetics as irreducible to individual bodies but also proceeding from them.

Flo went further in an attempt to describe what these affective stimuli prompted as a whole in response to *Antony and Cleopatra*, without ever arriving at a fixed meaning. She recalled Caesar (Luke Walsh) speaking to Octavia (Rebecca Livermore) and looking toward a choppy Atlantic Ocean as he wished his sister safe passage: "The elements be kind to thee" (*Antony and Cleopatra* 3.2.40):

> I think the first word that comes to me is provocative. Because the play in itself has a lot of provocative moments. And I think that the surrounding is very provocative because it really makes you come together with nature and with the sea and the sun and the seagulls. I mean it's ... I don't know. There's just something really provocative about nature generally and I think the two together are really beautiful.

Although Flo did not articulate what it was the atmosphere provoked, the idea of a provocative "beauty" was both more than and reliant upon its individual parts, weather included, encompassing mood, tone, and air: "determinate and indeterminate, present and absent, singular and vague," as Anderson puts it.[54]

Across the examples above, McCormack's warning against the "temptation to invoke atmosphere as shorthand for an empiricism that privileges presence, immediacy, and immersion [...] too easily affirmed as a concept for reclaiming some kind of authentic experience of a world" niggles.[55] He argues that "the terms of the

---

[54] Ben Anderson, "Affective Atmospheres," *Emotion, Space and Society* 2, no. 2 (2009): 77–81, 80.
[55] McCormack, *Atmospheric Things*, 8.

relations between different bodies, the infrastructures and devices that condition the atmospheres in which they move, and the capacities of these bodies to exercise some influence over these conditions" are at stake politically in atmospheres.[56] Open-air Shakespeares often appeared to reproduce atmospheres that evoked the pastoral in its pejorative sense. But they also and often seemed good for making the air felt as part of theatrical atmosphere, which ultimately seemed good for the recognition of humans as part of a swirling world with agency of its own. I venture that while meteorologically and affectively composed atmospheres, filtered through a green language, facilitated a nostalgic mythologizing of Shakespeare with echoes of the regressive or moralizing pastoral, they also produced affects, such as Richard Kerridge terms "green pleasures," that we might carefully consider contributing to what Kate Soper refers to as an "alternative hedonist" ecopolitics.[57]

Alternative hedonism represents a pragmatic, maverick position proposing "new forms of desire rather than fears of ecological disaster, as the most likely motivating force in any shift towards a more sustainable economic order."[58] What Soper summons as an emergent Williamsian structure of feeling advocates for a revision to the conditions for human prospering and flourishing in resistance to pressured neoliberalism and capitalist patterns of consumption. It is within Soper's framework of alternative hedonism that Richard Kerridge advocates for "green pleasures" that "follow the logic of environmentalism—by using less carbon, deepening one's love of things already at hand, appreciating cycles of growth and renewal in the local and global ecosystems, understanding and taking delight in interdependency."[59] Alternative hedonism describes a collective, demographically delimited structure of feeling, applicable to affluent practices of green consumption that can undertake "a distinctively moral form of [green, *pace* Kerridge] self-pleasuring" and "a self-interested form of altruism which takes pleasure in committing to a more socially accountable mode of consuming."[60]

Clearly, choosing to attend an open-air Shakespeare is not "alternative" in the same sense as choosing a bicycle—one of the examples Soper uses to sketch an alternative hedonism—over a fuel-guzzling vehicle (nor is the individual act of riding a bicycle particularly world-saving in isolation), but when Rachel

---

[56] McCormack, 8.
[57] Kate Soper, "An Alternative Hedonism," *Radical Philosophy* 92 (1998): 28–38; and "'Alternative Hedonism,' Cultural Theory and the Role of Aesthetic Revisioning," *Cultural Studies* 22, no. 5 (2008): 567–87.
[58] Kate Soper, Martin Ryle, and Lyn Thomas, eds. *The Politics and Pleasures of Consuming Differently* (Basingstoke and New York: Palgrave), 3.
[59] Richard Kerridge, "Green Pleasures," in *The Politics and Pleasures of Consuming Differently*, eds. Kate Soper, Martin Ryle, and Lyn Thomas (Basingstoke and New York: Palgrave), 130–53, 131.
[60] Soper, Ryle, and Thomas, *The Politics and Pleasures of Consuming Differently*, 5.

explained what the performance of the *Dream* meant for her in terms of savoring the atmosphere at Ripley Castle, her comments evoked a pleasurable experience that we might carefully think of as green:

> I get to see it with new eyes. So if I came to Ripley Castle, what would happen is I would be … I would have argued with my children beforehand, I will have needed to … at the wrong point one of them will have needed the toilet break, at which point my partner doesn't look as attractive because actually they're not pulling their weight and blah blah blah. Whereas with this you take a break from all of that and you shift state and because you shift state, you think "Isn't it good to be here and aren't the trees majestic?" rather than just quickly travelling through it because actually they've got to be in bed by seven kind of feeling. It's very much just to sit and be in a clearing in the wood. Like when do we actually have permission from ourselves to do that? The birds are singing and the wind is blowing and this incredible, astonishing stuff is happening in front of us.

It seemed not to be a lack of imagination or an incapacity to making meaning from the words alone that was behind Rachel's response to being at the *Dream* in the woods, but pleasure derived from the atmosphere of the cultural event in the open-air. She expressed pleasure in the time made available by the performance, a slowing down, a deepening her appreciation for "things already at hand," things she might have otherwise missed because of the pressures of motherhood and everyday life.[61] Rachel's generous sharing in the wind was also a reminder that future behavior depends upon the sensibilities people bring with them to a performance as much as anything that happens at a play.

Remembering the Weather

Atmospheres time travel on human bodies speaking in a green language, turning wildlife, light, landscape, weather, and Shakespeare into anecdotes. In sunshine at the Willow Globe, Ben recollected a performance of *Hamlet* he had seen years previously on "a warm day like today. Warm":

> My favourite memory was seeing our Hamlet doing his 'To be or not to be' (*Hamlet* 3.1.58) speech with a pair of blackbirds duelling across the willows really loud. So there's him doing this really … this really dark and difficult sort of angst ridden speech and these perfect blackbirds right over the audience's head. Really brilliant atmosphere.

---

[61] Kerridge, "Green Pleasures," 131.

More than others, Ben's comments recalled the pigeon that began this chapter, insofar as his memory was linked to a well-known speech. Ben's blackbirds differed from the pigeon at Shakespeare's Globe in that he neither suggested that the blackbirds were commenting on the Shakespeare nor that Shakespeare's text commented on the blackbirds particularly (unless we infer that he heard the blackbirds singing a "duet" that satirized *Hamlet*'s "duels"). The blackbirds retained their "blackbirdness" without being subsumed into the play. At risk of stating the obvious, Ben's blackbirds spoke blackbird, Hamlet spoke Shakespeare, and Ben was affected by them both in an atmosphere he remembered with the weather. Stretching out his arms to demonstrate pleasure in the warm sunshine—his expansive movement simultaneously performed his body's previous pleasure in the sunshine—he seemed to intuit that the world's speech did not start with him, nor with the actors, nor even with Shakespeare's famous soliloquy on human existence.

Just as Ben remembered the warm day around the blackbirds singing, across this study, as theatergoers recounted previous outdoor performances they had attended they usually referred to the past weather at least as much as they referred to whatever play it was that they remembered seeing. Always these spoken memories were accompanied by a performance of weathering that included a physical re-enactment of how that past atmosphere had affected their bodies.[62] Rebecca's comments about cold weather uttered at Minack as horizontal rain pelted our faces, recalled past discomfort caused by heat in present rain. As she spoke, her tightly held body expanded in the drizzle to reflect the warm weather she remembered, gesturing toward the other side of the auditorium.

> I've been here before in glorious sunshine. Not quite the damp weather we're having today. I was actually sat in the first seat down there. I melted into the stone it was that warm but it was magical. The scenery out there was stunning, the sea was blue and it was just a gorgeous day. It just added to the atmosphere of the theater.

Rebecca's memory of the past weathering was performed "transcorporeally," to utilize Stacy Alaimo's concept for thinking across bodies, extended to weathering by Astrida Neimanis and Rachel Loewen-Walker.[63] An embodied

---

[62] Anecdotally, over the years I have worked on this project and also away from the fieldwork, I have continued to meet with individuals spontaneously sharing unsolicited memories of attending outdoor theatre, accompanied without exception by physical performances of what it was like to be in that past weather.

[63] Stacy Alaimo, *Bodily Natures: Science, Environment, and the Material Self* (Bloomington: Indiana University Press, 2010); Astrida Neimanis and Rachel Loewen-Walker, "*Weathering*: Climate Change and the 'Thick Time' of Transcorporeality," *Hypatia* 29, no. 3 (2014): 558–75.

archive of past weathering surfaced as the performance of weathering and green pleasure in the present.

Mike Hulme proposes that "climate becomes reified through a rather unstructured assemblage of *remembered* weather" or "indexed memories" as much as climate is accepted and understood through scientific data.[64] For Hulme, today's weather only makes sense "through reference to the past."[65] Understanding climate change therefore demands understanding disruptions to weather memories. Hulme follows that "From the perspective of the mind then, a change in climate—'climate change' if you wish—becomes a dislocation of such weathered memories."[66] It is worth noting that Hulme locates weather memories in the "mind," although in later work he obliquely alludes to subjects "immersed" in the weather—that *feel* temperature and moisture on the body.[67] In an earlier piece on climate for *Environmental Humanities*, Hulme argues against "a false separation between a physical world (to be understood through scientific inquiry) and an imaginative one (to be understood in terms of meaningful narratives or human practices)."[68] Instead, he proposes that it is the "sensory experience of weather that conditions cultural responses to human dwelling *in* the atmosphere, whether these be celebratory rituals, material technologies, collective memories, social practices, and so on."[69]

But humans notoriously misremember past weather, as Hulme himself acknowledges. We also choose to misremember events for the sake of a good anecdote.[70] We might wonder then how it is that we can misremember the weather but still use memory to form a stable idea of what a climate *should* be. If spoken weather memories are fallible, are embodied weather memories performed in the present equally unreliable? Furthermore, how could we trouble the differences between imagined and embodied weather memories without resorting to re-instigating a mind/body split? It is possible that the human body can recuperate weathering as performance and reach toward a sense of understanding changes in climate. These questions are more than this chapter has evidence to answer, but, as inconsistencies across Hulme's work

[64] Mike Hulme, "Climate Change and Memory," in *Memory in the Twenty-First Century*, ed. Simon Groes (Basingstoke and New York: Palgrave, 2016), 160 (original emphasis).
[65] Hulme, "Climate Change and Memory," 161.
[66] Hulme, 161.
[67] Hulme, "Climate Change and Memory," 162–3.
[68] Hulme, "Climate," *Environmental Humanities* 6 (2015): 175–6.
[69] Hulme, "Climate," 176.
[70] Trevor A. Harley, "Nice Weather for the Time of Year: The British Obsession with the Weather," in *Weather, Climate, Culture*, eds. Sarah Strauss, and Ben Orlove (Oxford and New York: Berg), 116.

suggest, scholarship is only at the edges of grappling for where atmosphere made memory makes climate as performance.

But however much atmospheres—affective and meteorological—have some capacity to influence ethical sensibilities, Shakespeare on his own, performed outdoors in any kind of park, garden, wood, or by the sea, was not received as speaking with *explicit* force to our current ecological moment. The concluding chapter looks to open-air Shakespeares created specifically in response to anthropogenic climate change, finishing with performances of the weather at intentional productions that stir new kinds of reflection and conversation.

6

Shakespeare for a Changing Climate

This concluding chapter analyzes three contemporary approaches to Shakespeare in the open-air that explicitly address present-day environmentalisms, drawing attention to performances of weathering in the context of a changing climate. Do these latest works simply act as the latest iteration of concept Shakespeare catching up with climate change, continuing the long-standing trend of adapting Shakespeare to advance new causes—whether they be progressively queer, feminist, postcolonial, or simply costumed to emulate a fashionable period drama? Do they merely pay due diligence to—or capitalize upon—dire world circumstances in a carry-over of centuries of ideologically purposed efforts to keep Shakespeare relevant, or is there something more ecologically "useful" in their potential to foster dialogue, generate self-reflection, present complexity, and contribute to material change in the world?[1] By way of a conclusion, I consider three case studies, each production representing a different approach to staging Shakespeare outdoors in response to anthropogenic climate change. As with the rest of this book, this is not to propose that a production offers a micro-example of concerns that are automatically and universally applicable, but to tune into ideas that might be fruitful beyond the scope of time-limited performance contexts. What I find reinforces the need to be wary of easy assumptions that ecodramaturgical intentions elicit reliable affective responses. A chorus of dissonant voices sings that aesthetic acts never simply fulfil a predetermined "sender/receiver" relationship, and that reception—contingent upon what people bring with them to the performances, the performances themselves, and the weather—disperses beyond attempts to contain it.[2] Wariness does not mean

---

[1] Nicole Seymour, *Bad Environmentalism: Irony and Irreverence in the Ecological Age* (Minneapolis and London: University of Minnesota Press, 2018), 7, writes an excellent critique of "usefulness" as an environmental work's assumed "capacity to educate the public or spark measurable change."
[2] For the "sender/receiver" model of spectatorship, see Marco De Marinis, *The Semiotics of Performance*, trans. Áine O'Healy (Bloomington and Indianapolis: Indiana University Press, 1993), 158.

dismissing their accomplishments, however. Rather, these performances generate diverse cultures and responses, some of which seem to act in favor of biodiversity. No longer relegated to a theatrical backdrop for open-air performance, decorating human drama, the agency of the nonhuman world comes to the fore in each of these works.

All of the productions here use comedy—albeit in different ways—to counter the stereotype of the tedious, virtuous environmentalist. Each approach yields pleasures and pitfalls. I look first at *As You Like It* by The HandleBards in 2017, a Shakespeare company that tours by bicycle, drawing attention to green modes of transportation. With irreverent productions, The HandleBards obliquely contribute to the visibility of sustainable modes of production without being encountered as didactic. Second, I look at BP or not BP's unsanctioned Fossil Free Mischief Festival intervention outside the Royal Shakespeare Theatre at Stratford-upon-Avon in June 2018. This daylong protest performance challenged the greenwashed oil multinational Beyond (née British) Petroleum's corporate sponsorship of reduced price tickets for young people with an anarchic approach to creative activism, parodying Shakespeare's well-known texts and asking passers-by to join in dancing a participatory tempest. While BP or not BP has a serious manifesto and is in that sense unapologetically message-driven in intent, comedy costumed this pop-up campaign, which ultimately contributed to the RSC decision to drop BP as a sponsor. Lastly, I consider the 2018 production of *As You Like It* at Regent's Park's Open Air Theatre, directed by Max Webster. Webster's production addressed the theme of waste and the accumulation of rubbish in the court/forest landscapes with a pointedly ecological design. Reviewers received the potentially moralistic framing of Arden as an intentional permaculture community, countered, with relief, by the production's otherwise being good fun.

I continue to diversify the methodological exploration of thinking about reception, ending with an unstable commixture of possibilities for open-air storytelling. Continuing the ethnographic approach taken in Chapters 3 and 4, the first section on The HandleBards' *As You Like It* incorporates my own response to the piece into snatches of conversations with theatergoers: before performances, during intervals, and afterwards. The section on BP or not BP's Fossil Fuel Mischief Festival also combines ethnographic observation with autoethnography. This happened partly through necessity, as the activist context of the performance meant that many of the people to whom I spoke in Stratford-upon-Avon did not want to be interviewed for a book. Moreover, it feels fair to include the self as part of the autoethnography since I was also—in addition to undertaking the research—an audience member, corporeally present and performing my own weathering amongst others throughout. In Chapters 1 and 2, history prevented me from speaking to audiences in person. In July 2018, however, and at seven months pregnant, I was surprised to wake up one morning with Bell's palsy, a (temporary, in my case) form of facial paralysis, uncommon enough for doctors to compare it to being "struck by lightning," but more common in the third trimester of pregnancy and speculatively brought on by the hot summer.[3] I was unable to speak or blink for weeks. As a result, I finish the book with my own response to Webster's *As You Like It*, in conversation with the extensive reviews. The sequence of examples does not progress an argument for one way of doing Shakespeare in a changing climate as more environmentally efficacious than another, but I hope that they conclude the book by leaving the reader with a sense of the messy and generative cultural work that weathering Shakespeare "can do" in the anthropocenic open-air.[4]

No single approach in this chapter produces a stable set of responses, just as no single approach to addressing climate change and its attendant disasters is possible or would suffice if it was. What we will continue to need are plural actions and polyvocal conversations. Some may brighten things for human and nonhuman critters alike—make exposure more bearable. Small, everyday inter- and intra-actions may be where we can track shifting cultures, in changes to the ways we talk about the weather and what we "flag" when we perform with it.[5] Rain seeps into the edifice of the dramatic canon: melting the ink, altering the tone of an actor's voice, infiltrating histories of cultural signifiers. Wetted, the edifice sprouts "prismatic" mold.[6] Scraped under fingernails, here are a few of its colors.

I Can't Even Ride a Bike, Let Alone Do Shakespeare: The HandleBards *As You Like It*, 2017

The HandleBards is a touring Shakespeare company made up of teams of four actors who travel the UK on bicycles. Founding members Paul Moss and Tom Dixon belong to the generation of theater-makers who have grown up

---

[3] Any statistical connection between incidences of Bell's palsy and being struck by lightning is fanciful, but I was struck by the weather metaphor used by medical professionals. I considered removing this section from the book entirely. But as the ethnographer's presence in the field is central to a post-positivist approach, it felt as false to excise this part of the research as the methodology may seem weakened because of it.

[4] Carl Lavery, "Introduction," in *Performance and Ecology: What Can Theatre Do?*, ed. Carl Lavery (London and New York: Routledge, 2018).

[5] Michael Billig, *Banal Nationalism* (Los Angeles and London: Sage, 1995), 105.

[6] Jeffrey Jerome Cohen, ed., *Prismatic Ecology: Ecotheory beyond Green* (Minneapolis and London: University of Minnesota Press, 2013).

with knowledge of climate change. Since first getting on their bikes in 2013, The HandleBards have won the 2014 Award for Sustainable Practice at the Edinburgh Fringe and have been nominated for *The Stage*'s 2017 Sustainability Award. The company now includes separate male and female troupes who tow props, scenery, and costumes in trailers behind their bicycles. On windy August evenings in 2017, I attended the "girls'" *As You Like It* at the Vicarage Gardens, Great Torrington, and the square outside the Marine Theatre, Lyme Regis, in the South West of England. In the walled gardens at Great Torrington, gusts zoomed dark clouds across the sky, felling the tents and bicycles used as stage scenery in their wake. "I wish I had a blanket," Marie said, peering out from a tightly drawn hood and sipping from a tightly clasped flask. On the theater square at Lyme Regis, beachgoers-turned-theatergoers grew cold as afternoon sunlight glowed gold then pink, disappearing behind the Jurassic Coast cliffs. "I shouldn't have worn flip-flops," Vanessa said, cocooned in a light summer wrap. Bright bunting flapped loudly, failing to deter the seagulls in competition with the actors' voices. Averaging a bike ride of thirty miles a day over the summer, the actress Jessica Hern blogged about the tour: "We battled wind, rain, hail, sunburn, the Peak District, dislocated shoulders, un-bikeable paths, numerous falls, more than a handful of punctures … and we're still standing, because #thesegirlscan."[7]

The impulse greening The HandleBards' work is more attentive to modes of production than to the enactment of an ecocritical reading of the plays. Bicycle-themed props are integrated into staging choices. The ping of a bicycle bell routinely indicates character changes by four actors who play multiple roles. In *As You Like It,* Rosalind (Lucy Green) and Celia (Jessica Hern) donned bicycle helmets and backpacks to disguise themselves as Ganymede and Aliena. They cycled to Arden where they met Audrey's (Eleanor Dillon-Reams) goats, signified by curved handlebar horns on their heads. When Orlando (Lotte Tickner), a lisping and effeminate badminton player, was finally reunited with Green's well-spoken Rosalind, Rosalind revealed herself by removing her helmet and emerging from behind the "wings" (made of large signaling flags) of a high-pitched, ukulele-strumming Hymen. A masculine Rosalind and effeminate Orlando pranced toward one another, exclaiming audibly in time with their steps, taking hands and skipping in a delighted circle before consummating their reunion with an extravagant kiss. The uncontrollable flapping of Hymen's makeshift wings drew attention to the strength of the wind and the actors'

---

[7] Jessica Hern, "Cycling across the UK: A Bard Remembers," March 30, 2018, https://www.handlebards.com/cycling-across-the-uk/

struggle against it generated some of the scene's queer humor. Watching the four women perform, I thought of Eleanor Calhoun and Lady Archibald Campbell (coincidentally a champion of women's cycling and a noted advocate for the split skirt) improvising *As You Like It* on a warm day in Coombe Woods in 1884. Unlike The Pastoral Players in the late nineteenth-century, however, the labor of the female HandleBards was visible to the audience, who were impressed by their exertion. The HandleBards' *As You Like It* upheld the upper-class stereotypes for outdoor leisure pursuits (badminton racquets, heightened received pronunciation) through parody, but the whole enterprise was underscored by their physical, creative, improvisational, organizational, and empathetic capacities—presented to audiences as actors' performances of weathering.

Although at times the women's efforts were overtaken by the wind, they were always working within rather than attempting to harness the ecologies of the places in which they performed. Rather than evoking a sentimental pastoral, their performances of weathering depicted human fumbling and effort as ecology; their struggle was open to the world's meteorological contingencies—at times reveling in, embracing, despairing of, and surrendering to their part in blustery evenings. They reinforced the spirited and eccentric Englishness in evidence in responses to open-air Shakespeares since a commentator for *The Observer* first disparaged the women at Coombe's lack of business savvy, but they also performed the humility of weathering, creatively responding to the conditions with limited resources, buffeted by the wind.[8] Their individual physicalities showcased a restlessness more typically and historically associated with men in the wind[9]; which energized their pursuit of fun in the circumstances, making perceptible the energy and clarity of action needed to communicate in the weather. Always deferred was an unspoken but assumed later retreat to shelter and the wind's calming.

There was nothing serious about this camp production, except perhaps its earnest opening statement. The cast of four sang, "Come hither, Come hither, come hither! / Here shall he see no enemy / But winter and rough weather" (*As You Like It* 2.5.5–7). Met by wind, the last line of the chorus received a hearty laugh in both locations. Eleanor Dillon-Reams announced the exact figure of the hundreds of miles that the women had cycled so far that summer and her declaration was met with appreciative gasps, murmurs, and wows, followed by

---

[8] "No sane manager, […] would commit himself to such an undertaking as a matter of business, even though he were granted a pitch in Hyde Park for nothing." "Garden Theatricals at Coombe House," *The Observer,* May 31, 1885, 3.

[9] Lyall Watson, *Heaven's Breath: A Natural History of the Wind* (New York: New York Review of Books, 2019).

Figure 6.1 Eleanor Dillon Reams and Lucy Green in *As You Like It*, Maumbury Rings, Dorchester, 2017. Photograph courtesy of Richard Anders.

cheers and applause. I often heard words like "inspirational," "impressive," and "admirable" when speaking to audiences at *As You Like It*.[10] Gail said, "They're very brave. Because they're cycling for four months. It's a long time and a lot of weather. I mean, think of how windy it's been today." For Clare, the cycling was, "Motivating. Pretty amazing. I like the way the fact that they try to encourage us to do the same by offering a discount to cycle here." She hadn't cycled to the performance, as it wasn't "very practical for the geography we're in." Her companion Sean continued, "I'm a very keen cyclist myself. I thought it was a very cool novel idea certainly seeing how they've created everything with everything around them is very impressive." For George, the HandleBards' cycling epitomized endurance, "I think it's crazy. That's really cool. It's a lot of pressure. Every day. I have no idea how they do it." Felicity was also in awe of the demands of the tour, stating, "I can't even ride a bike, let alone do Shakespeare," suggesting that extensive cycling and speaking Shakespeare were extraordinary achievements rather than personally motivating or environmentally illuminating. Audiences

---

[10] Julie Hudson, "Bicycles on Stage—Shapeshifters or Scenery?" *The Environment on Stage: Scenery or Shapeshifter* (New York: Routledge, 2019). The ethnographic work I present here accords in many ways with Hudson's extensive qualitative and quantitative audience research at HandleBards' productions, which was published as my own book was reaching completion. Hudson identifies the environment as an "open secret" in The HandleBards' work. I recommend her complementary study of this company, which is more detailed than mine.

impressed by the HandleBards' resilience performed their own comparative weakness in response. These theatergoers received the tour as a feat, akin to climbing a mountain to fundraise for a charitable cause. Felicity encapsulated this kind of response when she proposed that "They should try and get sponsored to do this, like a charity. I know they get their bikes from a company. But they could raise money for charity by doing this." Despite the cheery tenacity that makes the HandleBards such fun, then, their work is unabashedly ableist even as it highlights the fragility of actors on the road: young and fit people go for a bike ride and perform Shakespeare whatever the weather—the healthiest of human bodies, tested against the elements, can still show up and present the play. If we don't (and they don't) say it aloud, it is clear that what they do isn't an option for everyone.[11]

Theatergoers responded to *As You Like It* without articulating connections between *As You Like It* and the HandleBards' thrifty approach, beyond suggesting that their mode of transportation recalled a vague Elizabethanism, similar to that found at the Willow Globe. Some ventured that Shakespearean touring might have been less resource hungry than contemporary touring. Amelia, for example, offered that "They give you the sense of a travelling company. They're a bit sort of Shakespearean in that sense, going around with their tents. That they would be travelling about without much stuff." For Mark, The HandleBards resembled "A modern day version of a Shakespearean troupe. Like, they don't use much scenery because they only use what they can carry." Kate contrasted her imagined sense of the sociability of early modern touring theater with a contemporary sense of alienation:

> I think the bikes provide a modern slightly kind of edgy parallel of what theater used to be with travelling troubadours. And they used to show up onto the village green and be welcomed into the community and steal their food and provide an atmosphere for the people who are there to interact and kind of remind each other of what it is to be human.

For Shakespeare, wheels were for potters, chariots, and Fortune. Bicycles were invented in the late 1800s. Like the rhododendrons decorating the Pastoral Players' *As You Like It* in Coombe Woods, and as far as historical transport is concerned, there is no connection between cycling and Shakespeare's touring companies. In addition to the ideological work that Susan Bennett associates with Shakespearean nostalgia, though, where theatergoers equated simplicity with an imagined past,

---

[11] Cognizant of their personal resources, The HandleBards spent the summer of 2020 delivering groceries and supplies by bicycle to people in need across London when their performances were postponed because of the Covid-19 pandemic.

the frugal aesthetic necessitated by bicycle touring also counterpointed early modern practices in a kind of "avant-garde nostalgia," such as that proposed by Kate Soper and identified at the Willow Globe.[12] Jenny, in Lyme Regis, remarked that the HandleBards had hit upon, "A very eco idea that is probably much more of how these plays were originally rehearsed and sometimes performed." Rob, at Great Torrington, said, "They [The HandleBards] encourage us to consider that mankind did much less environmental damage then." Commenting upon the staging, Sara remarked that "simplicity is not of detriment to our enjoyment and understanding." As Soper's proposition for an "alternative hedonism" hopes, less was more than enough in this production.[13] There was depth in the pared back performance, richly pleasurable and anathema to austerity.

Joy and environmentalism do not tend to keep company, as Nicole Seymour reminds us in *Bad Environmentalism* (2018), but nowhere was The HandleBards' *As You Like It* encountered as sanctimonious or pious.[14] Overwhelmingly, audience members framed the production in positive language, using bland superlatives. *As You Like It* was "brilliant," "exciting," "wonderful," "fantastic," and "memorable," evoking the affirmative "virtuous circle" of positive evaluation that Katya Johanson and Hilary Glow identify across arts-based audience research.[15] They also praised "accessibility" and "child friendliness," common areas of approval for open-air Shakespeares and outdoor performance more generally. Where responses to the HandleBards differed from their counterparts in my research, however, was where terms such as "clever," "unique," "novel," and "ingenious" described the bicycle-based approach to staging Shakespeare, blending the historical and contemporary. Coupled with compliments for innovative staging, words like "earthy," "green," "ecofriendly," and "sustainable" were common. Overwhelmingly audiences received the production as "fun" and "hilarious." A reference to "laughter" or "humor" appeared in every conversation I had. The laughter underscoring banal statements about "green" and "ecofriendly" theater begins to disclose the environmental reception of The HandleBards' work. Occasionally, but not inevitably, comments about ingenuity

---

[12] Susan Bennett, *Performing Nostalgia: Shifting Shakespeare and the Contemporary Past* (New York: Routledge, 1996); Kate Soper, "Passing Glories and Romantic Retrievals: Avant-garde Nostalgia and Hedonist Renewal," in *Ecocritical Theory: New European Approaches*, eds. Kate Rigby and Axel Goodbody (Charlottesville and London: University of Virginia Press, 2011), 23.

[13] Kate Soper, "An Alternative Hedonism," *Radical Philosophy* 92 (1998): 28–38; "Alternative Hedonism, Cultural Theory and the Role of Aesthetic Revisioning," *Cultural Studies* 22, no. 5 (2008): 567–87; Kate Soper, Martin Ryle, and Lyn Thomas, eds., *The Politics and Pleasures of Consuming Differently* (Basingstoke and New York: Palgrave Macmillan, 2009).

[14] Seymour, *Bad Environmentalism*, 4–5.

[15] Katya Johanson and Hilary Glow, "A Virtuous Circle: The Positive Evaluation Phenomenon in Arts Audience Research," *Participations Journal of Audience & Reception Studies* 12, no. 1 (2015): 254–70.

and green fun returned to the characteristics of British or English nationality, nuanced and compounded by phrases like "quirky," "mad," "curious but cute," "crazy, but witty and ethical," "admirable and bonkers," and "wacky and different."

As with all of the productions in this book, people made familiar allusions to open-air Shakespeares, reinforcing what Clare synthesized as a "Love of the magic of the natural world." More than love for nature and perceptions of Shakespeares in the open-air as "magical," Clare had a sense that the relationship between the production and the outdoor setting was "A thoughtful one, to consider how our travels affect the environment." Tim explained that while at the performance he "talked about impact on the planet with my children—a positive message to share." In some respects, the HandleBards touch something like validating instrumentalist approaches to arts-based environmental education. A social sciences survey undertaken in 2018 proposes a number of "climate change transformations processes possibly accessible through the arts," for instance.[16] For what the exercise is worth, many themes in the responses to the HandleBards' work can be mapped against these areas of potential.[17] While it would be pedantic to plough through the list item by item, noting some of the "transformations processes" alongside audience responses is a useful rejoinder to dogmatic positions either for or against the arts as an assist to climate-change communication. Are there "metaphors, imagery and narratives of alternative futures"[18] in these comments by Sarah, for example? "Performing outdoors in some of the most beautiful spots in the country and travelling there in such an environmentally friendly way is so encouraging for the environment. No technology needed on the day of the performance." Gemma said:

> Doing the shows outside brings a connection to nature and appreciation of how Shakespeare might have seen the world. The cycling from place to place is inspiring. I love that the promotion of 'if we can do this, you could do so much' is never said, but is a clear message.

Does her comment suggest quietly "attuning human perception" to the value systems required to respond to biospheric change?[19] George offered, "The environment played a part within the play and the actor's asides ... especially the peacocks and the hot air balloon taking off mid performance!" noting the actors' capacity in asides and ad-libs. In this respect, does he observe them "embrace uncertainty" and "open up alternative modes of relations to nature beyond

---

[16] Diego Galafassi et al., "'Raising the Temperature': The Arts on a Warming Planet," *Current Opinion in Environmental Sustainability* 31 (2018): 74.
[17] Galafassi et al., "Raising the Temperature," 74.
[18] Galafassi et al., 74.
[19] Galafassi et al., 74.

"command-and-control,'" modeling creative and responsive ecological relations.[20] The HandleBards "ham it up" and don't take themselves or Shakespeare seriously, hosting events that are staged to be haphazard in their embrace of uncertainty. The survey's claims are ambitious and the audience comments may seem relatively weak companions, but it feels worth letting them simmer side by side. At the very least, they suggest that critiques of instrumentalist approaches to ecodramaturgical theater—such as those which I outlined in the Introduction—need to remain open to the possibility that works can have environmentally positive effects. If there is less a transformation than a reinforcement of existing values at work, this blustery *As You Like It* unmoored skepticism.

Out, Damned Logo! Fossil-Free Mischief at the Royal Shakespeare Company, 2018

On a heavy, humid, and overcast June 16, 2018, approximately seventy "actorvists" from BP or not BP: Reclaim Our Bard staged a Fossil Free Mischief Festival outside the entrance to the Royal Shakespeare Theatre (RST) at Stratford-upon-Avon

Figure 6.2 Darragh Martin, Michelle Tylicki, and James Atherton in BP or not BP's Mischief Festival, 2018. Photograph courtesy of Ron Fassbender.

[20] Galafassi et al., 74.

protesting BP's sponsorship of a £5 ticket scheme for sixteen- to twenty-five-year-olds. BP or not BP's unsanctioned Mischief festival was organized in response to the RSC's official Mischief Festival, which was happening at The Other Place—the RSC's theater founded by Buzz Goodbody to present radical and experimental works—just a short walk up the road. This was BP or not BP's fiftieth performance and the festival set-up outside the theater featured a Shakespearean Insult Booth, with a blackboard of select insult words on magnets—resembling the Shakespearean insults and vocabulary fridge magnets sold inside the RSC shop; tents for food and costume changes; and a stage area for "rebel" performances with microphones and an amplifier. The headline act—a "Mischief" flash mob inviting participation in a "people's tempest" from passers-by—was repeated twice during the day. In the evening, the guerrilla projectionist Feral X lit up the outside walls of the RST with the following phrases: "BP also sponsors climate change"; "BP also sponsors: regressive regimes"; "BP also sponsors: colonialism"; "BP also sponsors: violence and corruption"; "BP: you smiling, damned villain." Unlike the other performances discussed in this book, the public space outdoors on the RST forecourt was not chosen for its bucolic qualities, but as a suitable site for protest. At the time of the BP or not BP action, the official Mischief Festival was presenting two new plays. The first, *#WEAREARRESTED* (adapted by Pippa Hill and Sophie Ivatts), told the story of Can Dündar, the Turkish journalist imprisoned in 2015 for publishing evidence of the government's unlawful actions. In this play, from the stage inside the theater, Dündar (Peter Hamilton Dyer) referenced the outdoor protest space from his prison confinement, imagining barbed wire framing a blue sky as he listened to protesters beyond the walls. The second Mischief production, *Day of the Living* (created by Darren Clark, Amy Draper, and Juliet Gilkes Romero), was a devised musical recounting the disappearance of forty-three male students in Ayotzinapa, Mexico, in 2014. Inside the theater, this production staged public space protests as young people clashed with the authorities. In an interview with the online magazine *Hyperallergic*, Sarah Horne, who is a member of BP or not BP, explained their response to plays of the RSC's official festival:

> The shows in the official Mischief Festival—*Day of the Living* and *#WeAreArrested*—tell vital stories of struggles against repression in Mexico and Turkey. But it is deeply upsetting to see these plays being used by BP to position itself as a champion of free speech while colluding with governments that silence people speaking out against the oil and gas industry around the world."[21]

[21] Isabella Smith, "Protest Performance Pressures Royal Shakespeare Company to End BP Sponsorship," June 18, 2018. https://hyperallergic.com/447680/bp-or-not-bp-protest-festival-royal-shakespeare-company-festival/.

I visited Stratford-upon-Avon for the weekend with my dad to attend both Mischief Festivals. We saw the RSC plays on the Friday night and spent the Saturday sitting on the steps of the theater, watching and participating in the BP or not BP activities. Actorvists handed out leaflets and engaged the members of the public in conversation about BP's corporate sponsorship of the RSC. Some of those who stopped to join in were supportive of the protestors, while others disagreed with the premise of the protest. Still others articulated that, while they did not necessarily like BP as an organization, they felt that it was right for the RSC to take whatever sponsorship money they could get. Some thought that it was good that BP was trying to take more social responsibility by supporting the RSC.

BP or not BP competed with others sharing the same open public space outside the theater. We heard large groups cheering excitedly for rowers on the River Avon, just out of sight. Members of an organization called Renewal Christian Centre also proselytized, handing out leaflets to anyone passing. From the steps, we glimpsed Arclight Theatre Company performing an abridged version of *Much Ado About Nothing* at the Dell amphitheater—the RSC's sanctioned amphitheater space for free, programmed performances. Tour guides led bewildered-looking groups through the Mischief activities, following flags. Young people on L-plated motorbikes zigzagged across BP or not BP's "performance" space. Not everyone in earshot realized that the flash mob was a protest. I heard one woman say to a man, "oh, it's BP doing a performance in opposition to BP's sponsorship of the RSC" and yelled, "Yeah cool!" "Go on!"—self-consciously performing their support for the performers and for their peers. When the festival paused for lunch, I walked into town and noticed a crowd outside a café mesmerized by a tenor in a tracksuit singing Andrew Lloyd Weber's "Memory" from the mega musical *Cats*. He received the most rapturous applause I heard all weekend.

Later activities included a lip-syncing battle in drag between the House of Renewables and the House of Fossil Fools, which featured the personification of "solar power" singing Katrina and the Waves' "Walking on Sunshine" as it began to rain. Umbrellas came out amongst those watching as the song carried on. After a second iteration of the Mischief Mob performance, the actorvists walked in a procession up to The Other Place for a somber protest outside that theater where the official Mischief plays were running, holding placards and making spoken declarations about BP's involvement in global atrocities and human rights abuses. The argument for why any arts organization should not accept sponsorship from a fossil fuel company was articulated as BP or not BP's key message:

Oil companies like BP are fueling runaway climate change, lobbying against environmental laws and blocking clean energy alternatives. BP also helps to fund governments that violently suppress protest and free speech – often in ways that benefit the oil giant.[22]

For BP or not BP, the point is the relationship between the environmental message and the Shakespeare. Campaigning is made palatable *through* Shakespeare. Aesthetically, BP or not BP pitch themselves as cultured lovers of Shakespeare and RSC musicals in their performance choices: culture "civilizes" the protest—what are we fighting for, after all. They take a camp and anarchic to "culture jamming" (the term for anti-consumerist, social activism that subverts hegemonic representations in art and media, first used by experimental music group NegativLand in 1984 and subsequently popularized by Mark Dery).[23] Will Platt notes that Liberate Tate (another member group in the Art Not Oil coalition)'s culture jamming at the Tate Modern in London exemplifies what Mike Sell calls a "vested vanguard,"[24] marrying its protest aesthetic to the in-house style of the Tate, thus rendering the performance work ultimately co-optable by the institution. Transferring Platt's argument to BP or not BP at the RSC, many of the actorvists were declared supporters of the theater and their blend of art and activism paid homage to the institution and likewise appealed to its audience.

The Mischief Mob played irreverently with Shakespeare's well-known characters and texts, with each character speaking familiar Shakespearean lines with oleaginous textual amendments. The flash mob featured Hamlet, dressed in black and pondering a skull ("and yet what to me is this quintessence of evil [BP])"; Macbeth, rubbing stained palms together ("will all great Neptune's oceans wash clean this oil from my hands?"); Lady Macbeth scrubbing her oily hands ("out damned logo!"); Juliet, dressed in angel wings like Claire Danes as Baz Luhrmann's Juliet, and clutching the BP logo to her heart ("What's in a name? That which we call BP, By any other words would be as rich. / Beyond or British Petroleum, who cares / When companies keep us stocked with ample shares!"); and Puck ("Let us put our best disguise on, forget the Deepwater Horizon"). BPRozencrantz and BPRilldenstern hosted the event ("*two BP executives, like Ant + Dec, but more terrible*"), drinking from champagne glasses filled with thick

---

[22] BP or not BP, Fossil Free Mischief Festival Leaflet, June 16, 2018, 1.
[23] Mark Dery, "The Merry Pranksters And the Art of the Hoax." *New York Times*, December 23, 1990; "Culture Jamming: Hacking, Slashing, and Sniping in the Empire of the Signs," Westfield, NJ: Open Magazine Pamphlet Series, 1993.
[24] Will Platt, "Subverting the Spectacle: A Critical Study of Culture Jamming as Activist Performance," (PhD thesis, University of Exeter, 2019), 242–3.

black liquid and dressed in large green and yellow ruffs matching the sun shape and colors of the BP Helios logo.[25]

Joining the Shakespearean characters, three performers played the character of Matilda, the young protagonist from the RSC's musical based on the Roald Dahl children's story of that name—her "innocent" presence in the protest extending Peter Marinelli's argument for the supposed simplicity of childhood as a new form of pastoral nostalgia, where the child replaces the shepherd.[26] BP or not BP's Fossil Free Mischief Festival leaflet informed us that the ticket sponsorship deal was especially insidious, since the younger generation whose tickets were offered at a reduced rate would feel the worsening effects of a changing climate. Matilda argued that the RSC could afford not to accept oil sponsorship because the profit made from *Matilda, The Musical* far surpassed BP's financial contribution to the theater (this financial aspect to her argument somewhat confused the scope of BP or not BP's environmentalism, sustaining the capitalist narrative that progress and growth can continue indefinitely).

The playwright Sarah Ruhl riffs on the trope of drama students in training, unwillingly performing the weather for teachers who are disconnected from the "real" world. She jokes, "I thought that once you got your Equity card, you refused on principle to ever make the sound of wind again."[27] The actorvists from BP or not BP harnessed this tired trope, not just performing weather themselves but asking us—the audience—to join in making the weather using our human bodies as resources. The flash mob therefore ended by inviting passers-by to perform not weathering but the weather itself. The actorvist playing *The Tempest*'s Caliban entreated the assembly: to "kick up a tempest: you can't have a decent tempest without a company willing to wreak havoc with the climate." We were taught dance moves for the participatory storm—simple gestures and movements devised to represent thunder claps, lightning strikes, and rolling winds performed in sequence. Pete the Temp improvised beatbox weather rhythms to accompany the movement as the people's tempest closed in on the BP executives, dancing the weather on the RSC forecourt. The participatory tempest dissipated when the Matildas smashed foam pies into the faces of the

---

[25] BP or not BP, "Mischief Mob draft," (Unpublished, 2018), 1.
[26] Peter Marinelli, *Pastoral* (London: Methuen, 1971), 81.
[27] Sarah Ruhl, *100 Essays I Don't Have Time to Write: On Umbrellas and Sword Fights, Parades and Dogs, Fire Alarms, Children, and Theater* (New York: Farrar, Straus and Giroux, 2014), 98. I briefly address ecopedagogies and the request that drama students "be the weather" in "Theatre for a Changing Climate" in *Posthumanism in Higher Education: A Lecturer's Portfolio*, eds. Carol Taylor and Annouchka Bailey (Basingstoke and New York: Palgrave, 2019); and Ian Morgan, Evelyn O'Malley, Ciaran Clarke, and Gey Pin Ang, "Answer the Question: How Does Nature Nurture Your Training," *Theatre, Dance and Performance Training* 83 (2017): 350–5.

BPRozencrantz and BPRilldenstern, ousting them from the RSC. If, as Astrida Neimanis and Rachel Loewen-Walker argue, we are always "intra-actively" (after Karen Barad) becoming-with weather in a "transcorporeal" (after Stacy Alaimo) process, then this participatory dance implicitly worked to "cultivate a sensibility that attunes us not only to the 'now' of the weather, but toward ourselves and the world as weather bodies, mutually caught up in the whirlwind of a weather-world."[28] The people's tempest acknowledged humans as weather-bodies in ways that extended beyond the metaphorical allusions to Prospero's tempest conjured by anyone willing to dance sides with the planet against the oil multinational.

My dad duly joined in with the people's tempest. He is so encouraging, I thought, and—reflecting on my own mortification at the prospect of participatory dance in this context—realized that part of what was so striking throughout the day was the encouragement that the actorvists gave to one another. The flash mob participants and audience for the protest performances often comprised actorvists as much as passers-by. Indeed, many of those who dressed up and entered the Shakespearean Insult Booth to "throw shade at BP" were actorvists rather than individuals stumbling across the installation from the street. They supported their peers when other potential audience members were thin on the ground. Performances of shared weathering evoked support and validation—although, to an observer like me at least, this support was quietly given, without veering toward self-satisfaction. Furthermore, the visible commitment to capturing performances on video and sharing them online was a reminder that the intended audience included not just the people present in Stratford-upon-Avon that day, but an online audience accumulating an archive of photographs and livestreamed footage on social media: for people who didn't share that afternoon's weather, but who shared the virtual winter of the actorvists' discontent.

Conducting previous fieldwork, I had better blended into audiences, only occasionally questioned about my residual Irish accent. Now I was conspicuous, sitting heavily on the concrete steps. Many people asked about the pregnancy, making well-meaning assumptions and offering advice. This changed the substance of the conversations I had throughout the day. I received kicks every now and again in response to loud noises, thumping reminders of the "next generation" to which actorvists and passers-by kept referring and which preoccupies so many environmentalisms (whether the ethical debate is around

---

[28] Astrida Neimanis and Rachel Loewen-Walker. "*Weathering*: Climate Change and the 'Thick Time' of Transcorporeality," *Hypatia* 29, no. 3 (2014): 561.

reproductive rights, population, inheritance, and responsibility; and where the narrative is often framed in terms of a future rather than a life that many are already living). Nuancing their argument for weathering, Neimanis and Loewen-Walker remind us of the "vast distances between differently situated humans that affect their vulnerability and accountability in the face of climate change."[29] A discarded newspaper reported on the separation of children from their families at the Mexico-US border by Immigration and Customs Enforcement. Migration already underway will continue as anthropogenic climate change makes some homes more unlivable than others: this was one of BP or not BP's messages and it resonated with me as an observer of their work, in conjunction with thoughts of the RSC's Mischief plays and slugging through the heavy day.

The Fossil Free Mischief Festival ended with an unscheduled intervention, breaking into the theater. Actorvists, led by BPRozencrantz and BPRilldenstern, stormed the indoor foyer of the RST and approached the BP logo on RSC sponsorship signage on a wall, singing the catchy version of the adapted Matilda's song that they had been singing all day.

> We are revolting players
> These are revolting times
> BP's revolting actions
> Make us revolt in rhyme
> We'll be revolting here
> Till BP's out the door
> RSC you'd better listen
> We're revolting.[30]

As Neimanis and Loewen-Walker argue, "We are not all swept up into some amorphous gust of wind and water. As weather bodies, we encounter boundaries of difference at every turn."[31] Breaking in to the theater, the actorvists diluted the outdoor/indoor performance binary, traipsing the day's weather across the threshold. If the building represented institutional security, safety, and shelter, and the street was the open-air, then the day's weather on their bodies, hair, and clothes—literally as well as figuratively—entered the theater, acknowledging the boundaries of difference as well as the continuity of the weather, and demonstrating the "mutually emergent, coextensive" nature

---

[29] Neimanis and Loewen-Walker, "*Weathering*," 564.
[30] BP or not BP, Fossil Free Mischief Festival Leaflet, June 16, 2018, 3.
[31] Neimanis and Loewen-Walker, "*Weathering*," 564.

Figure 6.3 Projection onto the Royal Shakespeare Theatre, Stratford Upon Avon, June 2018. Photograph courtesy of Feral X.

of "humans and nonhuman climate and weather."[32] Weathering Shakespeare at this protest acknowledged differences amongst people—those present as actorvists and audiences member and those whose lives to which they alluded— and the differences between weathered spaces in and out of doors, recognizing their "co-constitutive" continuities.[33] The tenacious, creative campaigning undertaken by BP or not BP—as one of many mounting pressures from varied sources—ultimately contributed to the RSC decision to "conclude" the BP partnership at the end of 2019 (when news of this outcome reached me in the privacy of my workplace, I danced what I could remember of the people's tempest.)[34]

Upcycling Arden: *As You Like It* at the Regent's Park Open Air Theatre, 2018

After the HandleBards put their bicycles into the garage at the end of summer 2017, and before BP or not BP arrived on the RST forecourt in spring 2018, autumn evenings of 2017 grew dark and UK television audiences listened to

[32] Neimanis and Loewen-Walker, 564.
[33] Neimanis and Loewen-Walker, 564.
[34] We are to conclude our partnership with BP, https://www.rsc.org.uk/news/we-are-to-conclude-our-partnership-with-bp [Accessed October 2, 2019].

David Attenborough narrate *Blue Planet,* growing increasingly incensed by images of plastic pollution—fishing nets, drinking straws, takeaway cups—floating discarded in the world's oceans. So vividly had the series brought these images to their living rooms, effecting almost-instantaneous changes amongst savvy, "ethically intentioned" retailers, that the comedian Nish Kumar dubbed David Attenborough "the first person in history to say 'This is the last straw,' and mean it literally."[35] By July 2018, as Max Webster's production of *As You Like It* played in scorching temperatures at the Open Air Theatre in Regent's Park, London, what came to be known as the *"Blue Planet* effect" meant that plastic waste troubled a new wave of environmentally concerned citizens, politely doing their bit by requesting "no straw, please" during England's (then) hottest recorded summer.[36] Even the then Conservative British Prime Minister Theresa May, notable for her absence from environmental conversations, was forced to promise a nationwide ban on plastic straws, stirrers, and cotton buds.

Webster's *As You Like It* at Regent's Park, designed by Naomi Dawson, tuned into this public preoccupation. Its court was a corporate city space of voracious consumption. Arden became an upcycled haven in the dump. Jane Bennett elucidates her now-prolific argument for the vibrant materiality of "thing power" by invoking trash, asking how "patterns of consumption [would] change if we faced not litter, rubbish, trash, or recycling but an accumulating pile of lively and potentially dangerous matter?"[37] Patterns of consumption and throwaway culture were central to an imagined court/Arden distinction in Webster's production, which commenced with the court characters holding takeaway cups and singing a rock version of "The Rain It Raineth Every Day" (*Twelfth Night* 5.1.376–95) composed by Charlie Fink of rock band Noah and the Whale. A steel frame rained water onto the undecorated stage where Duke Frederick was sheltered from the court's inhospitable climate under a large black umbrella. When the song reached the line "A great while ago the world began" (*Twelfth Night* 5.1.392), the performers on stage aggressively tossed their cups into a moat that separated the stage from the audience, punctuating

---

[35] Episode 5: The Mash· Report https://subsaga.com/bbc/comedy/the-mash-report/series-1-winter/episode-5.html. I taught a module at the University of Exeter on Theatre for a Changing Climate DRA3092 in the autumn term of 2017, concurrently with the showings of *Blue Planet*. I was already familiar with the images of plastic waste shown but struck by just how much students were affected by them. Such unquantifiable anecdotal evidence of affect is repeated in the reception of *Blue Planet* since.

[36] 2018 was the joint hottest summer on record for the UK as a whole, tied with those of 1976, 2003, and 2006 for being the highest since records began in 1910. https://www.metoffice.gov.uk/news/releases/2018/end-of-summer-stats.

[37] Jane Bennett, *Vibrant Matter: A Political Ecology of Things* (Durham and London: Duke University Press, 2010), viii.

the music with the physical gesture (and, temporally, alluding to the scale of the anthropocene and the beginning of the "world"). The detritus floated in the water for the remainder of the first half. Flanking the moat on either side of the playing area—on liminal land usually maintained as green lawn for overspill audience—were two mountains of garbage piled high, resembling images of the Pacific Garbage Patch that had so profoundly entered public consciousness by way of *Blue Planet*. A great while ago the world began and certain humans have been piling up the trash ever since.

As always, those less fortunate were left to clean up. Orlando (Edward Hogg) and Adam (Gary Lilburn) began their dialogue dressed in illuminated jackets, picking up litter as Orlando lamented his lack of education. Orlando entered exile by wading through the dirty moat: a hero leaving his uninhabitable home in search of somewhere better. Likewise, when Adam was forced to leave the place that had been his home, "From seventeen years till now almost fourscore" (*As You Like It* 2.3.72), it was no longer habitable. Like Orlando, he waded through the polluted moat, his aging body's vulnerability heightened by his physical presence in water, cups bobbing at his legs: "Here lived I, but now live here no more" (*As You Like It* 2.3.73). In leaving the court, Webster's staging, in concert with Dawson's setting, visually reiterated those dystopian or post-apocalyptic climate narratives that commence with an involuntary exodus from a ruined home place. The departures of Orlando, Adam, Rosalind (Olivia Vinall), and Celia (Keziah Joseph) from court evoked the forced migration already occurring as a result of food scarcity, political instability, and inequalities exacerbated by climatic change.

The climate of Arden was initially no more forgiving than the court. Snow fell from the steel structure and the performers acted cold in the sweltering summer sunshine. Trash was not absent from the Forest of Arden. Arden was precisely where the court's trash ended up. Arden was *in* the dump. Arden *was* the dump. As Bennett reminds us, "our trash is not 'away' in landfills but generating lively streams of chemicals and volatile winds of methane as we speak."[38] She warns, "a vital materiality can never really be thrown 'away', for it continues its activities even as a discarded or unwanted commodity."[39] Duke Senior's (Simon Armstrong) banquet was laid on a table constructed from car tires and wooden pallets. Lords sat on crates of Evian water bottles, indicating the moat as an undrinkable supply. A rusty oil barrel was used to bar-be-que. If it is too late for pristine nature, then Arden represented a way of approaching the mess rather

---

[38] Bennett, *Vibrant Matter*, 6.
[39] Bennett, 6.

than an escape from it. When the dump is all that is left, Arden became about finding ways to live well in a devastated landscape.

Steve Mentz posits that the Duke's key speech on "tongues in trees" (*As You Like It* 2.1.1–17) in Arden presents an argument that "loses purchase on the natural world" because "its polished rhetoric about unpolished nature could only have been learned at court."[40] The speech's ending is "pure abstraction," Mentz convinces us, partially because the metaphor escalates from spoken language ("tongues in trees"), to reading ("books in the running brooks"), to preaching "sermons in stones," only to end with the anthropocentric moralizing of "good in everything" that fails to acknowledge nonhuman nature's intrinsic worth. Thinking of the visual context for *As You Like It* at Regent's Park set out above, however, with Bennett's "thing power," the compound word every*thing* referenced the materials on stage beyond the biotic "things" contained within the Duke's lines. The "good" to be found in every "thing" capaciously encompassed not just trees, brooks, and stones, but takeaway cups, tires, straws, and all kinds of waste. Unlike Reinhardt's trees, discarded things—human trash—might be salvaged for new uses in Arden. In this reading of the performance, the Duke was a steward urging care and attention to commodities, as well as to trees, brooks, and stones.[41] His ability to see re-use potential was premised on human exceptionalism, but it proffered a human imagination with a keen sense of interdependence in the presence of the enduring trash object. Therefore, when Hogg as Orlando approached the banquet, starving and ready to fight for food, thinking "that all things had been savage here" (*As You Like It* 2.7.106) and the Duke not only offered to share but promised they would "nothing waste" until Orlando returned with Adam (2.7.133), the audience was encouraged to think about food hypothetically wasted in light of the waste witnessed at court and the trash piled either side of the stage.

Orlando's departure to retrieve Adam left Jacques (Maureen Beattie) to chastise the assembly with the "Seven Ages of Man" (*As You Like It* 2.7.138–65). In her (female) voice, the fatalistic lines sounded like an accusatory tirade, taking aim at *man*kind's commitment to capitalist progress and growth. Pointedly, and the sound of Beattie uttering this scathing admonishment on what economist Kate Raworth has referred to as the "Manthropocene"[42] resonated with the

---

[40] Steve Mentz, "Shakespeare, Ecological Crisis, and the Resources of Genre," in *Ecocritical Shakespeare*, eds. Dan Brayton and Lynne Bruckner (Farnham and Burlington: Ashgate, 2011): 162–3.
[41] There are many comparisons that could be made between theatrical portrayals of Duke Senior and David Attenborough, in terms of stewardship, patriarchy, and moral authority.
[42] Kate Raworth, "Must the Anthropocene Be a Manthropocene?" *The Guardian* 2014; Jennifer Hamilton and Astrida Neimanis, "Composting Feminisms and Environmental Humanities" 10, no. 2 (2018): 501–27.

feminist—and associated concerns of antiracist, political, and social justice—underpinnings of new materialist theory that Jennifer Hamilton and Astrida Neimanis argue have tended to be overlooked by environmental humanities scholars extracting their ecological arguments.[43] These resonances stayed with me beyond the end of the production, in the "compost" with the problems of the text faithfully rendered, as I sketch below.

When the audience returned after the interval, Arden had been upcycled. The trash either side of the stage had disappeared and in their place, lawn was visible. The forest's inhabitants had turned car tires into hanging baskets and a swing. Plants grew around the edges of the stage and greenery spilled out of rusty oil barrels. Lords in Arden rode bicycles, presumably replacing the vehicles from which the tires were leftovers. The moat had been cleared of litter and a bridge was constructed across it (notionally making things easier for people to come and go: build bridges not walls). Celia washed her knife in the water before chopping her apple, indicating a newly clean water supply. Arden for the anthropocene was not so much a "no place," such as the Utopia Thomas More envisages, but another way of being "in place," a celebration of human creativity.[44]

It was at this point that the production's environmental concept began to decompose, exposing the limits of the play's dramaturgy when it comes to contemporary environmental concerns (I think positively of "decomposition" after Haraway, and Neimanis and Hamilton's work on intersectional feminist "composting" in the generative sense a process of remaking, where some of the compost is efficacious and some of it is harmful to plants, but all of it steams in the same heap).[45] In his review of *As You Like It* for *The Times*, Sam Marlowe pointed out that Webster's concept wasn't "quite sustained."[46] My sense is that Marlowe's feeling had had less to do with the production (which did a creditable job of demonstrating the possibilities of upcycling) and more to do with the shape of the play, which veers toward a happy resolution in human time that eclipses even Jacques's unease ("I am for other than for dancing measures," *As You Like It* 5.4.182). True, the trash was not *all* there in the upcycled Arden: not everything can be reused. While choice objects proudly wore their origins as upcycled trash—and this is a concern about some of the limits of upcycling as much as a comment on the production—not all of the trash was present in the

---

[43] Jennifer Hamilton and Astrida Neimanis, "Composting Feminisms and Environmental Humanities," *Environmental Humanities* 10, no. 2 (2018): 501–27.
[44] Edward Casey, *Getting Back into Place*, 2nd ed. (Bloomington: Indiana University Press, 2009).
[45] Neimanis and Hamilton, "Composting Feminisms and Environmental Humanities."
[46] Sam Marlowe, "It's Very Nearly as We Like It," *The Times*, 2018, 107.

second part of the play (nor was it clear where it had gone). Rhetorically, barrels and tires make great garden features, but what can we do with the cups from the moat? As the play progressed toward its resolution and preparations were undertaken for the multiple weddings, the Lords of Arden cheerily wheeled remaining tires off the stage to clear the space for a country-dance. The play's resolution left little space for showing the "slow violence" that Robert Nixon so compellingly identifies, "a violence that occurs gradually and out of sight, a violence of delayed destruction that is dispersed across time and space, an attritional violence that is typically not viewed as violence at all."[47]

What I am digging for is not the environmental credentials of the materials used to make the pieces of scenery (although others usefully question the materials used in theater-making[48]), but what the trash's uncomplicated removal implied in terms of Shakespeare as ecotheater. Ultimately, the environmental concept was partially subsumed into the play's structure and into the legacy of pastoral conventions of summer performance in the open-air, which originate in the late-Victorian era and continue through to the creation of performance spaces like Regent's Park Open Air Theater in the 1930s and the reconstructed Shakespeare's Globe in 1997.[49] Costumes—long hair, floaty dresses, and dungarees—contributed to a scenographic affect that was as much flower- as thing-power, as much nostalgic merrymaking as anthropocene Arden: a hopeful, hippie summer of love in a summer of plastic. This is neither to dismiss "flower-power" as unenvironmentalist—as is too easily done—nor to disparage the environmental work of the hippie movement—also too easily done, as Timothy Morton points out—but to note the conflicted history of their association with ineffective environmentalists, sharing the stage with salvage from the wreck.[50]

Not unlike the emphasis that David Attenborough places on secular stewardship and care for the natural world by individuals in *Blue Planet*, Webster's production highlighted the problems of plastic consumption but didn't quite extend as far as climate change with this aspect of staging. Such an approach potentially bolsters the neoliberal emphasis on the individual's responsibility to the detriment of a

---

[47] Rob Nixon, *Slow Violence and the Environmentalism of the Poor* (Cambridge, MA: Harvard University Press, 2011), 2.

[48] For "ecoscenography" that attends to the "actual" materials used to create theatrical scenery and performance installations, see Tanja Beer's work. In particular, see "The Living Stage: A Case Study in Ecoscenography," *Etudes* 1, no. 1 (2015): 1–16.

[49] Michael Dobson, *Shakespeare and Amateur Performance* (Cambridge and New York: Cambridge University Press, 2011), 152–96.

[50] Timothy Morton argues that the New Left in 1960s America failed to take the environment seriously as part of an agenda that covered class, race, and gender because it was a "hippie" thing, "It Was a Hippie Thing," 2014 http://ecologywithoutnature.blogspot.com/2014/01/it-was-hippie-thing.html.

political awakening. Intended as additional reading and not a comment on the production, Jan Martin Bang's program note's emphasis on permaculture and intentional communities helps us into the ecopolitics of this aesthetic conundrum. Bang imagines permaculture (and Arden, by extension) to model socially and environmentally equitable communities. He cleanses permaculture of politics, however, by noting that "One way to deal with the perceived threats to our future is to object and protest, to organize socially and politically and stop things that are harmful. All honor to those that do this."[51] As an alternative, he suggests, "Another way is to scout out ways of doing things better" and cites Arden as one such place of better doing.[52] Permaculture that closes itself to the wider world might model more viable ways of living for some, but remains in danger of creating gated communities, whatever the intention. Who is out beyond the gates looking for Adam? Where is responsibility beyond the fringes of the Utopian republic? With no such thing as a clean slate, who is backstage picking up the historical trash? Dawson's bridge across the moat was significant in this respect but Shakespeare's play was only partially up to the task.[53] Ironically, the tension between the production concept and the structure of the Shakespearean text was a relief for the production's reviewers, who expressed reservations that an *As You Like It* they variously encountered as an "earnest," "ecoconscious," and "ecocharged" "ecoparable" or "ecocomedy" about "the sufferings of Mother Earth" and "environmental catastrophe" might have been "tediously virtuous." Thankfully, they found it to be a "riot" of "great fun" instead.[54]

---

[51] Jan Martin Bang, "This Way for the Forest of Arden," *As You Like It* program (2018): 12.
[52] Bang, "This Way for the Forest of Arden," 12.
[53] Todd A. Borlik, *Ecocriticism and Early Modern English Literature* (London: Routledge, 2011), 185, points out historical precedents for the Duke's generosity in an incident where an early modern dyer fed hundreds of people on carrots and cabbages from his garden for a week.
[54] "As You Like It, Open Air Theatre, Regent's Park, London—'bright, touching performances,'" *Financial Times*, July 13, 2018, https://www.ft.com/content/417e10f2-85c3-11e8-96dd-fa565ec55929; Andrzej Lukowski, "'As You Like It' Review," *TimeOut*, July 12, 2018, https://www.timeout.com/london/theatre/as-you-likeit-review-1; Fiona Mountford, "As You Like It Review: Warm, Charming and Perfect for the Park," *Standard*, July 12, 2018, https://www.standard.co.uk/go/london/theatre/as-you-like-it-review-warmcharming-and-perfect-for-the-park-a3885516.html; Heather Neill, "As You Like It, Regent's Park Open Air Theatre Review—Love among the Bucolic Hippies," *Theartsdesk*, July 13, 2018, https://theartsdesk.com/theatre/you-it-regents-park-open-air-theatre-review-love-among-bucolic-hippies; Matt Trueman, "Review: As You Like It (Regent's Park Open Air Theatre)," *WhatsOnStage*, July 12, 2018, https://www.whatsonstage.com/london-theatre/reviews/as-you-like-it-regents-park-open-air-olivia-vinall_47091.html; https://www.telegraph.co.uk/theatre/what-to-see/like-review-open-air-theatre-regents-park-embraces-craziness/; Michael Billington, "As You Like It Review – Captures Love's Exhilarating Madness," *Guardian*, July 12, 2018, https://www.theguardian.com/stage/2018/jul/12/as-you-like-it-review-regents-park; Rosemary Waugh, "As You Like It, Regent's Park Open Air Theatre, London, Review: Shakespeare's Summer Loving Gets a Nineties Makeover," *Independent*, July 13, 2018, https://www.independent.co.uk/arts-entertainment/theatre-dance/reviews/as-you-like-it-review-regents-park-open-air-theatreshakespeare-olivia-vinall-a8445876.html;

Juliet Dusinberre argues that the history of staging the Forest of Arden "tells of disappointment as often as delight."[55] I would like to finish by proposing that the nature of the open-air theater collaborated with the set design (whether it disappointed its designers or whether they anticipated it in light of global warming, I do not know, although the heat may well have disappointed audiences hoping for a comfortable experience) to enhance the production's emphasis on human interference with the natural world. After the visibly geoengineered weathers of the early scenes—rain at court and snow in the forest—the real summer weather was left to signify Arden's later climate as the steel frame was removed from the stage. For the most part of the summer of 2018, this meant unbroken sunshine and uncomfortable heat. Real rain or at least slightly cooler temperatures would have been welcome beyond the stage area. The cast performed characters performing weathering in the wet and cold conditions of the city and forest respectively for the first half of the play. The climate of Arden appeared to have changed for the better in as much as they danced at the end, but the actual weather showed them showing us the better weather as a thing of the past. They performed as though their characters were physically contented within the real summer weather to which audiences were also exposed (but discontented in the sweltering heat). Webster's *As You Like It* in the heatwave of 2018—a summer I will also remember mostly indoors, hoping for my left eye to twitch—was a poignant reminder that it will likely be unbearably hot at the best upcycled banquet and that no matter how many single-use cups are purged not everyone will make it to Arden.

---

[55] Juliet Dusinberre, "Introduction," *As You Like* It (London: Bloomsbury), 65.

Afterword

What kind of air isn't open? Any construction of what is "out-of-doors" is culturally contingent, and boundaries between what might be considered "in" and "out" of doors are inevitably porous. So much good fortune is inherent in the assumption of a door. Where is outdoors when I traipse leaves from the footpath into a house, or a window blows open unsettling papers in a room? What is the difference between the absence of a roof and the absence of walls? How does Shakespeare's Globe, where a portion of the sky is open to the weather, differ from an open-air theater space like Minack with no walls at all? Or differ from a theater structure where the walls are deciduous willow leaves, thresholds that act as homes for bugs, birds, moisture, and light and wind—passing through? And where is the weather when protesters cross the threshold of the Royal Shakespeare Theatre, carrying the day's drizzle on their shoes and in their hair?

Whilst working on this project, just before Christmas of 2015, Teresa Mannion's weather forecast on Radio Telifís Éireann went viral, as her real-life performance of braving Storm Desmond for Ireland's 9 o'clock news sparked watchers' imaginations.[1] Mannion performed weathering sensationally in pursuit of an in-situ weather-warning. Her weather outside instigated culture inside: a céilí remix received nearly two million YouTube views, schoolchildren learned the remix as a "song," and another school group choreographed a *Riverdance*-inspired dance tribute to the track.[2] Each subsequent performance contains traces of the memory of Mannion's weathering in an ongoing process of archiving enacted as a performance repertoire via bodies, words, and digitized responses. Turning from Mannion's report, I caught an ad for

---

[1] newsworthy.ie, "Teresa Mannion in Storm Desmond on RTÉ 9 O'clock News," YouTube video of original broadcast, December 5, 2015. https://www.youtube.com/watch?v=6ZldS9CiX88.

[2] SUPER CÉILÍ "Teresa Mannion Remix - SUPER CÉILÍ," YouTube video, December 5, 2015. https://www.youtube.com/watch?v=bzx3MeYonT8; Aine Usher, "Teresa Mannion's Weather Report ~ Irish Dancing," YouTube video December 14, 2015. https://www.youtube.com/watch?v=v9qbMRGxE5M.

a climate-controlled Peugeot SUV, "designed to master the elements."[3] This pinnacle of geoengineering weathers apocalyptic storms and tidal waves, whilst its white, hetero-occupant couple remain comfortable and in control of their biosphere, watching the weather as performance through the windows, unconcerned spectators of others' coping. Theirs is a mediatized performance of not-needing-to-weather thanks to a car that can buy its owner out of environmental disaster.

The performances of weathering that this book has identified are likewise tethered to the cultural embeddedness of Richard Mabey's "street theatre of daily coping."[4] As I have encountered these physical and discursive social and aesthetic practices, undertaken in response to Shakespeare's plays in the open-air—from my own position as an Irish person living in England, who spent a number of years performing in open-air Shakespeares after college, learning worlds, words, and weather—a particular performance of Englishness emerged, one that is geographically contingent and inflected by histories. In thinking carefully about the cultural work that Shakespeare does across spaces with respect to the weather, I have grasped at different ways of apprehending audience "experience," whilst also maintaining the impossibility of the catch. But if weathering denotes audience performance, then the ways in which these open-air Shakespeares instigate performances of weathering that also respond to theater architectures, community settings, and staging decisions reveal shifting attitudes toward nonhuman nature, particularly in relation to cultural constructions of climate. If an indoor/outdoor binary is as untenable as nature/culture always was, these theatrical events matter because they cling onto both distinctions: they frame weather as theater—the weather that people see with the play and the weather that they're in to see it. The meteorological is absorbed into the pastoral, and the pastoral is exceeded by the meteorological, which is often retrospectively memorialized into pastoral. Embodied archives of past weathering occasionally break through the green surface of these memories.

On climate tipping points—those already tipped passed repair or imminently so—the climate scientist Gavin Schmidt offers that, "there is no point after which it doesn't make sense to start making better decisions."[5] Schmidt's simply stated philosophy, uttered as an aside during a talk in which he advocated for

---

[3] Peugeot Citroën, "Designed to Master the Elements," YouTube video of original ad, March 10, 2017, https://www.youtube.com/watch?v=MCCik8ZXjZo.
[4] Richard Mabey, *Turned Out Nice Again: On Living with the Weather* (London: Profile Books, 2013), 90.
[5] Gavin Schmitt, "Adventures in Climate" (Alumni Auditorium, University of Exeter, January 10, 2017).

storytelling in climate science, was compelling. Better decision-making will require rigorous attempts to understand all kinds of human and nonhuman performance (whether or what we end up understanding matters less than the effort). Responses to the escalating effects of climate change are preceded by responses to naturecultures everywhere. Stories about performances of weathering can attest to erosion, continuance, and togetherness. Listening out for the work they do might mean reminding and uncouraging: relearning complex lessons for how to be around. It may be too late not to change the climate. But it will never be too late to make the fallout out better; to tell a better story.

Bibliography

Abram, David. "Afterword: The Commonwealth of Breath." In *Material Ecocriticism*. Edited by Serenella Iovino and Serpil Oppermann, 302–14. Bloomington and Indianapolis: Indiana University Press, 2014.

Abram, David. *Becoming Animal: An Earthly Cosmology*. New York: Vintage Books, 2010.

Abram, David. *The Spell of the Sensuous*. New York: Vintage Books, 1996.

Ahmed, Sara. "Happy Objects." In *The Affect Theory Reader*. Edited by Gregory J. Seigworth and Melissa Gregg, 29–51. Durham and London: Duke University Press, 2010.

Alaimo, Stacy. *Bodily Natures: Science, Environment, and the Material Self*. Bloomington: Indiana University Press, 2010.

Alaimo, Stacy. *Exposed: Environmental Politics and Pleasures in Posthuman Times*. Minneapolis and London: University of Minnesota Press, 2016.

Anderson, Ben. "Affective Atmospheres." *Emotion, Space and Society* 2, no. 2 (2009): 77–81.

Anderson, Ben and Paul Harrison. *Taking-Place: Non-Representational Theories*. Farnham: Ashgate, 2010.

Anderson, Benedict. *Imagined Communities: Reflections on the Origin and Spread of Nationalism*. Revised Edition. London and New York: Verso, 2016.

Angelacki, Vicki. *Theatre & Environment*. Basingstoke: Macmillan, 2019.

Arnold, Matthew. *Culture and Anarchy*. Edited by Jane Garnett. Oxford: Oxford University Press, 2006.

Arons, Wendy and Theresa J. May, eds. *Readings in Performance and Ecology*. Basingstoke: Palgrave Macmillan, 2012.

Aronson, Arnold. *The History and Theory of Environmental Scenography*. Ann Arbor, Michigan: UMI Research Press, 1981.

Auslander, Philip. *Liveness: Performance in a Mediatized Culture*. London: Routledge, 1999.

Bachelard, Gaston. *The Poetics of Space*. Edited by J. R. Stilgoe. Boston, MA: Beacon Press, 1994.

Barad, Karen. *Meeting the University Halfway: Quantum Physics and the Entanglement of Matter and Meaning*. Durham and London: Duke University Press, 2007.

Barker, Roberta, Kim Solga, and Cary Mazer. "'Tis Pity She's a Realist: A Conversational Case Study in Realism and Early Modern Theater Today." *Shakespeare Bulletin* 31, no. 4 (2013): 571–97.

Bassi, Anna. "Weather, Mood, and Voting: An Experimental Analysis of the Effect of Weather beyond Turnout." May 22, 2013, SSRN: https://ssrn.com/abstract=2273189

Bassi, Anna, Riccardo Colacito, and Paolo Fulghieri. "'O Sole Mio: An Experimental Analysis of Weather and Risk Attitudes in Financial Decisions." *The Review of Financial Studies* 26, no. 7 (2013): 1824–52.

Bauman, Zygmunt. *Community: Seeking Safety in an Insecure World*. Cambridge: Polity Press, 2001.

Behringer, Wolfgang. *A Cultural History of Climate*. Translated by Patrick Camiller, Cambridge and Malden: Polity Press, 2010.

Beer, Tanja, "The Living Stage: A Case Study in Ecoscenography," *Etudes* 1, no. 1 (2015): 1–16.

Belsey, Catherine. *Why Shakespeare?* Basingstoke and New York: Palgrave Macmillan, 2007.

Bennett, Jane. *The Enchantment of Modern Life: Attachments, Crossings and Ethics*. New Jersey: Princeton University Press, 2001.

Bennett, Jane. *Vibrant Matter: A Political Ecology of Things*. Durham and London: Duke University Press, 2010.

Bennett, Susan. *Performing Nostalgia: Shifting Shakespeare and the Contemporary Past*. New York: Routledge, 1996.

Bennett, Susan. *Theatre Audiences: A Theory of Production and Reception*. London and New York: Routledge, 1997.

Biehl, João. "Ethnography in the Way of Theory." *Cultural Anthropology* 28, no. 4 (2013): 573–97.

Billig, Michael. *Banal Nationalism*. Los Angeles and London: Sage, 1995.

Bishop, Claire. *Artificial Hells: Participatory Arts and the Politics of Spectatorship*. London: Verso, 2012.

Böhme, Gernot. "Atmosphere as the Fundamental Concept of a New Aesthetics." *Thesis Eleven* 36 (1993): 113–26.

Boecker, Bettina. *Imagining Shakespeare's Original Audience: 1660-2000: Groundlings, Gallants, Grocers*. Basingstoke and New York: Palgrave, 2015.

Boia, Lucian. *The Weather in the Imagination*. London: Reaktion Books, 2005.

Borlik, Todd. *Ecocriticism and Early Modern English Literature: Green Pastures*. London: Routledge, 2011.

Bottoms, Steve, Aaron Franks, and Paula Kramer. "Editorial: On Ecology." *Performance Research* 17, no. 4 (2012): 1–4.

Bourdieu, Pierre. *Distinction: A Social Critique of the Judgement of Taste*. Translated by Richard Nice. London: Routledge, 2010.

Bowen, Ursula. "The Shakespeare Meadow." Unpublished (2012): 1–2.

Bratton, Jacky, *New Readings in Theatre History* (Cambridge. Cambridge University Press, 2003).

Brayton, Dan. *Shakespeare's Ocean: An Ecocritical Exploration*. Charlottesville: University of Virginia Press, 2012.

Brokow, Katherine Steele and Prescott Paul. "Shakespeare in Yosemite: Applied Theatre in a National Park." *Critical Survey* 31, no. 4 (2019): 15–28.

Brook, Peter. *The Empty Space*. London: McGibbon and Kee, 1968.

Brown, John Russell. *Shakespeare and the Theatrical Event*. Basingstoke: Palgrave Macmillan, 2002.

Bruckner, Lynne and Dan Brayton, eds. *Ecocritical Shakespeare: Literary and Scientific Cultures of Early Modernity*. Farnham and Burlington: Ashgate Publishing Limited, 2011.

Buell, Lawrence. *The Environmental Imagination: Thoreau, Nature Writing, and the Formation of American Culture*. Cambridge, MA, and London: Harvard University Press, 1995.

Campbell, Janey Sevilla. "The Woodland Gods." In *The Woman's World*. 2 volumes. Edited by Oscar Wilde, 1–7. London: Cassell & Company, 1887.

Carlson, Marvin. *The Haunted Stage: Theatre as a Memory Machine*. Michigan: University of Michigan Press, 2001.

Carroll, Tim. "Practising Behaviour to Its Own Shadow." In *Shakespeare's Globe: A Theatrical Experiment*. Edited by Christie Carson and Farah Karim-Cooper, 37–44. Cambridge, Delhi, and New York: Cambridge University Press, 2008.

Casey, Edward. *Getting Back into Place*. Second Edition. Bloomington and Indianapolis: Indiana University Press, 2009.

Cave, Charles. "Popular Long-Range Weather Forecasts." *Nature* (January 1927): 52–5.

Chandler, Timothy. "Reading Atmospheres: The Ecocritical Potential of Gernot Böhme's Aesthetic Theory of Nature." *Interdisciplinary Studies in Literature and Environment* 18 (Summer 2011): 553–68.

Chaudhuri, Una. "Anthropo-Scenes: Theater and Climate Change." *JDCE* 3, no. 1 (2015): 12–27.

Chaudhuri, Una. "AnthropoScenes: Enduring Performance." Paper presented at Arts in the Anthropocene conference, Beckett Theatre, Trinity College Dublin, June 8, 2019.

Chaudhuri, Una. "'There Must Be a Lot of Fish in That Lake': Toward an Ecological Theater." *Theater* 25, no. 1 (1994): 23–31.

Chaudhuri, Una and Shonni Enelow. *Research Theatre, Climate Change, and The Ecocide Project*. New York: Palgrave Macmillan, 2014.

Cheng, Judith Chen-Hsuan and Martha C. Monroe. "Connection to Nature: Children's Affective Attitude Toward Nature." *Environment and Behavior* 44, no. 1 (2010): 31–49.

Chiari, Sophie. *Shakespeare's Representation of Weather, Climate and Environment: The Early Modern "Fated Sky."* Edinburgh: Edinburgh University Press, 2018.

Clapp, Brian W. *An Environmental History of Britain since the Industrial Revolution*. London and New York: Longman, 1994.

Clark, Timothy. "Derangements of Scale." In *Telemorphosis: Theory in the Era of Climate Change, Vol 1*. Edited by Tom Cohen, 148–66. London and Ann Arbor, MI: Open Humanities Press, 2012.

Clark, Timothy. *Ecocriticism on the Edge: The Anthropocene as a Threshold Concept*. London and New York: Bloomsbury, 2015.

Clark, Timothy. "Phenomenology." In *The Oxford Handbook of Ecocriticism*. Edited by Greg Garrard, 276–90. Oxford and New York: Oxford University Press, 2014.

Cless, Downing. *Ecology and Environment in European Drama*. New York: Routledge, 2010.

Clifford, James and George E. Marcus, eds. *Writing Culture: The Poetics and Politics of Ethnography*. Los Angeles and London: University of California Press, 1986.

Clifford, Sue and Angela King with Gail Vines, Darren Giddings and Kate O'Farrell for Common Ground. *England in Particular: A Celebration of the Commonplace, the Local, the Vernacular and the Distinctive*. London: Hodder and Stoughton, 2006.

Cochrane, Claire. *Twentieth-Century British Theatre: Industry, Art and Empire*. Cambridge: Cambridge University Press, 2011.

Cohen, Alexander. "Sweating the Vote: Heat and Abstention in the US House of Representatives." *Political Science and Politics* 45, no. 1 (2012): 74–7.

Cohen, Jeffrey Jerome, ed. *Prismatic Ecology: Ecotheory Beyond Green*. Minneapolis and London: University of Minnesota Press, 2013.

Cohen, Jeffrey Jerome and Lowell Duckert, eds. *Veer Ecology: A Companion for Environmental Thinking*. Minneapolis and London: University of Minnesota Press, 2017.

Cohen, Ralph Alan. "Directing at the Globe and the Blackfriars: Six Big Rules for Contemporary Directors." In *Shakespeare's Globe: A Theatrical Experiment*. Edited by Christie Carson and Farah Karim-Cooper, 211–25. Cambridge, Delhi, and New York: Cambridge University Press, 2008.

Conkie, Rob. "Nature's Above Art (An Illustrated Guide)." *Shakespeare Bulletin* 36, no. 3 (2018): 391–408.

Connolly, Marie. "Some Like It Mild and Not Too Wet: The Influence of Weather on Subjective Well-Being." *Journal of Happiness Studies* 14 (2013): 457–73.

Conquergood, Dwight. "Performance Studies: Interventions and Radical Research." *The Drama Review* 46, no. 2 (2002): 145–56.

Conville, David. *The Park: The Story of the Open Air Theatre*. London: Oberon Books, 2007.

Cook, John and Haydn Washington. *Climate Change Denial: Heads in the Sand*. London: Earthscan, 2011.

Cooper, David E. "The Idea of Environment," in *The Environment in Question: Ethics and Global Issues*. Edited by E. Cooper David and Joy A. Palmer, 165–80. London: Routledge, 1992.

Coult, Tony and Baz Kershaw, eds. *Engineers of the Imagination: The Welfare State Handbook*. Second Edition. London: Methuen, 1990.

Craig, Curtis, Randy W. Overbeek, Miles V. Condon, and Shannon B. Rinaldo. "A Relationship between Temperature and Aggression in NFL Football Penalties." *Journal of Sport and Health Science* 5 (2016): 205–10.

Craig, Edward Gordon. *Craig on Theatre*. Edited by J. Michael Walton. London: Methuen, [1910] 1999.

Cresswell, Tim. *Place: A Short Introduction*. Oxford: Blackwell, 2004.

Davis, Jim and Victor Emeljanow. *Reflecting the Audience: London Theatregoing, 1840–1880*. Hatfield: University of Hertfordshire Press, 2001.

Däwes, Birgit and Marc Maufort, eds. *Enacting Nature: Ecocritical Perspectives on Indigenous Performance*. Brussels: P.I.E. Lang, 2014.

Deakin, Roger. *Wildwood: A Journey through Trees*. London and New York: Penguin Books Ltd, 2007.

de Certeau, Michel. "Walking in the City." In *The Practice of Everyday Life*. Edited by S. Rendall, Berkeley, LA, and London: University of California Press, 1984.

Dessen, Alan. *Elizabethan Stage Conventions and Modern Interpreters*. Cambridge and New York: Cambridge University Press, 1984.

de Marinis, Marco. *The Semiotics of Performance*. Translated by Áine O'Healy, Bloomington and Indianapolis: Indiana University Press, 1993.

de Vet, Eliza. "Exploring Weather-Related Experiences and Practices: Examining Methodological Approaches." *Area* 45, no. 2 (2013): 198–206.

de Vet, Eliza. "Weather-Ways: Experiencing and Responding to Everyday Weather." PhD Diss., University of Wollongong, Australia, 2014.

Diamond, Elin. *Unmaking Mimesis: Essays on Feminism and Theater*. London and New York: Routledge, 1997.

Dionne, Craig and Lowell Duckert. "Introduction: Shake—Scene." *Early Modern Culture* 13, no. 5 (2018): 72–8.

Dobson, Michael. *The Making of the National Poet: Shakespeare, Adaptation, and Authorship, 1660–1769*. Oxford: Oxford University Press, 1992.

Dobson, Michael. *Shakespeare and Amateur Performance*. Cambridge: Cambridge University Press, 2011.

Dolan, Jill. *Utopia in Performance: Finding Hope at the Theater*. Ann Arbor: University of Michigan Press, 2005.

Dollimore, Jonathan and Alan Sinfield, eds. *Political Shakespeare*. Second Edition. Ithaca and London: Manchester University Press, 1994.

Drakakis, John, ed. *Alternative Shakespeares: Volume 1*. London: Routledge, 1985.

Dusinberre, Juliet. "Introduction" in *As You Like It* (London: Bloomsbury).

Egan, Gabriel. *Green Shakespeare: From Ecopolitics to Ecocriticism*. Oxon and New York: Routledge, 2006.

Egan, Gabriel. *Shakespeare and Ecocritical Theory*. London: Bloomsbury, 2015.

Estok, Simon C. "Afterword: Ecocriticism on the Lip of a Lion." In *Ecocritical Shakespeare*. Edited by Lynne Bruckner and Dan Brayton, 239–46. Farnham: Ashgate, 2011.

Estok, Simon C. *Ecocriticism and Shakespeare: Reading Ecophobia*. New York: Palgrave Macmillan, 2011.

Evernden, Neil, *The Natural Alien: Humankind and Environment*, 2nd edn. Toronto: University of Toronto Press, 1993.

Eversmann, Peter. "The Experience of the Theatrical Event." In *Theatrical Events. Borders-Dynamics-Frames*. Edited by Vicky Ann Cremona, Peter Eversmann, H. van Maanen, Willmar Sauter, and John Tulloch, 139–74. Amsterdam and New York: Rodopi, 2004.

Farabee, Darlene. *Shakespeare's Staged Spaces and Playgoers' Perceptions*. Basingstoke: Palgrave Macmillan, 2014.

Featherstone, Simon. *Englishness: Twentieth-Century Popular Culture and the Forming of English Identity*. Edinburgh: Edinburgh University Press, 2009.

Felton, Felix. "Max Reinhardt in England." *Theatre Research* 5 (1963): 134–42.

Fensham, Rachel, Eddie Paterson, and Paul Rae, eds. "On Climates." *Performance Research* 23, no. 3 (2018): 1–5.

Fiedler, Leonhard M. "Reinhardt, Shakespeare, and the 'Dreams'." In *Max Reinhardt: The Oxford Symposium*. Edited by Margaret Jacobs and John Warren, 79–95. Oxford: Oxford Polytechnic, 1986.

Flynn, Sean Masaki and Adam Eric Greenburg. "Does Weather Actually Affect Tipping? An Empirical Analysis of Time-Series Data." *Journal of Applied Psychology* 42, no. 3 (2012): 702–16.

Fortier, Mark and Daniel Fischlin, eds. *Adaptations of Shakespeare: A Critical Anthology of Plays from the Seventeenth Century to the Present*. London and New York: Routledge, 2000.

Fox, John. *Eyes on Stalks*. London: Methuen, 2002.

Fox, Kate. *Watching the English: The Hidden Rules of English Behaviour*. London: Hodder & Stoughton, 2004.

Freshwater, Helen. *Theatre & Audience*. Basingstoke: Palgrave Macmillan, 2009.

Fuchs, Elinor and Una Chaudhuri, eds. *Land/Scape/Theater*. Ann Arbor: University of Michigan Press, 2002.

Gaby, Rosemary. *Open-Air Shakespeare: Under Australian Skies*. Basingstoke: Palgrave, 2014.

Gaby, Rosemary. "Taking the Bard to the Bush: Environmental Shakespeare in Australia." *Shakespeare* 7, no. 1 (2011): 70–7.

Galafassi, Diego, Sacha Kagan, Manjana Milkoreit, María Heras, Chantal Bilodeau, Sadhbh Juarez Bourke, Andrew Merrie, Leonie Guerrero, Guðrún Pétursdóttir, and Joan David Tàbara. "'Raising the Temperature': The Arts on a Warming Planet." *Current Opinion in Environmental Sustainability* 31 (2018): 71–9.

Garrard, Greg. *Ecocriticism*. London and New York: Routledge, 2012.

Garrard, Greg. "Foreword." In *Ecocritical Shakespeare*. Edited by Dan Brayton and Lynne Bruckner, xxii–xxiv. Farnham and Burlington: Ashgate, 2011.

Geertz, Clifford. *The Interpretation of Cultures*. New York: Basic Books, 1973.

Ghosh, Amitav. *The Great Derangement: Climate Change and the Unthinkable*. Chicago and London: University of Chicago Press, 2016.

Gillies, John. *Shakespeare and the Geography of Difference*. Cambridge and New York: Cambridge University Press, 1994.

Gibson, James W. *A Reenchanted World: The Quest for a New Kinship with Nature*. New York: Holt, 2009.

Gifford, Terry. *Pastoral*. London and New York: Routledge, 1999.

Gifford, Terry. "Pastoral, Anti-Pastoral, and Post-Pastoral." In *The Cambridge Companion to Literature and Environment*. Edited by Louise Westling, 17–30. Cambridge: Cambridge University Press, 2014.

Golinski, Jan. *British Weather and the Climate of Enlightenment*. The University of Chicago Press: Chicago and London, 2007.

Golinski, Jan. "Time, Talk, and the Weather in Eighteenth-Century Britain." In *Weather, Climate, Culture*. Edited by Sarah Strauss and Ben Orlove, 17–38. Oxford and New York: Berg, 2003.

Gruffudd, Pyrs. "Reach for the Sky: The Air and English Cultural Nationalism." *Landscape Research* 16, no. 2 (1991): 19–24.

Guéguen, Nicolas. "Weather and Courtship Behavior: A Quasi-Experiment with the Flirty Sunshine." *Social Influence* 8, no. 4 (2013): 312–19.

Guéguen, Nicolas and Jordy Stefa. "Hitckhiking and the 'Sunshine Driver': Further Effects of Weather Conditions of Helping Behavior." *Psychological Reports: Sociocultural Issues in Psychology* 113, no. 3 (2013): 994–1000.

Gurr, Andrew and Mariko Ichikawa. *Staging in Shakespeare's Theatres*. Oxford: Oxford University Press, 2000.

Hadley, Bree. *Disability, Public Space Performance and Spectatorship: Unconscious Performers*. Basingstoke and New York: Palgrave Macmillan, 2013.

Hamilton, Jennifer Mae. *This Contentious Storm: An Ecocritical and Performance History of King Lear*. London: Bloomsbury, 2017.

Haraway, Donna. *Staying with the Trouble: Making Kin in the Chthulucene*. Durham and London: Duke University Press, 2016.

Harley, Trevor A. "Nice Weather for the Time of Year: The British Obsession with the Weather." In *Weather, Climate, Culture*. Edited by Sarah Strauss and Ben Orlove, 103–16. Oxford and New York: Berg, 2003.

Hartwig, David. "The Place of Shakespeare: Performing *King Lear* and *The Tempest* in an Endangered World." PhD diss., University of Warwick, 2010.

Harvie, Jen. *Staging the UK*. Manchester and New York: Manchester University Press, 2005.

Heddon, Deirdre and Sally Mackey. "Environmentalism, Performance and Applications: Uncertainties and Emancipations." *Research in Drama Education* 17, no. 2 (2012): 163–92.

Heim, Caroline. *Audience as Performer: The Changing Role of Theatre Audiences in the Twenty-first Century*. London and New York: Routledge, 2016.

Heim, Wallace. "Epilogue." In *Readings in Performance and Ecology*. Edited by Wendy Arons and Theresa J. May, 211–16. Basingstoke and New York: Palgrave Macmillan, 2012.

Heise, Ursula K. *Sense of Place and Sense of Planet: The Environmental Imagination of the Global*. Oxford and New York: Oxford University Press, 2008.

Hindson, Catherine. *London's West End Actresses and the Origins of Celebrity Charity, 1880–1920*. Iowa City: University of Iowa Press, 2016.

Hodge, Stephen and Cathy Turner. "Site: Between Ground and Groundlessness." In *Histories and Practices of Live Art*. Edited by Deirdre Heddon and Jennie Klein, 91–121. Basingstoke: Palgrave Macmillan, 2012.

Höfele, Andreas. *Stage, Stake and Scaffold: Humans and Animals in Shakespeare's Theatre*. Oxford: Oxford University Press, 2011.

Hudson, Julie. *The Environment on Stage: Scenery or Shapeshifter*. New York: Routledge, 2019.

Hughes, Donald J. *What Is Environmental History?* London: Polity Press, 2006.

Hulme, Mike. "Climate." *Environmental Humanities* 6 (2015): 175–8.

Hulme, Mike. "Climate Change and Memory." In *Memory in the Twenty-First Century*. Edited by Simon Groes, 159–62. Basingstoke and New York: Palgrave, 2016.

Hulme, Mike. *Weathered: Cultures of Climate*. Los Angeles and London: Sage, 2017.

Ingold, Tim. *Being Alive: Essays on Movement, Knowledge and Description*. Oxon and New York: Routledge, 2011.

Ingold, Tim. "Earth, Sky, Wind, and Weather." *Journal of the Royal Anthropological Institute* 13, no. 1 (2007): 19–38.

Jerolmack, Colin. *The Global Pigeon*. Chicago and London: Chicago University Press, 2013.

Johanson, Katya and Hilary Glow. "A Virtuous Circle: The Positive Evaluation Phenomenon in Arts Audience Research." *Participations Journal of Audience & Reception Studies* 12, no. 1 (2015): 254–70.

Jones, Gwilym. "Environmental Renaissance Studies." *Literature Compass* 14, no. 10 (2017): 1–15.

Jones, Gwilym. *Shakespeare's Storms*. Manchester: Manchester University Press, 2015.

Kämpfer, Sylvia and Michael Mutz. "On the Sunny Side of Life: Sunshine Effects on Life Satisfaction." *Social Indicators Research* 110 (2013): 579–95.

Kent, Alan M. "'Art Thou of Cornish Crew?' Shakespeare, *Henry V* and Cornish Identity." *Cornish Studies* 4 (1996): 7–25.

Kent, Alan M. *The Theatre of Cornwall: Space, Place, Performance*. Bristol: Redcliffe Westcliffe Books, 2010.

Keller, Matthew C., Barbara L. Fredrickson, Oscar Ybarra, Stéphanie Côté, Kareem Johnson, Joe Mikels, Anne Conway, and Tor Wager. "A Warm Heart and a Clear Head. The Contingent Effects of Weather on Mood and Cognition." *Psychological Science* 16, no. 9 (2005): 724–31.

Kerridge, Richard. "An Ecocritic's Macbeth." In *Ecocritical Shakespeare*. Edited by Lynne Bruckner and Dan Brayton, 193–210. Farnham and Burlington: Ashgate, 2011.

Kerridge, Richard. "Green Pleasures." In *The Politics and Pleasures of Consuming Differently*. Edited by Kate Soper, Martin Ryle, and Lyn Thomas, 130–53. London: Palgrave, 2009.

Kershaw, Baz. *Theatre Ecology: Environments and Performance Events*. Cambridge and New York: Cambridge University Press, 2007.

Kiernan, Pauline. *Staging Shakespeare at the Globe*. London: Macmillan Press, 1999.

Klein, Naomi. *This Changes Everything*. London and New York: Allen Lane, Penguin, 2014.
Kulmala, Dan. "'Is All Our Company Here?': Shakespeare Festivals as Fields of Cultural Production." *English Language and Literature Studies* 5, no. 1 (2015): 1–12.
Kwon, Miwon. *One Place after Another: Site-specific Art and Locational Identity*. Cambridge, MA: MIT Press, 2004.
Lack, Martin. *The Denial of Science: Analysing Climate Change Scepticism in the UK*. Bloomington: AuthorHouse, 2013.
Lakoff, George. "Why It Matters How We Frame the Environment." *Environmental Communication: A Journal of Nature and Culture* 4, no. 1 (2010): 70–81.
Latour, Bruno. *We Have Never Been Modern*. Translated by Catherine Porter. Cambridge, MA: Harvard University Press, 1993.
Lavery, Carl. "Introduction." In *Performance and Ecology: What Can Theatre Do?* Edited by Carl Lavery, 1–8. London and New York: Routledge, 2018.
Lavery, Carl. "From Weather to Climate." *Performance Research* 23, no. 4–5 (2018): 6–10.
Lavery, Carl. "Rethinking the *Dérive*: Drifting and Theatricality in Theatre and Performance Studies." *Performance Research* 23, no. 7 (2018): 1–15.
Lawson, Helen. *A Summer Hamlet* Documentary Produced by Dusthouse, 2013.
Lazarovich-Hrebelianovich, Princess (Eleanor Hulda Calhoun). *Pleasures and Palaces; The Memoirs of Princess Lazarovich-Hrebelianovich*. New York: The Century Company, 1915.
Leddy, David. *Susurrus*. Glasgow: Fire Exit Ltd, 2009.
Lefebvre, Henri. *The Production of Space*. Oxford: Basil Blackwell, 1991.
Levine, George. "High and Low: Ruskin and the Novelists." In *Nature and the Victorian Imagination*. Edited by U. C. Knoepflmacher and G. B. Tennyson, 137–52. London and Los Angeles: University of California Press, 1977.
Lopez, Jeremy. "Small-time Shakespeare: The Edinburgh Festival Fringe, 2003." *Shakespeare Quarterly* 55, no. 2 (2004): 200–11.
Lucas, John. *England and Englishness: Ideas of Nationhood in English Poetry, 1688–1900*. London: The Hogarth Press, 1990.
Mabey, Richard. *Turned Out Nice Again: On Living with the Weather*. London: Profile Books, 2013.
Mackey, Sally and Sarah Cole. "Cuckoos in the Nest: Performing Place, Artists and Excess." *Applied Theatre Research* 1, no. 1 (2013): 43–61.
Madison, D. Soyini. *Critical Ethnography: Method, Ethics, and Performance*. Thousand Oaks, London, and New Delhi: Sage, 2005.
Maitland, Sara. *Gossip from the Forest: The Tangled Roots of Our Forests and Fairy Tales*. London: Granta Publications, 2012.
Maley, Willy and Philip Schwyzer. *Shakespeare and Wales: From the Marches to the Assembly*. Farnham and Burlington: Ashgate, 2010.
Maloney, Alison. *And Now the Weather: A Celebration of Our National Obsession*. London: Penguin, 2017.
Marcus, Sharon. *Between Women: Friendship, Desire, and Marriage in Victorian England*. Princeton and Oxford: Princeton University Press, 2007.

Marinelli, Peter. *Pastoral*. London: Methuen and Co. Ltd, 1971.
Martin, Randall. *Shakespeare & Ecology*. Oxford: Oxford University Press, 2015.
Martin, Randall and Evelyn O'Malley. "Introduction: Eco-Shakespeare in Performance." *Shakespeare Bulletin* 36, no. 3 (2018): 377–90.
Mason, Bim. *Street Theatre and Other Outdoor Performance*. London and New York: Routledge, 1992.
Massey, Doreen. "A Global Sense of Place." In *Reading Human Geography*. Edited by T. Barnes and D. Gregory, 315–23. London: Arnold, 1997.
Massie-Blomfield, Amber. *Twenty Theatres to See before You Die*. London: Penned in the Margins, 2018.
May, Theresa J. "Tú eres mi otro yo—Staying with the Trouble: Ecodramaturgy & the AnthropoScene." *The Journal of American Drama and Theatre* 29, no. 2 (2017): 1–18.
Mayer, F. Stephan F. and Cynthia McPherson Frantz. "The Connectedness to Nature Scale: A Measure of Individuals' Feeling in Community with Nature." *Journal of Environmental Psychology* 24, no. 4 (2004): 503–15.
McAuley, Gay. *Space in Performance: Making Meaning in the Theatre*. Ann Arbor, Michigan: University of Michigan Press, 2000.
McConachie, Bruce A. *Engaging Audiences: A Cognitive Approach to Spectating in the Theatre*. Basingstoke: Palgrave Macmillan, 2008.
McCormack, Derek. *Atmospheric Things On the Allure of Elemental Envelopment*. Durham and London: Duke University Press, 2018.
McCormack, Derek. *Refrains for Moving Bodies: Experience and Experiment in Affective Spaces*. Durham and London: Duke University Press, 2013.
Mentz, Steve. *At the Bottom of Shakespeare's Ocean*. London and New York: Continuum, 2009.
Mentz, Steve. "Shakespeare, Ecological Crisis, and the Resources of Genre." In *Ecocritical Shakespeare*. Edited by. Dan Brayton and Lynne Bruckner, 162–3. Farnham and Burlington: Ashgate, 2011.
Mentz, Steve. "Strange Weather in *King Lear*." *Shakespeare* 6, no. 2 (2010): 139–52.
Merchant, Carolyn. *Reinventing Eden: The Fate of Nature in Western Culture*. New York: Routledge, 2004.
Merleau-Ponty, Maurice. *Phenomenology of Perception*. Translated by D. A. Landes. London: Routledge, 2012.
Milne, Richard I. and Richard J. Abbott. "Origin and Evolution of Invasive Naturalized Material of *Rhododendron Ponticum* L. in the British Isles." *Molecular Ecology* 9 (2000): 541–56.
Minton, Gretchen E. "'… The Season of All Natures': Montana Shakespeare in the Parks' Global Warming *Macbeth*." *Shakespeare Bulletin* 36, no. 3 (2018): 429–48.
Mitman, Greg. "Reflections on the Plantationocene: A Conversation with Donna Haraway and Anna Tsing." June 18, 2019, https://edgeeffects.net/haraway-tsing-plantationocene/.
Monks, Aoife, *The Actor in Costume* (Basingstoke and New York: Palgrave, 2013).

Moores, Shaun. *Interpreting Audiences: The Ethnography of Media Consumption*. London: Sage, 1993.
Morgan, Ian, Evelyn O'Malley, Ciaran Clarke, and Gey Pin Ang. "Answer the Question: How Does Nature Nurture Your Training." *Theatre, Dance and Performance Training* 83 (2017): 350–55.
Morton, Timothy. *Ecology without Nature: Rethinking Environmental Aesthetics*. Cambridge, MA: Harvard University Press, 2007.
Morton, Timothy. *The Ecological Thought*. Cambridge and London: Harvard University Press, 2010.
Morton, Timothy. *Hyperobjects: Philosophy and Ecology after the End of the World*. Minneapolis: University of Minnesota Press, 2013.
Mulryne, J. R. and Margaret Shewring. *Shakespeare's Globe Rebuilt*. Cambridge: Cambridge University Press, 1997.
Munroe, Jennifer and Rebecca Laroche. *Shakespeare and Ecofeminist Theory*. London: Bloomsbury, 2017.
Nardizzi, Vin. *Wooden Os: Shakespeare's Theatres and England's Trees*. Toronto, Buffalo, and London: University of Toronto Press, 2013.
Neimanis, Astrida and Jennifer Mae Hamilton. "Composting Feminisms and Environmental Humanities." *Environmental Humanities* 10, no. 2 (2018), 501–27.
Neimanis, Astrida and Jennifer Mae Hamilton. "Open Space Weathering." *Feminist Review* 118, no. 1 (2018): 80–4.
Neimanis, Astrida and Rachel Loewen-Walker. "*Weathering*: Climate Change and the 'Thick Time' of Transcorporeality." *Hypatia* 29, no. 3 (2014): 558–75.
Nicholson, Helen, Nadine Holdsworth, and Jane Milling. *The Ecologies of Amateur Theatre*. London: Palgrave Macmillan, 2018.
Nixon, Rob. *Slow Violence and the Environmentalism of the Poor*. Cambridge, MA: Harvard University Press, 2011.
Nobbs, Patrick. *The Story of the British and Their Weather: From Frost Fairs to Indian Summers*. Gloucestershire: Amberley, 2015.
Norgaard, Kari M. *Living in Denial: Climate Change, Emotions, and Everyday Life*. Cambridge, MA: MIT Press, 2011.
O'Dair, Sharon. "Slow Shakespeare: An Eco-critique of 'Method.'" In *Early modern Ecostudies: From the Florentine Codex to Shakespeare*. Edited by Thomas Hallock, Ivo Kamps, and Karen L. Raber, 11–30. Basingstoke: Palgrave Macmillan, 2008.
O'Malley, Evelyn. "Imagining Arden: Audience Responses to Place and Participation at Taking Flight Theatre Company's *as You Like It*." *Participations: Journal of Audience and Reception Studies* 13 (2016): 512–29.
O'Malley, Evelyn. "Theatre for a Changing Climate." In *Posthumanism in Higher Education: A Lecturer's Portfolio*. Edited by Carol Taylor and Annouchka Baile, 55–71. Basingstoke and New York: Palgrave, 2019.
O'Malley, Evelyn. "'To Weather a Play': Audiences, Outdoor Shakespeares, and Avant-Garde Nostalgia at The Willow Globe." *Shakespeare Bulletin* 36, no. 3 (2018): 409–27.

O'Malley, Evelyn. "You Do (Not) Assist the Storm." *Performance Research* 21, no. 2 (2016): 81–4.
Oreskes, Naomi and Erik M. Conway. *Merchants of Doubt: How a Handful of Scientists Obscured the Truth on Issues from Tobacco Smoke to Global Warming*. New York: Bloomsbury, 2010.
Palmer, Scott. *Light*. Basingstoke and New York: Palgrave Macmillan, 2013.
Pearson, Mike. *In Comes I: Performance, Memory and Landscape*. Exeter: University of Exeter Press, 2006.
Pearson, Mike. *Site-Specific Performance*. Basingstoke and New York: Palgrave Macmillan, 2010.
Pearson, Mike and Michael Shanks. *Theatre/Archaeology*. London: Routledge, 2001.
Pevsner, Nikolaus. *The Englishness of English Art*. London: The Architectural Press, 1955.
Philips, Dana. "Review Article *Ecology without Nature*." *The Oxford Literary Review* 32, no. 1 (2010): 151–61.
Platt, Will. "Subverting the Spectacle: A Critical Study of Culture Jamming as Activist Performance." PhD Diss., University of Exeter, 2019.
Powell, Kerry. *Acting Wilde: Victorian Sexuality, Theatre, and Oscar Wilde*. Cambridge: Cambridge University Press, 2009.
Purcell, Stephen. *Popular Shakespeare: Simulation and Subversion on the Modern Stage*. Basingstoke: Palgrave, 2009.
Purcell, Stephen. *Shakespeare and Audience in Practice*. Basingstoke: Palgrave, 2013.
Purcell, Stephen. "A Shared Experience: Shakespeare and Popular Theatre." *Performance Research* 10, no. 3 (2005): 74–84.
Preedy, Chloe. *Theatres of the Air: Representing Aerial Environments on the Early Modern Stage, 1576-1609*. Forthcoming.
Prescott, Paul. *Reviewing Shakespeare: Journalism and Performance from the Eighteenth Century to the Present*. Cambridge: Cambridge University Press, 2013.
Radbourne, Jennifer, Hilary Glow, and Katya Johanson, eds. *The Audience Experience: A Critical Analysis of Audiences in the Performing Arts*. Bristol: Intellect, 2013.
Rancière, Jacques. *The Emancipated Spectator*. London and New York: Verso, 2009.
Reason, Matthew. "Asking the Audience: Audience Research and the Experience of Theatre." *About Performance* 10 (2010): 15–34.
Reason, Matthew and Anja Molle Lindelof, eds. *Experiencing Liveness in Contemporary Performance: Interdisciplinary Perspectives*. London: Routledge, 2016.
Reason, Matthew and Kirsty Sedgman. "Editors' Introduction: Themed Section on Theatre Audiences." *Participations* 12, no. 1 (2015): 117–22.
Rebellato, Dan. "When We Talk of Horses: Or, What Do We See When We See a Play?" *Performance Research* 14, no. 1 (2009): 17–28.
Reinelt, Janelle. "What UK Spectators Know: Understanding How We Come to Value Theatre." *Theatre Journal* 66, no. 3 (2014): 337–61.

Rose, Deborah Bird. "Slowly Writing into the Anthropocene." In *TEXT Special Issue 20: Writing Creates Ecology and Ecology Creates Writing*. Edited by Matthew Harrison, Deborah Bird Rose, Lorraine Shannon, and Kim Satchell (October 2013). http://nla.gov.au/nla.arc-10069-20160717-0026-www.textjournal.com.au/speciss/issue20/content.htm.

Ruhl, Sarah. *100 Essays I Don't Have Time to Write: On Umbrellas and Sword Fights, Parades, Dogs, Fire Alarms, Children, and Theater*. New York: Farrar, Straus and Giroux, 2014.

Rushdie, Salman. "Introduction." In Angela Carter, *Burning Your Boats: Collected Short Stories*, ix–xiv. London: Vintage Books, 1996.

Ryan, Richard M., Netta Weinstein, Jessey Bernstein, Kirk Warren Brown, Louis Mistretta, and Marylène Gagné. "Vitalizing Effects of Being Outdoors and in Nature." *Journal of Environmental Psychology* 30, no. 2 (2010): 159–68.

Ryle, Martin and Kate Soper. *To Relish the Sublime?* London and New York: Verso Books, 2002.

Sager, Jenny. *The Aesthetics of Spectacle in Early Modern Drama and Modern Cinema: Robert Greene's Theatre of Attractions*. Basingstoke: Palgrave, 2013.

Salazar, Rebecca. "A Rogue and Pleasant Stage: Performing Ecology in Outdoor Shakespeares." *Shakespeare Bulletin* 36, no. 3 (2018): 449–66.

Sanders, Julie. *The Cambridge Introduction to Early Modern Drama, 1576–1642*. Cambridge: Cambridge University Press, 2014.

Sauter, Willmar. "The Audience." In *The Cambridge Companion to Theatre History*. Edited by David Wiles and Christine Dymkowski, 169–83. Cambridge: Cambridge University Press, 2013.

Schechner, Richard. "6 Axioms for Environmental Theatre." *The Drama Review* 12, no. 3 (1968): 41–64.

Schmiedeberg, Claudia and Jette Schröder. "Does Weather Really Influence the Measurement of Life Satisfaction?" *Social Indicators Research* 117 (2014): 387–99.

Schwyzer, Philip. "Shakespeare's Arts of Reenactment: Henry at Blackfriars, Richard at Rougemont." In *The Arts of Remembrance in Early Modern England: Memorial Cultures of the Post Reformation*. Edited by Andrew Gordon and Thomas Rist, 194–7. Farnham and Burlington: Ashgate, 2013.

Scollen, Rebecca. "Does the 'Shakespeare' in Shakespeare-in-the-park Matter? An Investigation of Attendances at and Attitudes to the University of Southern Queensland Shakespeare in the Park Festival." *Applied Theatre Researcher/IDEA Journal* 12, no. 6 (2011): 1–16.

Sedgman, Kirsty. "Audience Experience in an Anti-expert Age: A Survey of Theatre Audience Research." *Theatre Research International* 42, no. 3 (2017): 307–22.

Sedgman, Kirsty. *Locating the Audience: How People Found Value in National Theatre Wales*. Bristol: Intellect, 2016.

Sedgman, Kirsty. "On Rigour in Theatre Audience Research." *Contemporary Theatre Review* 29, no. 4 (2019): 462–79.

Sedgman, Kirsty. "We Need to Talk about (How We Talk about) Audiences." October 2019, https://www.contemporarytheatrereview.org/2019/we-need-to-talk-about-how-we-talk-about-audiences/.
Serres, Michel. *The Natural Contract*. Translated by E. MacArthur and W. Paulson, Michigan: University of Michigan Press, 1995.
Seymour, Nicole. *Bad Environmentalism: Irony and Irreverence in the Ecological Age*. Minneapolis and London: University of Minnesota Press, 2018.
Shepherd-Barr, Kirsten E. *Modern Drama: A Very Short Introduction*. Oxford: Oxford University Press, 2016.
Simmons, Ian G. *An Environmental History of Great Britain: From 10,000 Years Ago to the Present*. Edinburgh: Edinburgh University Press, 2001.
Skey, Michael. *National Belonging and Everyday Life: The Significance of Nationhood in an Uncertain World*. Basingstoke: Palgrave Macmillan, 2011.
Small Wonders Frequently Asked Questions. Arts Council England, 2012: 1–3.
Smith, Bruce R. "Within, without, Withinwards: The Circulation of Sound." In *Shakespeare's Theatres and the Effects of Performance*. Edited by Farah Karim-Cooper and Tiffany Stern, 171–94. London: Bloomsbury, 2013.
Smith, Philp. "Turning Tourists into Performers: Revaluing Agency, Action and Space in Sites of Heritage Tourism." *Performance Research* 18, no. 2 (2010): 102–13.
Smith, Philip and Nicolas Howe. *Climate Change as Social Drama: Global Warming in the Public Sphere*. New York: Cambridge University Press, 2015.
Solnit, Rebecca. *Wanderlust: A History of Walking*. London: Verso, 2001.
Soper, Kate. "Passing Glories and Romantic Retrievals: Avant-garde Nostalgia and Hedonist Renewal." In *Ecocritical Theory: New European Approaches*. Edited by Kate Rigby and Axel Goodbody, 17–29. Charlottesville and London: University of Virginia Press, 2011.
Soper, Kate. "An Alternative Hedonism." *Radical Philosophy* 92 (1998): 28–38; and "Alternative Hedonism, Cultural Theory and the Role of Aesthetic Revisioning," *Cultural Studies* 22, no. 5 (2008): 567–87.
Soper, Kate. *What Is Nature?* Oxford: Blackwell, 1994.
States, Bert O. *Great Reckonings in Little Rooms: On the Phenomenology of Theater*. London and California: University of California Press, 1981.
Strauss, Sarah and Ben Orlove, eds. *Weather, Climate, Culture*. Oxford and New York: Berg, 2003.
Styan, J. L. *Max Reinhardt*. Cambridge: Cambridge University Press, 1982.
Taylor, Diana. *The Archive and the Repertoire: Performing Cultural Memory in the Americas*. Durham and London: Duke University Press, 2003.
Thornes, John E. "Cultural Climatology and the Representation of Sky, Atmosphere, Weather and Climate in Selected Art Works of Constable, Monet and Eliasson." *Geoforum* 39 (2008): 570–80.
Thrift, Nigel. *Non-representational Theory: Space|Politics|Affect*. Oxon and New York: Routledge, 2008.

Tilley, Christopher. *Interpreting Landscapes: Geologies, Topographies, Identities*. Walnut Creek, California: Left Coast Press, 2010.

Tollini, Frederick Paul. *The Shakespeare Productions of Max Reinhardt*. Lewiston, Queenston, and Lampeter: The Edwin Mellon Press, 2004.

Tomlin, Liz. *Political Dramaturgies and Theatre Spectatorship: Provocations for Change*. London and New York: Methuen, 2019.

Tribble, Evelyn. *Cognition in the Globe: Attention and Memory in Shakespeare's Theatre*. Basingstoke: Palgrave Macmillan, 2013.

Tsing, Anna, Heather Swanson, Elaine Gan, and Nils Bubandt, eds. *Arts of Living on a Damaged Planet*. Minneapolis and London: University of Minnesota Press, 2017.

Tulloch, John. *Shakespeare and Chekhov in Production and Reception: Theatrical Events and Their Audiences*. Iowa City: University of Iowa Press, 2005.

Vanek, Morgan. "Where the Weather Comes From." *The Goose Journal* 17, no. 1, 46 (2018): 1–13.

Walmsley, Ben. *Audience Engagement in the Performing Arts: A Critical Analysis*. Basingstoke and New York: Palgrave Macmillan, 2019.

Watson, Lyall. *Heaven's Breath: A Natural History of the Wind*. New York: New York Review of Books, 2019.

Watson, Robert N. *Back to Nature: The Green and the Real in the Late Renaissance*. Philadelphia: University of Pennsylvania Press, 2006.

Watson, Robert N. "The Ecology of Self in a *A Midsummer Night's Dream*." In *Ecocritical Shakespeare*. Edited by Lynne Bruckner and Dan Brayton, 33–56. Farnham and Burlington: Ashgate, 2011.

Weber, Susan. *E. W. Godwin: Aesthetic Movement Architect and Designer*. New Haven: Yale University Press, 1999.

Welton, Martin. "Making Sense of Air: Choreography and Climate in *Calling Tree*." *Performance Research* 23, no. 3 (2018): 80–90.

White, Gareth. *Audience Participation in Theatre. Aesthetics of the Invitation*. Basingstoke and New York: Palgrave Macmillan, 2013.

Wilkie, Fiona. "The Production of 'Site': Site-Specific Theatre." In *A Concise Companion to Contemporary British and Irish Drama*. Edited by Nadine Holdsworth and Mary Luckhurst, 87–106. Oxford: Blackwell, 2008.

Williams, David. "Weather." *Performance Research* 11, no. 3 (2006): 142–4.

Williams, Gary Jay. *Our Moonlight Revels: A Midsummer Night's Dream in the Theatre*. Iowa: University of Iowa Press, 1997.

Williams, Raymond. *The Country and the City*. London: Hogarth, 1985.

Williams, Raymond. *Culture and Materialism*. London and New York: Verso Books, 1980.

Williams, Raymond. *Keywords: A Vocabulary of Culture and Society*. London: Fontana Press, 1976.

Williams, Raymond. *Marxism and Literature*. Oxford and New York: Oxford University Press, 1977.

Woods, Penelope. "Globe Audiences: Spectatorship and Reconstruction at Shakespeare's Globe." PhD Diss., Queen Mary University of London, 2012.
Woynarski, Lisa. "A Brief Introduction to the Field of Performance and Ecology." March 10, 2015. https://performanceandecology.wordpress.com/2015/03/10/a-brief-introduction-to-the-field-of-performance-and-ecology/.
Wylie, John. *Landscape*. London and New York: Routledge, 2007.
Zhong, Bu and Yong Zhou. "'Under the Weather': The Weather Effects on U.S. Newspaper Coverage of the 2008 Beijing Olympics." *Mass Communication and Society* 15, no. 4 (2012): 559–77.

Index

Abram, David 41, 96, 108, 129, 156, 165
activism 40, 178, 189
adaptation 16, 125, 137, 139, 141
Aesthetic movement 46, 53
affect 13, 155, 185, 192, 198
After the Tempest 123, 146
 Teatro Vivo 137–44
Ahmed, Sara 155
Aires, Ben 108, 111
Alaimo, Stacy 17, 174, 191
Allen, Connor 136–7
All's Well That Ends Well 4, 27, 41, 109
 at Willow Globe 109, 157–8
amateur 5, 46, 58, 69, 77, 98–9
Anderson, Ben 155, 171
anthropocene 1, 3, 38, 40, 69–70, 111, 113, 156, 195, 197–8
anthropomorphizing/anthropomorphized 60, 115, 117, 132, 144
Antony and Cleopatra 158, 160, 165, 170–1
 at Minack 158, 165
arcadia 47, 62, 65
Arclight Theatre Company 188
Arden, Forest of 35, 38, 52, 54–9, 61–2, 64, 88, 125, 131–3, 135–6, 146, 178, 180, 193–200
aristocracy 65, 89
Armstrong, Simon 195
Arnold, Matthew 37
 Culture and Anarchy 35
Aronson, Arnold 12, 37
Arons, Wendy, *Readings in Performance and Ecology* 27
Arts Council England 7
assemblage 81, 104–5
As You Like It 5, 38, 40, 46–62, 64, 66–70. See also Pastoral Players, The
 audience research 46–7, 55, 57, 59–60, 62, 64, 81, 130–2, 181–2, 184, 200
 at Coombe 38, 46–64, 66–70, 80
 HandleBards, The 40, 178–86

Taking Flight Theatre Company 130–9, 143, 146
Atherton, James 186
Atlantic Ocean 5, 50, 98, 171
atmosphere 8, 39, 49, 57, 66, 74, 81, 104, 114, 152–61, 163, 166, 170–6
Attenborough, David 120, 198
 Blue Planet 194
audience research 167–8
 All's Well That Ends Well 158
 As You Like It 46–7, 55, 57, 59–60, 62, 64, 81, 130–2, 181–2, 184, 200
 class 35, 48, 89
 ethnography and 28–34
 green language 154–7
 Hamlet 173
 Merry Wives of Windsor, The 112–13
 Midsummer Night's Dream, A 65–70, 72–3, 75–7, 79, 81, 125–6, 132–3
 Tempest, The 82–3, 101–3, 105, 107
 weathering performance 60, 65, 80–1, 84, 92, 120–2, 146–7, 151–2, 179
Austin, Alfred 56, 58
Austin, Sophie 123, 138, 142, 143 n.38

Bachelard, Gaston 162
Barad, Karen 17, 191
Barking Park 139, 141
Beattie, Maureen 196
beauty/beautiful 38, 45, 48, 53, 55, 60, 62–3, 70, 77, 81–2, 84–5, 114, 138, 140, 142, 154, 164–5, 167, 171, 185
 Minack's landscape 96–101
Behringer, Wolfgang, *A Cultural History of Climate* 21
Belsey, Catherine 124
Bennett, Charlotte 123
Bennett, Jane 100, 104, 106, 145, 194
 Enchantment of Modern Life, The 145
 Vibrant Matter: A Political Ecology of Things 100 n.13

Bennett, Susan 118, 183
Best, Sue 108, 110, 112
Billig, Michael 23–4, 61
Blaise Castle 131, 133
blustery 26, 60, 181, 186
bodies 16–17, 19–20, 32, 59, 73–4, 81, 96, 129, 155–6, 171–4, 183, 190–2, 201
Bogdanov, Michael 110
Böhme, Gernot 154–6
Boia, Lucian 20, 91, 157
  The Weather in the Imagination 21
Borlik, Todd 121
Bottoms, Steve 14, 27
Bourdieu, Pierre 35
Bowen, Philip 108, 110, 112
BP (British Petroleum) 178, 186–93
BP or not BP 40, 178, 186–90, 192–3
Brayton, Dan 102
Bread and Puppet Theatre 6
breeze 60, 175, 171
British Empire/imperialism 23–4, 39, 55, 78, 107, 110
Britishness 23, 39, 168. *See also* Englishness
Britton, Jasper 152
Broad, Leah 89
Brook, Peter 11
Brown, John Russell 6
Buell, Lawrence 47–8, 57

Cade, Rowena 98–9, 121, 166
Calhoun, Eleanor 38, 46, 50, 89, 181
Californian Shakespeare Festival 85
Campbell, Janey Sevilla, Lady Archibald 38, 45, 49–50, 59, 69, 89, 181
  "The Woodland Gods" 49, 53 n.32, 67
Campbell, John 22
Carlson, Marvin 11 n.39, 38
Carroll, Madeleine 84
Carroll, Sydney 80–1, 81 n.37, 83–5
Carroll, Tim 8–9, 110, 152
Carter, Angela, *Burning Your Boats* 124
Casey, Edward 100, 146
Cave, Charles 79
Chandler, Timothy 156–7
Chapter Arts Centre 131
Chaudhuri, Una 4, 13, 27, 40, 128, 164–5
Chiari, Sophie 9
chilly 8, 60, 167

Clark, Timothy 4, 156–7, 187
Cless, Downing 5, 13, 98
Clifford, James 31
Clifford, Sue 24
climate change
  anthropogenic contexts 91, 144, 151, 154, 156, 176–7, 192
  human reaction to 21, 41, 175
  lobbying 187, 189
  scientific facts 2, 74
  as social drama 19–20, 179–80
Cochrane, Claire 39
Cohen, Ralph Alan 169
comfort 59–60, 80, 83
confidence 32, 74
control 41, 59–61, 64, 74, 77, 79–80, 84, 90–2, 106, 139, 145, 180, 186, 202
Conkie, Rob 26
Conquergood, Dwight 20
Cornishness 95, 99. *See also* Cornwall
Cornwall 5, 95, 98, 106, 109, 152
costumes 51, 59–60
Craig, Gordon Edward 40
Craven, Hawes 45
Cresswell, Tim 32, 100
culture/nature dualism 15, 34–7, 41, 53, 57, 70
cultural materialism 6, 32, 34–5, 73–4
Cyfarthfa Castle 131, 133, 136, 157–8
Cymbeline 4, 111

dance 15, 87, 190–1, 198, 201
Daniel, John 144–5
Davis, Jim 30
Davison, Elise 123, 131
Dawson, Naomi 194–5, 199
Deakin, Roger, *Wildwood: A Journey through Trees* 124
Dell amphitheater, Stratford-upon-Avon 188
depth 96–7, 130–1
Dery, Mark 189
Dessen, Alan 160
de Vet, Eliza 16
Diamond, Elin 128–9
Dillon-Reams, Eleanor 180–1
disability 99, 136
disjuncture 10, 64, 104
ditch vision 146–7

Dixon, Tom 179
Dobson, Michael 5–6, 35, 46, 68, 98–9, 106, 132, 134–5, 167
Dolan, Jill 33
Draper, Amy 187
drizzle 174, 201
dry 19, 46, 59, 68, 81, 119
Dündar, Can 187
Dusinberre, Juliet 200
dusk 66, 108, 143, 157, 159–60

ecocriticism 3, 10, 25–8, 41, 47
ecodramaturgy 27
ecomimesis 51, 125, 147
ecophobia 168
Elizabethan Stage Society 69
Elizabethan theater 1, 6, 11–12, 118, 127, 152, 159–60, 183. *See also* original practices
Emeljanow, Victor 30
enchantment 39, 77, 144–5
Englishness 23, 65, 95, 132, 181, 202. *See also* Britishness
English Shakespeare Company 110
Enlightenment 21–2, 167
entanglement/entangled 34–5, 130
environment 2–3, 12–14, 21–2, 28, 30, 34–7, 54, 70, 76, 89, 92, 103, 110, 114, 120–1, 125, 127–9, 133–4, 139, 155, 161, 170, 185
Escolme, Bridget 13
Estok, Simon 168
ethnography 20, 28–9, 96, 125
Evernden, Neil 74
Eversmann, Peter 30, 33
excess 87, 91, 98, 106, 117, 166
exposure/exposed 1–2, 17, 21, 41, 64, 66, 70, 74, 90, 102, 128, 153, 179, 200

Factory, The 110
Faculty Glade 85
Faculty Grove 88
fairy/fairies 54, 72–3, 76–7, 81–2, 87–8, 102–3, 113–17, 124–30, 132–3, 136, 141, 143, 146–7, 163
fairy tales 35, 124–30, 133, 136, 141, 143, 146–7, 163
Felton, Felix 76, 89, 89 n.84
Feral X 187
Fink, Charlie 194

fireflies 71–3, 86, 90, 92
forest 13, 55–6, 58–9, 61–2, 64, 67, 72, 84, 88, 113–14, 124–7, 129–34, 141, 145, 163, 178, 195, 200
Fossil Fuel Mischief Festival 178, 186, 188
  Day of the Living 187
  #WeAreArrested 187
Fox, Kate, *Watching the English* 24
frame 4, 14–15, 23, 28–9, 35, 37, 48, 53, 55, 58, 61, 69, 72, 102–3, 108, 117–18, 121, 126, 130, 134, 136, 146, 152–3, 166, 169, 172, 184, 192, 194, 200, 202
Franks, Aaron 14
Freshwater, Helen 33

Gaby, Rosemary 13
Garrard, Greg 3, 47–8
Garrick, David, Jubilee Parade 35
Geertz, Clifford 20, 31
gesture 4, 10, 103
Gersch, Emma 102
Ghosh, Amitav 21, 38
  The Great Derangement 51 n.23
Gibson, James 144–5
Gifford, Terry 48, 69–70
Gillies, John 98
Glow, Hilary 184
Godwin, Edward 46, 49, 58, 64, 66–7, 69
Golinski, Jan 20–2, 79, 145, 167
Goodbody, Buzz 187
Goode, Nathan 153
granite 81, 100, 102, 105
grass/grassy 50, 56, 63, 80, 82, 88, 91, 105, 114, 131, 143–4, 163
Greek Theatre 85
green language 39, 145, 151–6, 164, 168, 170, 172–3
Green, Lucy 180–1
Greet, Ben 46, 68–9
Groundweather 163

habitat 2, 62, 71, 90, 109
Hadley, Bree, *Disability, Public Space and Spectatorship* 135
Halstead, Alison 136–7
harmony 47, 54–5, 62–3, 66–7, 78, 88, 121. *See also* disjuncture; rupture
Hamilton, Jennifer Mae 17, 26, 66, 187, 196–7

Hamlet 26, 90, 173–4, 189
HandleBards, The 40, 193
　　As You Like It 40, 178–86
　　Award for Sustainable Practice 180
Haraway, Donna 16, 34, 197
Harrison, Paul 155
Hearst Greek Theatre, University of
　　California 88
Heim, Caroline 19
Heise, Ursula K. 111
Henry V 5
Her Majesty's Theatre 45
Hern, Jessica 180–1
Hill, Pippa 187
historiography 29, 73
Holland Park 139–41, 143–4
Hooker, Jeremy 146
Horne, Sarah 187
Howe, Nicolas 19
hubris 28, 74, 84, 106
Hulme, Mike 21, 23, 59, 175
Hume, David 21
humility 106, 181

Imperial Theatre 51
indoor theatre 7, 12–13, 15, 17–18, 34, 47,
　　51, 54–7, 64, 69–70
Ingold, Tim 17–18, 33, 37, 100–1, 130,
　　156, 159, 163
Ivatts, Sophie 187

Jackson, Phil 98, 161
Jauregui, José Antonio 110
　　Humans on Trial: An Ecological Fable
　　110–11
Jerolmack, Colin 158
Johanson, Katya 184
John, William Goscombe 131
Jones, Gwilym 8–10, 26, 102–3, 106
　　Shakespeare's Storms 8
Joseph, Keziah 195
journey 58, 71–2, 125, 130–6, 140–2
Jubilee Parade, 1869 35

Kent, Alan 98–9, 106, 110
Keown, Eric 81, 88
Kerridge, Richard 147, 172–3
Kershaw, Baz 27, 164
King Lear 5, 8, 26, 47, 59
Kipling, Rudyard, *Puck of Pook's Hill* 11

Knox, E. V. 82–3
Kramer, Paula 14
Kulmala, Dan 36, 123
Kwon, Miwon 11

Labouchere, Henrietta 45–8, 65–70, 160
Lakoff, George 37
landscape 14, 31, 34, 39, 48, 51, 54–9, 63–5
　　Minack 96–101
　　as performance space 164–6
Lane, Margaret 80
Latour, Bruno 22
Lavery, Carl 14, 28
lavish 38, 74, 85, 91–2
lawn 80, 84–5, 125, 131, 195, 197
Leddy, David, *Susurrus* 123
Lefebvre, Henri 107
Levine, George 51
Liberate Tate 189
light 6, 39, 60, 66–7, 71
　　audience research 159–60, 162–4
　　daylight performance 64, 66–7, 131,
　　　160–2, 164
　　electric lighting 39, 67, 71, 81, 84, 86,
　　　88, 90, 97, 159–60
Livermore, Rebecca 171
local 31, 37, 95, 98, 106, 108, 111, 113,
　　115, 121, 128, 131, 140–1, 147, 157,
　　161, 165, 172
Loewen-Walker, Rachel 17, 20, 163, 174,
　　191–3
Lopez, Jeremy 36
Lucas, John 65
Luhrmann, Baz 189

Mabey, Richard 16, 202
Macbeth
　　Birnam Wood 5
　　wildfire smoke 26
Madison, D. Soyini 31
magic 102–3, 114–15, 117, 124–5, 141,
　　185
Magigi, Natasha 141–2
Maitland, Sara 124, 126, 129, 147, 163
　　Gossip from the Forest 124
Mannion, Teresa 201
Marinelli, Peter 116, 190
Marlowe, Sam 197
Martin, Darragh 186
Martin, Randall 26, 111, 113, 115, 162

Mason, Bim 12
Massie-Blomfield, Amber, *Twenty Theatres to See before You Die* 5
mastery 78, 88, 91–2, 102–3, 121. *See also* control
Matilda, the Musical 190
May Festival 72
May, Theresa J., *Readings in Performance and Ecology* 27
Mazel, David 3
McAuley, Gay 124
McCormack, Derek 155–7, 171–2
meander 32, 20, 70
memory/remembering 19–20, 45, 50–1, 62–3, 89, 111, 153, 173–6, 201
Mentz, Steve 47, 58, 196
Merchant, Carolyn 63
Merleau-Ponty, Maurice 163
Merry Wives of Windsor, The 39, 90, 96, 115–17
    audience research 112–13
    at Willow Globe 109–10, 158
metaphor/metaphorical 17, 19, 29, 57, 74, 90, 105, 115, 129, 133, 165, 169, 185, 191, 196
Meyer-Eppler, Werner 152
Midsummer Night's Dream, A 1–2, 5, 9, 11, 38. *See also* Labouchere, Henrietta; Reinhardt, Max
    audience research 65–70, 72–3, 75–7, 79, 81, 125–6, 132–3
    landscape 164
    Pope, Alexander, Villa 45, 48, 65, 67, 70, 160
    at Ripley Castle 125–6, 128–9, 141, 157
    Sprite Productions 123, 125–30, 132–3, 146
Miller, Arthur 88
Minack 5, 106–13, 117, 121–3, 152, 157–8, 161, 165–6, 169, 174, 201
    Antony and Cleopatra 158, 165
    audiences 95, 97–8, 100–4, 112, 121
    landscape 96–101
    location 95
    Tempest, The 39, 96, 98–9, 101–8, 161
Minton, Gretchen 26
Mischief Mob 188–9
moon 66, 72, 113, 153
More, Thomas 197

Morton, Timothy 18, 28, 51, 129, 144–5, 168, 198
Moss, Paul 179
Much Ado About Nothing 188

Nardizzi, Vin 113, 116, 129, 147
nationalism 5, 18, 24, 74, 118, 168
naturalism 125, 128
nature 1, 18, 34–5, 47, 53–4, 63, 68. *See also* Minack; Willow Globe
    culture/nature dualism 15, 34–7, 41, 53, 57, 70, 96
Neimanis, Astrida 17, 20, 163, 174, 191–3, 196–7
Nicholson, Helen, *The Ecologies of Amateur Theatre* 8
Nixon, Robert 198
Noah and the Whale 194
nostalgia 35, 47, 70
    avant-garde nostalgia 118–19, 184

open-air
    aesthetic qualities of a production 151–2
    aleatory effects 152–3, 155
    alternative hedonism 172–3
    arts funding politics 5, 7, 29
    English climate 24–6
    environmental significance 2, 47, 52–4, 58–67
    green atmospheres 154–9
    pastoral performances 69–70
    small-scale performances 5–6
    stage scenery 57, 62–3
    under trees 124–47
original practices 1, 6, 11–12, 26, 117–18, 120, 127, 152, 159–60, 183. *See also* Elizabethan theatre
Orlove, Ben 169
outdoor 2, 5–7, 9, 11–16, 27, 36–7, 46–7, 53, 56–7, 61, 67, 69. *See also* Minack; open-air; Regent's Park Open Air Theatre; Willow Globe
    green atmospheres 152–4, 161, 167, 174
    weather conditions 181, 184, 187, 192, 202
Oxford University Dramatic Society 75, 89–90

Palmer, Scott 159, 162
participation/participatory 29, 105, 135–6, 178, 187, 190–1
  participants 32–3, 73, 105, 169, 191
Pastoral Players, The 46, 49–50, 57–61, 64–8, 73, 89
  As You Like It 121, 132, 160, 181, 183
pastoral 25, 34, 38, 45–9, 51–70
  classical literary form 47–8
  cultural context 62, 68
  literary 116
  nineteenth-century 160
  pejorative 48, 172
  sheep 59, 109, 121, 157, 159
  twenty-first-century 54–5
  Victorian 6, 51, 54, 69
  weather conditions 52, 59–60, 62, 65, 181, 198
  weathering 121–3
Pearson, Mike 32, 96, 104, 146
Performance Research (journal) 15
Pericles 90
Pevsner, Nicolas 23
Philips, Ambrose, *Pastorals* 65
physical exertion 16, 18–19, 24, 34, 47, 57, 60, 80, 83, 91, 99–100, 103, 112, 115–17, 122–3, 135, 163, 166–7, 169, 174–5, 181, 195, 200, 202
place 11, 13, 32, 35, 55, 67–8, 75, 77, 100, 102, 104–6, 108, 110–11, 122, 123–47, 157, 162, 164, 166, 185, 187–8, 195, 197, 199
Platt, Will 189
pleasure/pleasurable 19, 53, 59, 67, 80, 84, 104, 118–21, 133, 178, 184
  green pleasures 170–5
Poe, Edgar Allan 63
Poel, William, and the Elizabethan Stage Society 69
pollution 25, 49, 57, 156, 194
Powell, Kerry 69
power 3, 22, 39, 41, 51–2, 54, 86, 103, 110, 134, 139, 188, 194, 196, 198. *See also* powerlessness
powerlessness 64, 169
Prescott, Paul 27
presentism 10, 26, 30
Price-White, F.G. 80
professional 5, 8, 12, 29, 58, 68–9, 95

promenade 72, 88, 123, 127, 134–5, 140
Purcell, Stephen 6, 29, 36, 168
  Popular Shakespeare 8

rain 8–10, 24, 59–62, 82, 97, 138, 145, 165, 167, 174–5, 179–80, 188, 194, 200
Rancière, Jacques 15, 134
  The Emancipated Spectator 8, 134
Rand, Alex 102–3
Raworth, Kate 196
Realism 13, 125, 128. *See also* naturalism
Reason, Mathew 29
Rebellato, Dan 129
Regent's Park Open Air Theatre 5, 12, 38, 40, 72–4, 78–81, 85–6, 160. *See also Midsummer Night's Dream, A*; Reinhardt, Max
  As You Like It 193–200
Reinhardt, Max
  audiences 76–7, 79, 81
  Boboli Gardens, Florence 71–2, 75, 86
  electric lighting 160
  forest scene 72, 76–7
  Headington Gardens, Oxford 72
  Hollywood Bowl 71, 73, 85, 86–8, 90
  lighting effects 76
repertoire 1, 5, 19–20, 60, 83, 201
resourcism 18, 55, 73–4
Richard III 8
Romeo and Juliet 5, 160–1
  wildlife 159
Royal Shakespeare Theatre 40, 178, 186–93, 201
Ruhl, Sarah 190
rupture 63, 128
Rushdie, Salman 124
Ryle, Martin, *Culture and Anarchy* 35

Salazar, Rebecca 26
Sanders, Julie, *The Cambridge Introduction to Early Modern Drama* 8
San Francisco Memorial Opera House 85, 88
scenery/scenographic 14, 34–5, 55–7, 59, 64–6, 174, 180, 182–3, 198
scenography 12, 45, 52
Schechner, Richard 37
Schmidt, Gavin 202
Schwyzer, Philip 11, 95 n.2

Scollen, Rebecca 36
Scott, Clement 56
sea 87, 95–106, 111, 120–2, 166–7, 171, 174, 176
Second World War 23, 92, 168
Sedgman, Kirsty 29
Serres, Michel 82
Sewell, J. E. 82
Seymour, Nicole, *Bad Environmentalism* 184
Shakespearean Insult Booth 187, 191
Shakespeare Link 110–12
Shakespeare's Globe 5, 8, 30, 108, 117, 152–3, 169, 174, 198, 201
   Macbeth 152
   pigeon, anecdote 152–4, 158, 170, 174
Shanks, Michael 96, 104
Shklovsky, Victor 101
Sibley, Catharine 71–3, 75, 78, 85–8, 92
Simmons, Ian 49
Sinfield, Alan 35–6
site-specific performance 12, 32, 124, 138
Skey, Michael 24
sky 9–10, 45, 56, 58, 82, 101, 104, 108, 114, 145, 152–3, 159, 162, 169, 180, 187, 201
slow violence 198
Smith, Philip 12, 19
Soper, Kate 34–5, 118–20, 172, 184
   Culture and Anarchy 35
sound 4, 76, 97, 103–5, 110, 112, 115, 117–18, 133, 144, 156–9, 170, 190, 196
spectacle 38, 58, 91, 152, 164
Sprite Productions 123, 125–30, 132–3, 146
stars 13, 75, 144, 164
States, Bert 11, 101
Strauss, Sarah 169
sun 52, 55, 59–60, 80, 99, 144, 153, 162, 164, 167, 170–1, 190

Taking Flight Theatre Company 130–9, 143, 146
Taming of the Shrew, The 110, 169
Taylor, Diana 19–20
Teatro Vivo 123, 125, 137–44, 141, 146
   After the Tempest 123, 137–44, 141, 146
   Tempest, The 125
tears 62–3, 88
Tempest, The 5, 6 n.17, 8–9, 26 n.118, 82–3, 96, 98–9, 101–3, 105–7, 112–14, 121, 123, 125, 137–44, 146, 161, 166, 190
   audience research 82–3, 101–3, 105, 107
   at Minack 39, 96, 98–9, 101–8, 161
   Moving Stories' production 102, 104, 106–7
   Regent's Park 82–3
Terry, Ellen 66
theatergoers 8, 10, 16, 19, 23, 28, 33–5, 38–40, 47–8, 55, 59–60, 63, 66. *See also* audience members; participants; spectators
   weathering performance 83, 121, 124, 126, 131, 151, 166–7
Theilade, Nini 72–3, 77, 81, 87–8, 92
Thompson's Park 131, 133
Thrift, Nigel 31
thrifty 183
thunderstorms 81
Tickell, Alison 2
Tilley, Christopher 100, 118
tradition 35, 95, 114, 124–5, 128, 130, 132, 163
Tree, Herbert Beerbohm 45–7, 57, 67
trees 25, 39, 45, 52, 55, 57, 59, 67, 72, 75–6, 86–91, 108, 114, 116, 124–36, 141–4, 147, 158, 166, 173, 196
Tribble, Evelyn 33
Twelfth Night 8, 78, 80–1, 118, 194
Tylicki, Michelle 186

Vanek, Morgan 17
Venus and Adonis 90
vibrant matter 26, 32
Victorian theaters 52, 54
Vinall, Olivia 195

Walsh, Luke 171
warm 45–6, 60, 65, 71, 81, 99, 133, 153, 161, 173, 181
Warner Brothers 89
Warrington, George 85
waste 25, 40, 48, 91, 178, 194, 196. *See also* trash
Watson, Robert 52, 56, 64, 114
weather. *See also* blustery; breeze; chilly; drizzle; dry; hot; rain; sun; thunderstorm; warm; wind
   affective capacities 8–10
   everyday life 16

forecasting 79
green language 170–3
historical attitudes 30
memories 173–6
national character 20–5, 38
outdoor productions 47, 49–52, 55, 58–70
unreliability 61, 175
weathering 166–9
  audience research 60, 65, 80–1, 84, 92, 120–2, 146–7, 151–2, 178–9
  behavior 14, 18–19, 81–2, 45, 173
  pastorals 121–3
  as performance 16–20, 38, 47, 55, 64–6, 68–70
  theatergoers 83, 121, 124, 126, 131, 151, 166–7
Weber, Andrew Lloyd 188
Webster, Max 40, 178–9, 194–5, 197–8, 200
Weissberger, Felix 75
Welfare State International 6
Welshness 95, 110
Welton, Martin 15
wet 5, 8, 64, 81–2, 84, 109, 167–9, 200
Whistler, James 46
wildlife 39, 119, 143–4, 151, 154–5, 157–9, 170–1, 173
Wilkie, Fiona 96
Williams, David 15, 18
Williams, Gary Jay 72, 74 n.11

Williams, Raymond 35, 39, 118, 128, 151
  The Country and the City 165
  "Social Environment and Theatrical Environment: The Case of English Naturalism" 128
Williams, Tom Ross 141–2
Willow Globe 27, 39, 41, 95–6, 108–23, 141, 157–8, 160, 166, 173, 183–4
  All's Well That Ends Well 109, 157–8
  audiences 95–6, 111–12, 118–19, 121
  blackbirds 109, 157, 173–4
  green ethos 108–10
  location 108
  Merry Wives of Windsor, The 96, 112–20
  touring 110
wind 8, 19, 27, 41, 60–2, 75, 87, 102–3, 108, 110–11, 130, 157–8, 167–8, 170–1, 173, 180–1, 186, 190, 192, 201
Wolf-Ferrari, Ermanno, *I gioielli della Madonna* 140
woodland performances
  As You Like It 46, 52–3, 55, 68
  Shakespeare's pastoral play 52
Woods, Penelope 152–4, 159–60, 181, 183
wood 86–8, 91, 124–47, 158, 166, 173, 196. *See also* forest; trees
Wylie, John 96

www.ingramcontent.com/pod-product-compliance
Lightning Source LLC
Chambersburg PA
CBHW072151290426
44111CB00012B/2029